CREATING BETTER FUTURES

CREATING BETTER FUTURES

Scenario Planning as a Tool for a Better Tomorrow

James A. Ogilvy

OXFORD
UNIVERSITY PRESS
2002

OXFORD
UNIVERSITY PRESS

Auckland Bangkok Buenos Aires Cape Town
Chennai Dar es Salaam Dehli Hong Kong Istanbul Karachi
Kolkata Kuala Lumpur Madrid Melbourne Mexico City Mumbai Nairobi
São Paulo Shanghai Singapore Taipei Tokyo Toronto

an associated company in

Berlin

Copyright © 2002 by Oxford University Press, Inc.

Published by Oxford University Press, Inc.,
198 Madison Avenue, New York, New York 10016

Library of Congress Cataloging-in-Publication Data
is available at the Library of Congress
ISBN 0-19-514611-5

3 5 7 9 8 6 4 2
Printed in the United States of America
on acid-free paper

CONTENTS

Contents

Jay Ogilvy's *Creating Better Futures* brings the powerful tools of scenario planning, long applied successfully to business firms and other organizations, to the challenge of making the world a better place for all of us. Let me explain.

When executives of large companies like Ford and ATT or generals and admirals at the Pentagon make decisions about the future, they use the best planning tools at their disposal. Today they build their judgments about tomorrow using a tool known as scenario planning. It enables them to explore the unknowable future and chart a favorable course. For them, it is not difficult to know what a better future is. In the world of business, the metrics of success are well known. If your sales and profits are up, shareholders will be happy. If customers are happy, if employment is growing and there is a pipeline of future products, then the odds of continuing success are high. Success for the Pentagon is measured in a more prepared military and wars prevented or won.

Scenario planning is not a tool for making predictions. The future remains as unpredictable as ever. Rather, it is a tool for better decision making. The test of good scenario planning is not whether the scenario accurately predicts the future. Rather, the measure of good scenario planning is whether we made a better decision as a result of having considered the possible scenarios. Businesses and governments employ this tool because it helps them to make better strategic decisions.

What about the rest of us? What's a better future for us? For the world? This is a much harder problem. Is a better future for America a better future for the world? Is a better future for India the same as the one for Ghana? Is a better future for today's pensioners the same as for today's kids? Is a better future for people of deep religious faith the same as the better future for scientific humanists? Scenario planning can be a tool for handling these very hard questions. But social creativity calls for a philosophical context that is different from the simpler world of business. *Creating Better Futures* frames that new context and then shows how to apply scenario planning creatively to guide our shared future.

If we are to influence the future for the better, we need to have some idea of where we may be headed. We need to know how much maneuvering room we have. What are our options? What are the consequences of our choices? Who benefits and who loses? If the future were really predictable and inevitable, then human choice and freedom would be an illusion. Uncertainty and freedom go together. The indeterminacy of the future means that our choices actually might mean something. What we believe can happen influences what we do, and what we do actually influences the outcome of events. There is no better example than the collapse of Communism. When the people who supported Communism lost faith in its promise of a better future, their loss of faith destroyed the system.

Our aspirations and beliefs about the future matter. But when we think about big questions like the future of the world, the problem is that we have many aspirations and beliefs. Is there some single truth that subsumes all the others? Or is there some hierarchy of values and beliefs that will somehow enable us to sort our possibilities and priorities? *Creating Better Futures* does an excellent job of showing how naïve and simpleminded a universalistic approach to a singular future is, how it has failed in the past and, at the extreme, how it has been profoundly destructive. The thousand–year Reich of Nazi Germany was a future vision born of such a singular worldview.

Our understanding of how the world works shapes our views of the future. Our worldview tells us what's possible and what's not. How do things fit together? What are the connections of cause and effect? Why do events unfold as they do? Over time our worldview has evolved from beliefs in mystical forces to a science illuminated by rational and comprehensible forces. But even the scientific worldview has evolved. Once, a mechanistic billiard–ball like model of structures and dynamics was a perceptive metaphor for reality. Today, in an uncertain world woven together by elaborate networks of information, it is the relationships among things and forces that matter most. Hence this book builds the case for a relational worldview as a foundation for understanding how to frame coherent views of the future.

Even if we understand how the world works more clearly, we still have the problem of multiple and highly varied aspirations for a better future. Here *Creating Better Futures* provides a powerful argument for ethical pluralism. In a highly interconnected world, there is not one better future that we will all agree is best for us all. Is a Sudanese animist less ethical than his Muslim brothers to the north? Is a devout Christian more ethical than a serious scientist studying cloning? Obviously, each would claim to have a set of ethics and values, yet they lead to very different visions of the future. In the Sudan they are killing each other over their competing visions; and in the United States Christians and scientists disagree about many of the possibilities of new biological discoveries. Is a future with human clones better than one without them? The answer is not obvious or automatic.

It is here that scenarios become a vital tool for furthering the dialogue among differences. Each of the ethical perspectives has the opportunity to define its scenarios of the future, their hopes and fears embodied in stories about the future. Scenarios can foster understanding of and empathy for others' visions for tomorrow. Scenarios are only stories after all. They are not ideologies or matters of faith. They are simply ways of exploring possibilities. Scenarios provide a way of having a more imaginative and coherent conversation about the future. And since there is more than one plausible scenario, scenario planning enables a conversation that does not end with one side winning and the other losing. Indeed, the differences among us are among the most important tools for creating a diversity of possible futures, giving real meaning to human freedom.

Peter Schwartz
Chairman
Global Business Network

PREFACE

Whence and whither? Where does this book come from? For whom is
it intended?

This book is the result of 40 years of experience split almost equally
between studying and teaching philosophy and pursuing a career in social research and corporate consulting. During this time I pondered how
things *ought to be*; then I studied how things *are*; and finally I focused
on how things *might be*. I can't claim definitive answers from any of
these quests, but I can claim a unique perspective developed along the
peculiar path I've been gratefully privileged to tread, from the ivied walls
of Yale and Williams to the boardrooms of many of the world's largest
and most influential organizations.

"Philosophy bakes no bread," said Socrates, by which he meant that
nothing practical can be accomplished by philosophizing. Philosophy
has no utility. You certainly can't make a living at it. Billionaire George
Soros started out as a philosopher. He claims that he built his fortune
by testing in the marketplace certain ideas for which he could find no
hearing among fellow philosophers. But his success in the marketplace
came as a result of his acting as an investor, not as a philosopher. As
philosophers would put it—in pompous Latin—he was acting *qua* investor, *as* an investor, not *qua* philosopher. At best, he is a philosopher
gone wrong.

Even without Soros's billions, I sometimes feel like a philosopher
gone wrong. I started out as an academic. I studied philosophy for four
years as an undergraduate, then for another four years as a graduate student. I then taught philosophy for 12 years, mostly at Yale. Two decades
ago I turned to social research and corporate consulting, first at SRI In-

ternational (formerly Stanford Research Institute), and for the past dozen years at Global Business Network (GBN), a company that four friends and I founded in 1987. For the past 20 years I've had an opportunity to test in the marketplace certain ideas that I picked up from my training in philosophy.

This book is the result of this odd mix of philosophy and consulting. I can't say that I've always consulted *qua* philosopher. At times I've probably committed the sin that anthropologists call *going native*. That is, like Soros, but with far less success, I've simply acted *qua* consultant, but as a consultant who just happened to have in his bag of tricks some concepts picked up from my study of philosophy.

In mythology, Hermes (as he was known to the Greeks) or Mercury (as he was known to the Romans), was the gods' messenger, he of the winged heels. You may have seen his picture in ads for FTD florists. I often feel that I'm operating under the influence of Hermes as I carry messages from philosophy into the realm of business. Hermes was not only a messenger. He was also something of a trickster. Only days old, he stole a herd of cattle from Apollo by fashioning shoes from the bark of a fallen oak, then tying them to the cows' hooves with plaited grass to hide the cows' tracks. Hermes' outlaw cleverness was put to use in his role as a messenger. In order that his messages might get through to those to whom he was carrying them, he sometimes had to reframe them to suit the manners of his hearers.

I've learned that I have to go light on philosophizing in the boardroom. My colleagues kid me for dragging Hegel into too many conversations. I have to beware of intimidating clients with too much talk about corporate existentialism, the epistemology of knowledge management, or the ontology of bits and bytes as opposed to molecules and metals. But I can't help it. The applications of philosophical ideas to the world of business simply cry out to be made if you happen to wander into the marketplace carrying a bag of tricks like mine.

What I cannot presume—and do not presume in this book—is that anyone I'm talking with has actually read those impossible tomes I spent years studying. There is probably no writing as bad as that of German philosophers like Kant, Hegel, Heidegger, and Habermas, or their French heirs, Derrida, Foucault, Deleuze, and Guattari. No one should have to read that stuff. It's very nearly impenetrable. There's a need for a messenger who can translate the insights of these very obscure philosophers into language that ordinary mortals can understand.

Although philosophy can not actually bake bread, it can help us run our bakeries a little better. Smart business people should always be on the lookout for new ideas—or very old ideas that are new to the marketplace. I know I'm not alone in operating as a sort of Hermes. In recent years we've seen no end of books with titles advertising the Zen of this or the Tao of that. Perhaps it's time to mine the wisdom tradition of the West in addition to the more mystical traditions of the East. The word philosophy, meaning love of wisdom, is built from the Greek words for love (*philo*) and wisdom (*sophia*).

As Socrates argues in Plato's *Symposium*, his dialogue on love, just because you love something doesn't mean you have it. To the contrary, love often derives from what you lack. Love is like a heart-shaped hole seeking to be filled. The object of your desire fits the contours of your lack of self-sufficiency. So likewise, in playing the role of messenger from the wisdom tradition of Western philosophy, I do not purport to be wise. I may at times be intoxicated with the love of wisdom, but I lay no claim to wisdom.

While teaching philosophy at Yale, I found myself compelled to specialize. I was backed into the odd corner of becoming a specialist on Hegel—the preeminent generalist! But my real interest lay in accomplishing today something akin to what Hegel achieved in 1807: creating a holistic view to show how the different parts of our human endeavor relate to one another in the dance of history. During the 1980s at SRI International, I got my chance to Hegelize the world of today and tomorrow. I enjoyed the privilege of learning about scenario planning from Peter Schwartz, author of the widely read *Art of the Long View*, and co-author of *Seven Tomorrows, The Long Boom, China's Futures,* and *When Good Companies Do Bad Things*. While at SRI, I also worked as willing understudy to Arnold Mitchell, who invented the Values and Lifestyles (VALS) Program, a system for describing nine different lifestyles in terms of the values held by different groups of Americans. In 1987 Peter Schwartz and I invited three of our friends—Napier Collyns, Lawrence Wilkinson, and Stewart Brand—to join us in creating Global Business Network, a firm that practices strategic thinking using scenario planning. Since then we've had an opportunity to apply this tool in the service of over one hundred major corporations and government agencies, from Royal Dutch/Shell, where scenario planning took root under the guidance of Pierre Wack and Ted Newland, to scores of other organizations, from the National Education Association to companies like Motorola, AT&T, BellSouth, Nissan, American Express, IBM, General Mills, State Farm, Cisco Systems, Ford, Hewlett-Packard,

and many more. GBN has recently joined the Monitor Group of companies founded in 1983 by a group of colleagues from Harvard Business
School. Together with our colleagues at Monitor, we anticipate many
more years of scenario building for many more organizations and communities.

For whom is this book intended? The intelligent, inquisitive reader
who is concerned about the future, not the specialized scholar preoccupied with some narrow piece of the past. This book has footnotes, but
it is not really a work of scholarship. Its reach is far too broad to per-
suade specialists to change their minds about matters in their own disciplines. Instead the quotes and notes are introduced as evidence for what
is in most cases obvious to specialists within a given discipline, but interesting news to inquisitive minds who are relative strangers to that discipline. My method is one of presenting relatively uncontroversial high-
lights rather than digging up esoteric insights from the dark recesses of
scholarship. Anthropologists will learn nothing new about Lévi-Strauss
or Clifford Geertz from my treatments, but literary critics might. Literary critics will learn nothing new about Roland Barthes, but sociologists might. Businesspeople may learn little that is new about their own
industries from a factual point of view, but they may learn how to see
the same old stuff in brand new ways, and to think about strategy in a
way that is very different from traditional strategic planning.

My aim here is not so much one of popularizing brand–new discoveries in various disciplines. I don't dumb down the achievements of the
human sciences. Nor do I assume any familiarity with the texts I discuss. Instead I make use of textual quotation as a way of demonstrating
that people really do think and talk and write the way I say they think
and talk and write. I'm not making this stuff up. The point of representing scholars with their own words is to *show* rather than merely *say*
the points I want to make, to demonstrate rather than speculate.

I do not make original contributions to the scholarship in particular
fields, but rather make a series of new connections, joining some fairly
familiar dots in some relatively unfamiliar ways. I use quotations and
footnotes to display the dots on their own terms, but I then connect
those dots in ways that their original authors might never have imag-
ined.

My debts are legion. I would like to thank in particular those friends
and colleagues who have read and commented on earlier versions of all
or part of this book: John Seely Brown, Manuel Castells, Gerard Fairt-
lough, Robert Fuller, Charles Hampden-Turner, Paul Hawken, Stuart

Henshall, Andy Hines, Jack Huber, Eric Hughes, David Ing, Richard Lanham, Pete Leyden, Ron Loeb, Tatyana Mamut, Michael Marien, Brian Mulconrey, Michael Murphy, Jacob Needleman, Richard O'Brien, John O'Neil, Jim Pelkey, Jeremy Sherman, Bob Solomon, Marsha Vande Berg, Kees van der Heijden, and Steve Weber. For their help in introducing me to some of the intricacies of health care, I would like to thank in particular David Reynolds and Will Straub. For his help in educating me about education, I would like to thank Peter Arum. I would also like to thank Joe McCrossen and Lori Shouldice for their help in tracking down sources.

Parts of Chapter 2 appeared as an issue of GBN's *Deeper News* series under the title "This Postmodern Business," which was edited by Jim Smith from a longer article published in *Marketing and Research Today*, Vol. 18, No. 1, February 1990, pp. 5–22. Parts of Chapter 5 appeared as a chapter of *Revisioning Philosophy*, James Ogilvy, ed., State University of New York Press, 1991. Chapters 6, 7, and 10 include bits and pieces of three essays: "Reconstructing Genius," in *Social Creativity II*, edited by Alphonso Montouri, Hampton Press, 1999, pp. 219–233; "Future Studies and the Human Sciences: The Case for Normative Scenarios," *Futures Research Quarterly*, Vol. 8, No. 2, Summer 1992, pp. 5–65; and "Scenario Planning as the Fulfillment of Critical Theory," *Futures Research Quarterly*, Vol. 12, No. 2, Summer 1996, pp. 5–33. I want to thank Tim Biggs for soliciting and editing these last two articles, which include much of the scholarly research behind this book.

These last two essays, and much of this book, continue work that started with an invitation from Peter Schwartz to collaborate on an SRI report entitled *The Emergent Paradigm: Changing Patterns of Thought and Belief* (1979). Ever since we met in 1978, Peter has been a treasured friend and colleague. I cannot thank him enough for his inspiration and encouragement.

As he has done with so many books, Napier Collyns is largely responsible for escorting this book into print. Though not strictly my agent, Napier, the consummate networker, made the match between an earlier manuscript and Herb Addison at Oxford University Press, who is simply the best editor I've yet met. I would also like to thank another fine editor, Eric Best, formerly of GBN, now at Morgan Stanley, for his help in prying my prose away from the bad influence of those European philosophers. Though not directly involved with this book, Eric helped with an earlier book, *Living Without A Goal*, whose title raises the question, Doesn't creating better futures entail the setting of goals?

How do I square the message of *Living Without A Goal* with the manifestly aspirational message of this book? The answer lies in the consistently pluralistic philosophy behind both books. Like normative scenarios, goals are fine, even necessary to get you through a day, to say nothing of a life. It's the single Goal (capital G) and the single-point forecast that turn highly purposive people into fanatics and send narrowly focused companies down strategic dead ends. Likewise, this book is about what it takes to create many better futures, not just one. This book does not provide a blueprint for utopia. Instead it introduces a set of ideas and tools that others can use to build their own better futures. But here we move beyond the whence and whither and into the heart of the matter. . . .

CREATING BETTER FUTURES

CHAPTER ONE
———————

AIMING HIGHER

The future could be better than the present. The future *should* be better than the present. A large part of the glory of being human lies in our ability to imagine better futures and make them happen. But a large part of our history records the suffering of people who were sold a bill of goods about a better future—holy wars in the name of building the kingdom of God on earth, failed revolutions fought in the name of a better life after the revolution, the final solution that would bring the thousand–year Reich. Idealism can be dangerous. We know this.

But today we suffer from a lack of sufficient idealism. Popular images of the future tend toward the grim: blasted landscapes populated by barbarians, *Blade Runner* interiors by Ridley Scott, leaden landscapes by post-Holocaust German artist Anselm Kiefer. Polls on consumer confidence may reveal a high level of optimism about the short–term future, but when you ask young people about their hopes for the longer term, you hear more about their fears. When you ask intellectuals about their aspirations for a better society, you get cynicism in response. You find vivid images of environmental disaster, Third–World hunger, inner–city decay, the decline of community. On the upside . . . precious little. It is as if optimism were unfashionable. Cynicism sounds so *deep*. Hope sounds so superficial and naïve.

This book is unabashedly hopeful. It is aimed at restoring faith in the longer–term future. But this is not a feel–good book. It is not about some new age of spiritual enlightenment or some imminent era of inevitable prosperity. There is nothing inevitable about better futures. We have to create them.

This book is about what it takes to build better futures, and how much we already have at hand. Together with my friends and colleagues, I try to help people create better futures. We do this by helping them to frame alternative scenarios that are customized to their particular situations. We call it scenario planning. Sometimes our client is a corporation that wants to compete more effectively in the marketplace. Sometimes it is a union that wants to do a better job of serving its members. Sometimes it is a government agency that wants to do its job more effectively. Sometimes it is a state or nation that wants a better future for its citizens. We try to help them think ahead and do what's right.

There are so many ways of going wrong and we humans have tried most of them. History chronicles extraordinary cruelty and foolishness, from witch hunts and clitorectomies to wars and tortures. Why should we have faith that we can do better in the future?

Here's why. We now have reason to know better than to go down paths that lead to disaster. Unlike other animals, we humans can not only imagine better futures, but we have memories of bitter pasts that we can pass on to our children. We have histories inscribed in more than human memory. We have libraries. We have computers. We have databases. We have analytic tools that allow us to take what we have learned and turn it to the task of improving the future.

This all sounds so very obvious, but somehow the tenor of the times has led us to neglect our higher aspirations. Talk of a better future runs the danger of being dismissed as utopian. The word *utopia* is part of a vocabulary of knowing cynicism. The word is built from syllables—*ou* meaning not, and *topos* meaning place—literally meaning no place, nowhere. We are all supposed to know better than to believe in some story about a better future. Plato's *Republic,* Thomas More's *Utopia*— these are tales told to college students for various instructive purposes. But surely no one should believe that we could bring about a better future in which hope and happiness prevail.

I happen to agree with many of the criticisms of utopian thinking. That is why this book is called *Creating Better Futures* and not *A Better Future,* much less *The Best Future* or *A Perfect Future.* This book does not purport to have all the answers. But the pool of collective knowledge has grown immensely in recent centuries and there is no reason why we should not tap that pool to steer our way more wisely into a range of better futures . . . if not the *best* future of a perfect utopia.

It is said that the good has a way of driving out the better. *Good enough* solutions keep us from finding better solutions. Social scientists call this *satisficing*. But the *best* also drives out the better. Our worldly wisdom about the foolishness of chasing after false utopias has led many of us to lower our sights from the best and the better to the merely *good enough*. We think we know better than to aspire to radical improvement. So we settle for the status quo or, at best, incremental improvement.

There's nothing wrong with incremental improvement in many situations. The Japanese have shown us just how much can be accomplished by taking something good and making it, by small increments, better and better. But sometimes systems need a jolt to shake them out of self-reinforcing equilibrium. Like houses with heating and cooling systems controlled by thermostats, complex social systems get locked into self-correcting syndromes that are hard to break. The more we learn about complex systems (and the science of complex systems has made leaps and bounds recently) the more we learn how *lock in* is responsible for the *good enough* preventing the *better*—especially when well-grounded skepticism about the *best* is there to keep us from even trying.

When vast social systems get locked into one way of doing things, nothing short of systemic reform will do. The end of the Cold War was one radical improvement that is, for the most part, succeeding. It's rough on Russian pensioners, but the rest of the world rests easier knowing that the Cold War is over. National health care reform has, for the most part, failed. The systemic reforms envisaged by the Clinton team were pecked to death in Congress by piecemeal criticisms that ignored the needs of the whole system. Now incremental reforms leave us muddling toward managed care. As I'll suggest in the concluding chapter, we could do better.

This book is about the tools we need to create better systems: better health, better education, better business, better lives. I refuse to believe that we've exhausted our opportunities for progress. There is nothing inevitable about progress. It takes hard work and smart choices. But we have what it takes to make better choices about some of the vast systems that shape our lives. This book can change your life because its subject is the tools we have at hand for changing the systems that affect our lives. Some of these systems seem so vast that no individual could possibly change their course. They confront us with a massed might that renders each individual impotent by comparison. But the tools I'll describe, when placed in the hands of relatively small groups of individuals, can bend the course of very large organizations.

CREATING THE FUTURES WE WANT

The future is not predictable. Nor is it so open that absolutely anything is possible. The past and the present place conditions and constraints on what is and is not possible. For individuals, for corporations, and for communities, coming to terms with those conditions and constraints while exercising choice in the face of uncertainty is a large part of what a creative and fulfilling life is all about. We are not bound by our past to live out a future that is predetermined and therefore predictable. Nor are we so free that we can be anything we want to be. These simple truths define the boundaries of a fairly large space between total freedom and calculable determinism, for both individuals and communities.

Likewise for corporations: living without a single-point forecast does not mean doing away with strategy. But strategy should not be based on a calculation for closing the gap between a corporation's single vision of what it wants to be and a single prediction of what the future environment might force it to be. That kind of strategic planning got many companies into trouble during recent decades. When their predictions of the future proved false, their plans for realizing their visions proved useless. Look at the Detroit auto companies that expected low fuel prices, then got creamed by the Japanese and the Germans who had small, fuel-efficient cars. Recall the case of IBM, whose planners expected a demand for fewer than 300,000 personal computers during the 1980's, when Apple and Compaq stole the market for PCs that turned out to be around 100 times larger than IBM's forecast.

Single-point forecasts are as risky for corporations as singular, all-consuming goals are for individuals. Because time is real, and the future unpredictable, the challenge of carving a path into the future calls for a different way of thinking than the old, mechanical methods of strategic planning. In order to anticipate wholly new industries like the personal computer industry, it's not enough to make predictions based on old assumptions. You need to imagine alternative scenarios based on new assumptions. Those new assumptions need more than new numbers. It would not have been enough for IBM's executives to double or triple their estimate from 300,000 up to nearly a million. They still would have missed the significance of the PC revolution. They needed a qualitatively new way of thinking about computing. They needed a new paradigm for computing, one that values decentralized control over the desktop more highly than the power and speed of the centralized mainframe.

Fresh thinking about the future calls for alternative scenarios based on new assumptions that differ from the old, not just quantitatively but qualitatively. A coherent set of qualitatively new assumptions amounts to a new paradigm, a new way of looking at something we thought we knew. The creators of the personal computer industry had a new way of thinking about computing. Hence they saw an alternative scenario for the future of the PC, a scenario that was invisible to the executives at IBM. Alternative scenarios are often driven by new paradigms. For another example illustrating the relationship between paradigm shifts and qualitatively distinct scenarios, consider the challenge of anticipating a new regime in the future of telecommunications.

I recall a meeting in Paris in January 1988. The leaders of the world's telecommunications industry gathered for a meeting to plan the deregulation of telecommunications. Directors of strategic planning, senior vice-presidents, high–level government officials, several chairmen and presidents of technology companies or research institutes assembled from Belgium, England, France, Germany, Japan, and United States.

Over the course of two very intense days, 51 speakers revealed their very different perspectives. What became blatantly apparent was the inadequacy of the old distinctions between the public sector and the private sector, between state control and competitive markets, and between a regulated industry and an unregulated industry. Many of the major actors knew they had a lot to lose as long as we remained in the age of incompatibility. Plainly this diversity of standards is a bad joke, the twentieth century version of the nineteenth-century scenario in which different train companies ran on different gauges of railroad track. You couldn't travel long distances without cumbersome transfers from one railroad line to another, each one as quaint as the next. Then we left it to monopolies to gobble up the competition and impose their own standards. But if you hand over a vital public service to a private monopoly, you risk the return of robber barons who can extract any rent they desire for communications services that have no competition. This is what worries people about Bill Gates and Microsoft.

In the new millennium we face a dilemma: monopoly control is no longer an idea in good favor, but neither is government control. Countries are moving toward the privatization of publicly controlled telecommunications systems, mainly because government monopolies tend to become as slow–moving and inefficient as the U.S. postal system. In an era when time is money, private companies have mastered the use of new technologies more quickly than government bureaucrats could switch from typewriters to word processors. So no one wants to entrust the rapid deployment of new information and telecommunications technology to central governments or publicly sanctioned private monopolies. Only the sizzle of competition will keep pace with the crackle of new communications.

Having said that, no one wants to leave communications up to a band of competing companies with competing systems either. Then we're back to the inconvenience of different railroad gauges. Unlike the clothing industry, where diversity is obviously preferable to dressing everyone in the same size of the same uniform, in the world of communications some degree of uniformity is essential. Who wants a telephone so stylish and unique that it can't talk to any other telephones? The very idea of a universal communications system that lets anyone talk to anyone seems to require something like government control or private monopoly. But neither of these traditional approaches is acceptable. So what is to be done?

This puzzle was the focus of this gathering on the future of telecommunications: how to gain the efficiencies of common standards without handing the whole game over to governments or private monopolies? The world needs something close to a single communications system. But what will it be, and who will run it? How will it be capitalized, and to whom will the rent be charged? What is the best pipeline, satellites or fiber optic cable? Where in the system will the intelligence available from microprocessors be located—in centralized mainframe computers, in distributed networks of very clever personal computers, or in the switches of the communications network itself?

No wonder that, halfway through the second day of this conference, Midhat Gazale, President of AT&T France, declared, "We need a new paradigm for telecommunications." Monsieur Gazale was saying, in effect, that we need a whole new approach to telecommunications. The old models won't work. Neither regulated state monopolies run by the public sector, nor competitive businesses in the private sector can do the job. We need a new model. And that is the original meaning of this word *paradigm:* a model or exemplar. A new paradigm is another way of getting at the concept of a new set of beliefs organizing modern life.

FROM THE OLD PARADIGM TO A NEW WORLDVIEW

A paradigm is a way of seeing that is shared by many people over many years. A paradigm shift is a radical change in the way a society sees the things that shape every part of life. A paradigm shift changes the way we look at the so-called facts. For example, what counts as real health or real prosperity? Does the gross domestic product (GDP) accurately represent the facts about our economy? Does the absence of disease as recognized by the American Medical Association adequately represent real health?

Common sense tells us that knowledge is the result of combinations of facts and that our organs of perception pipe those facts, undistorted, from the world "out there" to our minds "in here." But common sense always lags the paradigm–breaking discoveries being made in laboratories and universities. Lettvin, Maturana, McCulloch, and Pitts wrote a famous article entitled "What the Frog's Eye Tells the Frog's Brain." The frog's eye is constructed so as to sort out the straight paths of insects in flight and ignore the curved paths of what is less likely to be lunch. As for higher levels of perception and intelligence, we know too much about our capacity for self-deception to share a naïve faith in the accuracy of our perceptions.

Paradigms are a bit like myths in being both pervasive and formative. Myths structure the lives of those who embrace them. Myths are far more powerful than the quaint fictions they are sometimes taken to be. It is part of the pretension of the eighteenth-century Enlightenment to imagine that modern rationality has transcended mythological thinking. But this ideal of undistorted rationality could just as well be characterized as the myth of mythlessness.

Like lenses that are invisible to the eyes that see through them, myths are not recognized as myths in their own times. The ancient Greeks did not think of their stories about Zeus and Athena and Hermes as *myths*, at least not in the sense that we use the term myths to mean fictions.

To appreciate the abiding power of myths we would do better to confront contemporary myths, as does James Oliver Robertson in *American Myth, American Reality*. Robertson defines myth to mean something very close to paradigm.

> Myths are stories; they are attitudes extracted from stories; they are "the way things are" as people in a particular society believe them to be; and they are the models people refer to when they try to understand their world and its behavior. Myths are the patterns—of behavior, of belief, and of perception—which people have in common. Myths are not deliberately, or necessarily consciously, fictitious.[1]

Thomas Berry picks up on the notion of stories, and describes our current situation as a time "between stories."

> It's all a question of story. We are in trouble just now because we do not have a good story. We are in between stories. The Old Story— the account of how the world came to be and how we fit into it—is not functioning properly, and we have not learned the New Story. The Old Story sustained us for a long period of time. It shaped our emotional attitudes, provided us with life purpose, energizing action. It consecrated suffering, integrated knowledge, guided education. We awoke in the morning and knew where we were. We could answer the questions of our children. We could identify crime, punish criminals. Everything was taken care of because the story was there. It did not make men good, it did not take away the pains and stupidities of life, or make for unfailing warmth in human association. But it did provide a context in which life could function in a meaningful manner.[2]

Where Thomas Berry talks about the Old Story and the New Story, I'll speak more often of the *old paradigm* and, in place of the new paradigm, which no one has yet articulated, I'll speak of the *relational worldview.* Why *relational?* Three reasons: First, at the heart of the difference between the old paradigm and this new worldview is a shift in focus from things and substances to relationships and structures. It is as basic as the difference between a Euclidean geometry that sees a line as the shortest distance between two given points, and a Hilbertian geometry that sees a point as resulting from the intersection of two lines. The old paradigm starts with the dots, then tries to connect the dots in patterns of secondary relationships. The relational worldview starts with the relationships and interprets the points in the context of their relationships.

The second reason for choosing the term *relational* to describe this worldview is to highlight its difference from relativism. While the relational worldview is pluralistic—tolerant of different values—it is not relativistic to the point of allowing any and all values. The Achilles' heel of pluralism is the danger of sliding down a slippery slope to (im)moral relativism. Once you abandon the old absolutes, once you let go of that old–time religion that's supposed to guide everyone everywhere, then what's to stop you from allowing anything anywhere? Relativism separates one from another. What's good for you is good for you; what's good for me is good for me. If ever we chance to meet, so be it, but nothing says that we owe each other anything. Relativism breeds indifference and disconnectedness. The relational worldview features our connectedness, our relatedness. It is precisely in our relationships that we find the rationales for both our differences and our identities. Just as a man and a woman can love one another across the difference of genders and find common ground in the identity of their relationship, so different cultures can retain their differences in the face of homogenizing globalization, yet find common cause in their identity as members of a human species sharing a common ecology.

Difference and identity, relatedness versus relativism—these sound like very abstract ideas until we see them acted out in the concrete struggles between peoples with different worldviews. Much of this book is devoted to making the connections between the ways these ideas have led to tragic conflicts in the past, and how changes in the ways these ideas are being developed on the forefront of the human sciences can help us use those revised ideas to build better futures.

The third reason for choosing the word *relational* for this new worldview is its timeliness. A quarter century ago I tried to introduce the idea of relational thinking.[3] But it was before its time—the occupational hazard of future-oriented thinking. Now I see the word *relational* popping up in others' writings,[4] so I'd like to think that the phrase *relational worldview* is right for these times.

Timing is everything. Part of the problem with the Old Story's way of connecting the dots was its claim to universal reach across all times despite its very particular, even parochial, origins in eighteenth–century Europe. The Enlightenment paradigm purported to replace primitive superstitions with the One True Story for all time. But there are many stories for making sense of the past and present, and many scenarios for the future. The One True Story proposed by the rationalists of the Enlightenment leaves out the abiding differences we find in a multicultural world. Ignoring those differences gets us in trouble when it comes to conflicts among different values.

VALUES IN A PLURALISTIC WORLD

Perhaps the most significant part of the paradigm shift unfolding before our changing eyes involves a change in the way we think about values. There was a time when teachers like Plato and Jesus and Mohammed taught us that values were beyond our choosing. They were altogether beyond the realm of change, partaking, as Plato said, of Being rather than mere Becoming. Or they were God–given, like the Ten Commandments. In any case, they were eternal, fixed, and far beyond man or woman ever to change by an act of will. As Plato argued in *The Republic*, justice was not a function of the ephemeral will of the stronger. Justice, in order to be a real value, must transcend the whims of tyrants. Not a bad idea. No wonder it prevailed for many centuries.

But Platonism and Christianity are on the run in the modern world. They still have millions of adherents, and with Islam included, the ranks of fundamentalists rise to the billions. But among most thoughtful people (e.g., tens of millions of college graduates) there is something quaint and old-fashioned about the very idea that there is some great blueprint in the sky that fixes the difference between right and wrong once and forever for everyone everywhere. Morality isn't like mathematics. It's more like art. Yes, there's a difference between the beautiful and the ugly, but fixed rules are hard to come by, and tastes change over time and across cultures.

From the perspective of the Old Story, this demotion of ethics from the realm of universal science has the unhappy consequence of relegating morals to little more than private opinions. The old paradigm makes a series of sharp distinctions between facts and values, the objective and the subjective, the given and the merely opined. And if values can't take their stand solidly on the ground of objective truths knowable by science, then they devolve into subjective relativism: "I like what I like, you like what you like. Whatever . . ."

Of course this is nonsense. No society can survive a bunch of whimsical, selfish, short-sighted me-firsters. Hedonism does not a social order make. Just look at crack addicts and the chaos in our inner cities. Nothing could be more obvious than the fact that individual human beings need some restraints on their impulses if they are to come together in anything resembling a civil society. What is not at all obvious is the source of legitimacy for those restraints. Does the source of that legitimacy lie in Plato's realm of eternal Ideas, in the will of Allah, in the consent of the governed, or in the laws of nature? What gives values their force? Why should we feel obliged to honor a given value such as honesty? Because our mothers told us to?

These are not simple questions. To answer them we need to dig even deeper than we already dig when trying to figure out whether one value or another is most important in a given instance, say, whether honesty or loyalty to a friend should rank higher when that friend breaks a law and you've been asked to give evidence. Morality is easy for zealots and simpletons. For the rest of us, values are complex constructions that don't usually fit together according to simple rules for assembly. Honesty strains against tact, courage struggles against prudence, ambition conflicts with modesty, and so on. Particular moral quandaries are hard enough; finding the source of legitimacy for morals in general is even harder, especially when the old paradigm forces hard distinctions that leave no room for the ambiguities that are intrinsic to moral conflicts.

As individuals trying to get along with our immediate neighbors, and as members of an increasingly multicultural society, we need a deeper understanding of *ethical pluralism*. The path of ethical pluralism wanders among all forms of absolutism—whether Platonic, Christian, Muslim, or scientific—on the one hand, and the pernicious relativism to which we children of the Enlightenment are heirs, on the other hand. The problem with pluralistic values is one of *ethical inflation:* too many values chasing too few goods, and, consequently, a devaluing of values in general. So it falls to us in our secular, postmodern, pluralistic times to undertake what the philosopher-poet Friedrich Nietzsche foretold as a *revaluation of all values.* Toward the end of this book I'll use the lenses of the relational worldview to take a new look at norms and a fresh look at values. The objective is to defend pluralism without sinking into relativistic amorality. We need a pluralism that is genuinely *ethical.*

SCENARIO PLANNING

Scenario planning is the third pillar on which this book stands, the first being a description of the current paradigm shift to a relational worldview, and the second, ethical pluralism. Scenario planning is a technique for steering ourselves and our institutions toward better futures—not the best future, not a single utopia, but one of several possible futures suggested by a pluralistic ethic.

Scenario planning turns out to be one of the best tools for drawing out the social creativity of communities. Scenarios are stories—narratives with beginnings, middles, and ends. As such they can provide us with the kind of New Story that Thomas Berry imagines. Normative scenarios—stories about what *ought* to happen—can offer new ways to think about the private sector and the public sector. Privatization has been a very popular idea in recent decades. From the demise of Communism to the privatization of communications, people are discovering that there are a lot of jobs that governments don't do very well. Marketplace mechanisms seem to be better at satisfying needs and allocat-

ing scarce resources. But are we ready for the privatization of everything? Health care? Education? Prisons? National security?

What are the limits of privatization? Are there things that markets
cannot do? These are some of the questions for which scenarios can be
useful as they help us think ahead and see the results of actions that
might have looked like a good idea at the time . . . but then yield unintended consequences we don't like at all. As this book goes to press,
Californians are suffering sky-rocketing prices for electricity and natural gas as the result of the deregulation of their utilities. The current crisis with its rolling blackouts could have been avoided. Scenario planning
can amount to something like anticipatory disaster relief. Much better
to rehearse a disaster in your mind and thus avoid it than to live through
it to learn from it. I'm reminded of a friend whose wife asked him, "Dear,
can we afford another 'learning experience'?"

Scenario planning differs from other ways of steering organizations.
One of the old ways relies on tradition. As our forefathers managed, so
shall we manage. Islam and Confucianism provide examples of such traditionalism. Modern industrial societies have adopted another method
of steering. Assuming that progress is possible, that the future can be
better than the past, modern planners have often assumed that, with
enough Enlightenment science in the budget, the future can be predicted
and/or controlled. Scenario planning is based on a contrary assumption,
that the future cannot be predicted and that belief in the possibility of
total control is a dangerous delusion. Because all things are interrelated,
you'll never keep surprises in one part of the universe from affecting
some other part you're trying to control.

Scenario planning breaks sharply from the kind of strategic planning
that starts with a single-point forecast of the future—a single prediction—and then tries to control things well enough to win in that future.
True to the Enlightenment paradigm from which it derives, this older
form of strategic planning makes an overly sharp distinction between
the objective facts in the external environment, and the internal wishes,
wants, and aspirations of an institution—what is often referred to as its
vision. This older form of strategic planning consists primarily in pre-
dicting the future, shaping a vision, then plotting the steps to fulfill that
vision in the context of the future as predicted.

Consider a concrete example in miniature: planning tomorrow's hike.
If you know it's going to rain, but you want to go anyway, take rain
gear. If you know it's going to be sunny, take sunscreen. Your internal
"vision" is to take a hike. The external environment includes weather

over which you have no control but which, presumably, you can predict. The fulfillment of your internal vision will require you to equip yourself for the external environment that science, in the person of the weatherman, has predicted.

Corporations go through similar reasoning when deciding, say, to develop a new product line. What will be the size of the total available market for a new widget? Let's conduct some scientific market research. What share of that market are competitors likely to take? Call in some consultants to conduct a rigorous competitive analysis. How many widgets does it then make sense for us to produce? Just run the numbers for the business case.

As reasonable as this sort of reflection may sound, it is based on fundamentally faulty assumptions, the first being that the future is predictable. Who predicted the fall of the Berlin Wall? Who can predict even the weather? Scenario planning is based on the assumption that the future is not predictable. Unlike traditional belief systems like Islam and Confucianism, however, scenario planning assumes that the future will *not* be like the past. Therefore, in thinking ahead over the long term, as a sense of responsibility demands, we need to think about several possible futures, not just one. We need a strategy for all seasons, not just one.

That strategy may require us to change our vision in light of changes in the external environment. The so-called external and internal are not so clearly independent of one another. Indeed, if our vision is truly remarkable, and our energy sufficient, we may succeed in significantly altering that environment, possibly for the worse. Rather than assuming that the environment is so external that we have no control over it, we need to assume responsibility for the degree to which our acts can influence the environment. We need to think hard enough about our acts that we do not provoke unintended consequences that might run contrary to our wishes, as through the overharvesting of fisheries and forests so that further harvests are reduced.

Once you assume some responsibility for steering—and this responsibility for steering is at the very heart of human freedom—then the ethical dimension of planning becomes obvious. Once we acknowledge the future is not predictable, it is not enough to create a set of scenarios for what *might* happen altogether independent of our will. Once we see that we're part of the picture, that the internal and the external are not that distinct, then it is incumbent upon us to conceive at least some scenarios of what *ought* to happen. And at this point ethical pluralism is es-

sential lest we fall into one of these equal and opposite errors: on the
one hand, arrogantly imposing some absolute standard; on the other
hand, abdicating ethics altogether and settling for pernicious relativism.

This is how the parts fit together. The relational worldview supports
ethical pluralism. That ethical pluralism gives meaning to the norms that
guide normative scenarios. Without troubling to consider the relational
worldview, normative scenarios would run the risk of depending on the
same old heavy–handed morality that led utopians and their followers
into so much trouble. We now know better than to trust people pushing the One True Path to the best future. But without normative scenarios that articulate the shared hopes of a community, we risk adopting a pernicious relativism where anything goes. Without hope, the
people perish.

PLAN OF THE BOOK

Having given this preview of where the trail is leading, and having out-
lined the three main ideas—the paradigm shift to a relational worldview,
ethical pluralism, and scenario planning—let me offer a brief overview
of how the rest of the book is structured. The five parts are titled *New
Game; New Players; New Lenses; New Rules, New Tools;* and finally,
Scenario Planning in Action. Part One, *New Game,* sets the stage by
showing how the political "game" is giving way to an economic "game."
The second chapter offers an interpretation of the end of left–wing politics (e.g., the fall of Communism) not as a swing to the Right by the
old political pendulum, but as the replacement of the pendulum by the
digital watch of the new information economy. Lest we rush toward the
privatization of everything, however, Chapter 3 looks at "The Limits of
the Marketplace"—what markets cannot do—and concludes that those
industries that labor under a mandate to universal service, such as communications, education, and health care, call out for some regulation by
the public sector. The problem is that once you've moved from the political game to the economic game, governments suffer a loss of legitimacy as many believe the market may be more democratic than the ballot box. Chapter 4, "Rethinking Representative Government," calls for
a new approach to democratic representation, one that is informed
by what we've learned about representation in the philosophy of
knowledge.

Once Part One, *New Game,* has set the stage in terms of the shift to
an economic game in which politics is only as powerful as the Church

was in the political game, then Part Two, *New Players,* locates the primary sources of agency in the economic arena. When the main game was politics, the major conflicts pitted the rights of individuals against the power of the collective, Right against Left, conservative versus liberal, Republican against Democrat. In the New Game, where the marketplace takes the foreground and politics slips into the background, new players take to the field. You don't send a baseball slugger out onto a football field. Likewise, the shift from the game of politics to the game of economics calls for different players. The marketplace does not pit individuals against collectives; now it's team versus team. Part Two is about this change in the roster: not individualistic free agents, not the entire human species, but teams, groups, communities, corporations.

Who are the main players in the making of history? Is it the individuals we've come to know and love in the Western libertarian tradition (Chapter 5, "Beyond Individualism and Collectivism")? Is it the entire human species, or the collective so idealized by Oriental cultures and Marxist ideology? Or could it be that communities—not one, not all, but *some*—are the subjects and agents of history? Chapter 6, "Social Forces and Creativity," challenges the American myth of the rebellious individual, the familiar tale of heroic individualism. Without wishing to discount the courage of many heroes and heroines, in those pages I reinterpret those acts in the context of a worldview that gives credit where it is due: to the communities and cultures that motivate and give meaning to those acts of heroism.

The burden of Part Two, *New Players,* is to show that the real heroes of history are groups and communities—more than one, less than all. *The social philosophy of some,* as I call it, is a story about the way creativity can reside in a group, not just in the soul of the solitary, romantic genius. Novelist Ken Kesey was fond of asking the question, Whose movie is this anyway? Social philosophy asks an equivalent fundamental question, Who is the subject of history? Is it solitary individuals who come together later to form groups? Or is it the entire species, which only occasionally extrudes "individuals"? Are social classes the subjects of history, as Marx thought? Or are our genes, our language, or our cultures the creators of history? Whose movie is this? *The social philosophy of some* makes the case for groups—companies or communities—as the primary agents of history.

Throughout Part Two, the story builds by borrowing bits and pieces from leading-edge research in psychology, sociology, and political theory. We have what it takes to make better futures, but we have to as-

semble the tools we need to build better futures. Part Three is about
New Lenses. The old game and the old players relied on a set of ideas
and processes that need to be updated for the new game and the new
players. Chapter 7, "From Worldviews to Better Worlds," tells the tale
of what is right and what is wrong about much of the talk about paradigms: what they are, how they shift, why it took so long for Americans to understand this very old idea, and how it is that many still get
it wrong. After separating the wheat from the chaff in all the talk about
paradigms, Chapter 8, "The Features of the Relational Worldview," takes
an inventory of new developments in anthropology, literary criticism,
and philosophy to show how the old laws-and-causes paradigm is shifting toward a more interpretive worldview, one that reads cultures the
way critics read texts. By harvesting leading–edge discoveries in the human sciences, we can assemble the pieces of a relational worldview that
can steer a course between overzealous fundamentalism on the one hand
and listless nihilism on the other.

Part Four, *New Rules, New Tools,* begins with a chapter on values—
how to hold one's own dear while letting others hold theirs dear. This
is important for the overall argument because we need a worldview that
will allow both passion and pluralism. If our passions derive only from
absolutism and monotheistic faith, then we'll have real trouble getting
along with one another in a multicultural world. If, on the other hand,
our pluralism is so permissive that it empties out into a flatland of indifference, then we'll have trouble getting out of bed in the morning.

What makes a better future "better"? When religion ruled, the will
of God provided the ultimate source for moral authority. When politics
ruled, might made right; moral history was written by the victors. Now
that the game has shifted from politics to economics, we are in danger
of knowing the price of everything but the value of nothing. When the
main game is economics, where is there a source of value that transcends
economic values set by the market? Chapter 9, "Facts, Values, and Scenario Planning," uses the features of the relational worldview to give
shape to a genuinely pluralistic ethic. After all, if it's better futures we're
after, we need to know the criteria we'd use to determine that one future was better than another. And in a pluralistic, multicultural world,
coming up with an answer to that question is not easy. Ultimately, the
moral fulcrum for lifting the better over the worse turns out to be *the
shared hopes of a community.* This is why it was important to show in
Part Two, *New Players,* how groups—companies and communities—
serve as the creative agents of historical change.

The concluding chapters pull together the several lines of argument running throughout the book. The moral fulcrum for prying a better future away from the actual present is to be found in the shared hopes of a community, as articulated through the process of scenario planning, using the new tools of a new worldview. Chapter 10, "Scenario Planning: A Tool for Social Creativity," shows how the practice of scenario planning elicits the shared hopes of a community that will serve as a moral fulcrum.

Finally, Part Five, *Scenario Planning in Action,* applies the tool to reflections on health, education, and politics. There I offer some hints for creating normative scenarios, value-laden scenarios for what *ought* to be. Specifically, I'll use what we learn about representation in the theory of knowledge to revise our view of representation in politics.

For those who decide whether or not to read a book by flipping through its footnotes, later chapters show the intellectual origins and name some of the sources for a number of the ideas I've used to build this book. Since those chapters will be of interest mainly to academics and intellectuals who like some scholarly heavy lifting, I've placed them toward the back where busy executives won't have to wade through them to get to the good stuff. In Chapters 6–10 you'll find the evidence and the justification for some of the sweeping generalizations I make in Chapters 2 and 3 in order to get the book off to a faster start. Those who want the treasure but lack the patience to read the map may want to skip from Chapter 5 to Chapter 11 for an accelerated read.

There, then, is a sketch of the argument this book will make. It is not that difficult an argument when taken step by step, but neither is it simple. It has many steps, a lot of supporting evidence, many examples, and several important implications, the most significant of which should be pretty obvious: we will get the future we deserve! It's largely (though not entirely) up to us. This thing called human history is something we're making up as we go along. We can do it well or we can do it poorly. The decisions we make *will* make a difference. Even if our different cultures cannot agree on every aspect of the difference between right and wrong, or a single ideal of the *best* future—utopia—we can all agree that there is a difference between better and worse, and we can all aspire to better futures.

Part One
New Game

CHAPTER TWO

RELIGIOUS, POLITICAL,
AND ECONOMIC PASSIONS

Back in the fabled sixties, many of us felt that politics were important. Social justice ranked high on our list of priorities, and political institutions seemed to be the right targets for our efforts. The bright kids in school didn't go into business. They chose teaching or the professions or God knows what. Anything but *business!*

Now the best and the brightest are getting MBAs, and many of us who spurned business have found our way into the corporate world. For some this seems like a swerve on the path. Nay, a sell out. For others the suit still feels like a costume, and they themselves feel like infiltrators in a place they don't belong. This kind of cognitive dissonance is not good for people. It is frustrating and deadening. Too much energy is wasted on denial, and there is too little energy left for playful creativity or passionate dedication.

I would like to make a defense for the worthiness of business. My defense will be bold—no mumbling about working from within, as if the corporate world were still regarded as an enemy whose ranks we must infiltrate. Nor will I attempt a defense of the ideological correctness of corporate work, as if politics were the only court of appeal for corporate legitimacy. Instead I'll make a case based on the broad sweep of a philosophy of history. I'll suggest that political ideology no longer provides an adequate foundation for claims to corporate legitimacy or illegitimacy. Or, to put the point in more extreme terms, political ideology must now go the way of religious theology when it comes to justifying our career choices. The arena in which businesses—and their employees—can find their legitimacy is an economic arena partly of their own making.

Does this mean that the defense of the legitimacy of business is a bootstrap—even self-serving—operation? Yes and no. Yes, but only in as much as political legitimacy was best defended by its own self-making through the invention of the nation-state and the historical development of civil society. Attempts at legitimation based on a religious rhetoric of the divine right of kings were ultimately self-defeating. So, likewise, I want to liberate the defense of business from an obsolete political rhetoric. No, this defense is not entirely self-contained in a tight circle of self-justification, for it requires an independent view of history that would convincingly demonstrate the near obsolescence of most political ideology.

Maybe it was my contrarian nature, maybe it was my (mistaken) certainty that I would spend my life as a poorly paid professor of philosophy, but I never shared my academic friends' disdain for business. I remember scandalizing a Nietzsche seminar I was teaching at Yale by telling them that the closest approximations to Nietzsche's supermen today were investment bankers—the characters that Tom Wolfe called "Masters of the Universe" in *Bonfire of the Vanities*. Talk about will to power! Investment bankers now wield the kind of power that political leaders held most recently, and religious leaders before them.

Theology meant a lot once upon a time. When Constantine converted to Christianity, he tipped the axis of history. Prior to the Reformation, the popes were in the driver's seat of history. Questions about the allocation of resources were decided on advice from the scriptures. The best education was found in the monasteries. The Church was the dominant institution in society.

People will continue to vote, as they continue to pray. But the real action has moved from the ballot box to the marketplace, just as it once moved from the cathedral to the town hall. The older institutions do not die; they just recede in historical significance.

It is like a sea change, or a shift in the tectonic plates. The figures in the foreground remain the same—churches still dot the landscape, and governments go about their daily business—but beneath all of the visible hubbub there has been a shift as fundamental as the Reformation. It is called privatization. The public sector is ceding power to the private sector.

There's a vocabulary people use for talking about these epochal changes: "from the modern era to the postmodern era." Enter *postmodern* in your Amazon.com search and you'll come up with dozens of entries. For many readers, one more treatise on postmodernism is bound to elicit a monstrous yawn. Been there, already read about that. And what's worse, the very name looks backward toward the modernism we've left rather than forward to better futures. One more treatise about postmodernism would take us forward into the new millennium with our eyes fixed firmly on the rearview mirror toward the modernity to which we're *post*. What's even worse: There is now a certain world-weariness associated with the very idea of postmodernism. It connotes the exhaustion of modernity, a tiredness, a cynicism about proud but callow aspirations toward modern progress.

So rather than talking a lot about a postmodern era or a postmodern consciousness, I'm going to focus on a relational worldview and the mood of the millennium. In this next section I want to clarify what I mean by a new millennial worldview by comparing and contrasting my ideas with what others have said about postmodernism.

THIS POSTMODERN BUSINESS

The title, "This Postmodern Business," is ambiguous—as are most things postmodern. Is the subject to be business in the postmodern era? Or is the subject to be this business—in the theatrical sense of a choreography of gestures—called postmodernism?

The answer is, of course, both. As citizens of a new millennium, we want to know something about the intellectual currents moving our time. We want to catch the momentum of history. And as businesspeople we need to know about those deep currents that are changing the tastes of our customers and the needs of our employees; we must keep abreast of the changing technologies of production and the changing structures of organization. For all four of these areas of change—consumption, work, technology, and organization—reading the mood of the millennium and differentiating it from postmodernism is important.

What are the defining features of so-called postmodernism, at least as the term is used in literary criticism? A sense of irony? A rhetoric of indirection? A lack of linearity? A preference for narrative in place of theory? A playful evasion of the literal that at times amounts to an escape from reality? All of these elements and more are reflected in the passage from modernism to postmodernism.

The features of the postmodern worldview aren't just in our heads. When people *see* differently, they do things differently. And then the things they do, and the way they do them, become what we see. So it goes: Philosophers call it "the hermeneutic circle." People see as people do, and people then do as people see. Seeing is believing, but there are some things you just can't see unless you believe them. Believing leads to seeing.

FROM THE IDEA OF PROGRESS TO HISTORICAL DRIFT

It is now fashionable to affirm that history is going nowhere. There is no preordained path of "development," no single ladder on which cultures can be ranked as higher or lower. To the contrary, the very idea of a single universal history is thought to be the self-serving invention of Western historians.

The attack on the idea of progress has two separate components, both of which have import for business. The first is an attack on cultural bias toward your own people, otherwise known as ethnocentrism. The second challenges the idea of progress altogether.

The charge of ethnocentrism is hardly new. What *is* new are the intellectual foundations added by anthropologists and others who are saying that the so-called underdeveloped cultures of the "Third World" are not necessarily "less developed" along a trajectory defined by European culture. They are simply on different trajectories. They are not lower down on *our* ladder. They are long ways up ladders that are *other*.

This challenge has several implications for business. In the realm of marketing it poses a direct threat to Theodor Levitt's ideas about global marketing. If we are all parties to a single Universal History, then it makes perfect sense for those furthest along the trajectory to pave the earth with products that are mass-produced, marketed with identical packaging, and advertised using identical slogans and appeals around the world, as Levitt recommends. If, on the contrary, different countries and cultures are on different trajectories, then it would make sense to consider each cultural segment of the global market and adopt more of a niche-marketing strategy. The same products might still be marketed the world over, but minor variations in production, such as slight changes in the taste of soft drinks, could be introduced. Information technology already allows for shorter production runs without sacrificing economies of scale, so the same brands can be customized to different cultures.

The second component of the attack on the idea of progress puts at risk the whole idea of economic development. If history is seen as a disease and the compulsion to progress as a neurosis,[1] then "modern conveniences" are Trojan horses whose appeal only conceals the agents of destruction of traditional ways of life. This disaffection from progress is part of postmodernism. This disaffection is also the part of postmodernism that invites a disaffection from postmodernism and calls for a new way of describing the mood of the millennium. The disaffection from progress will gain strength from its systematic interconnection with other features of postmodernism. And as it gains strength it will lessen the appeal of the "new and improved," making new product introductions more difficult. The value of well–established brands will increase. If so-called progress is too disorienting for traditionalists, they'll revert to that old–time religion and those old familiar brands. Coca-Cola isn't just colored sugar water: it represents stability in a turbulent world.

FROM THE RISE OF SCIENCE TO POST-SCIENTIFIC INQUIRY

The rise of modern science is another feature of modernity. Politicians and scientists may have replaced popes and priests in the driver's seat of history, but religion has hardly disappeared from the face of the earth. And the stubbornness with which religious fundamentalism hangs on in the face of science must give some indication of the inadequacy of a wholly secular worldview that is neither morally nor psychologically satisfying.

As effective as science may be at manipulating our physical environment to satisfy material needs, it has little to offer when it comes to giving meaning to life. Science gives us the means to realize ends, but it has no way of determining those ends. Science can tell us what we need—the physical necessities of life, our minimal daily requirements. But science cannot tell us what we *want*, or what a better way of life wants from us—what we *ought* to be and do.

These postmodern criticisms of science are not entirely new. They have been uttered by priests, poets, and philosophers for centuries. What is new is the shift from premodern reaction to postmodern critique. The romantic resistance to science makes the nostalgic mistake of denying science's truth value, as in the creationists' denial of evolution. The postmodern critique can accept science's achievements and its truth value on its own turf; it simply limits science's turf and acknowledges that, beyond that limit, other ways of knowing may be required. Call it religion, call it spirituality, or, if orthodox religions seem too superstitious to swallow, call it an intuitive, empathetic way of knowing.

The epistemology (the theory of knowledge) of both postmodernism and the relational worldview is still in formation, but some of its outlines are becoming increasingly clear. Rather than requiring a clear sep-

aration of subjective knower from objective facts, it accepts an intimacy
with the objects of knowledge, the involvement of the participant–
observer rather than the distance of purely objective, value-free inquiry.

Of course it would be a mistake to deny the virtues of unbiased re-
porting, objectivity, or methodological rigor in the laboratory. But
where human beings are concerned, there is a growing recognition of
the need for narratives in addition to facts, stories in addition to theories, if the human drama is to be usefully or adequately portrayed and
understood. And when it comes to inspiring hopes for better futures,
here's where scenarios, since they are *stories,* do a better job than theories of social change. Part of the appeal of premodern religions to the
postmodern mind may lie not so much in *what* those religions say about
the human condition as in *how* they say it—with myths and stories.

There is more to the postmodern critique of science than the opposition between objective distance and intimate participation, or the opposition between abstract theories and narrative stories. There is also an
opposition between an analytic approach that divides the world into its
smallest parts and a synthetic approach that tries to see the world as an
organic whole. Each of these oppositions plays into a further critique of
science for the havoc its technological tools have wreaked on the natural environment.

It is becoming increasingly clear that the damage inflicted on the natural environment is not just the result of a few unhappy accidents, a few
unintended side effects. The postmodern critique of the scientific worldview has identified in scientism a systematic and pervasive inability to
see things whole, to look for relationships, the tissue of interconnections
that constitute an ecology—the complexity of things.

FROM INDUSTRIAL MASS MANUFACTURING
TO THE KNOWLEDGE ECONOMY

Apart from the ravages inflicted on the environment by heavy industry
and consumerism, there are other reasons for moving beyond industrial
mass production. Information technology allows it and aesthetics demand it. In the use of information technology for flexible manufacturing, postmodern business meets postmodern aesthetics.

Postmodernity is a symbol–infested world filled with signs of signs
of signs . . . This symbolic universe does not function according to the
laws of physics but according to the laws of grammar and semantics.
What's more, there are real doubts about the degree to which these sym-

bols can be unambiguously tied down to a physical reality that stands beyond the realm of signs. Instead, one text is an interpretation of another text, one symbol a sign of another sign.

Unlike increasingly accurate measurements of some physical weight or length, interpretations do not necessarily converge on some single reality. Instead we make interpretations of interpretations without ever realizing our hope of reaching a foundational bedrock of non-symbolic reality.

An Indian tale illustrates the dilemma. An English gentleman is told that the world rests on a platform which rests on the back of an elephant which rests in turn on the back of a turtle. When the English man persists in asking what the turtle rests on, he is told, *another turtle*. And after that? "Ah, Sahib, after that it is turtles all the way down."[2]

In the postmodern worldview, it's interpretations all the way down with no bedrock of non-symbolic reality. Postmodern art and architecture both exhibit an ironic detachment from stolid functionality or steadfast representation. Narrow interpretations of utility give way to playful ornamentation in postmodern architecture, as in Robert Graves' references to Disney characters on his buildings in Orlando, Florida. Abhorrence of photographic representation gives way to ironic repetitions in postmodern art, as in Andy Warhol's repetitions of Marilyn Monroe's face. What is Reality? Who knows? And what's more important, who cares? The scientific quest for Truth has given way to a sometimes desperate, sometimes ironic, sometimes humorous search for *meaning*. But the meaning may be ambiguous, multiple, multifaceted. Physical things maintain their identity; they do not appear in two places at the same time. Symbols are inherently two-faced, like the statues of Janus. Symbols call out for multiple interpretations, while things invite the literalism of accurate measurement.

Postmodern art, architecture, and literary criticism are all in league to the extent that they occupy a symbolic space of meaning in addition to a literal space of physics with its mechanical pushes and pulls. To this extent they are also in league with the information revolution—the use of microprocessors and computers in the postmodern economy of information and services. Metal bending and mass production are yielding to information processing and services as the principal means of adding value in the postmodern, millennial economy.

The information and service sectors of the millennial economy are as different from the mass-manufacturing modern economy as postmodern art and criticism are from their modernist predecessors—and in some of the same ways. Instead of relying on the tool–and–die shop of mechanical reproduction, the postmodern arts rely on the rag–and–bone shop of the imagination. Instead of relying on literal repetition and slavish representation, the information and service sectors of the millennial economy call for innovation and customization to the different wishes and desires of different consumers.

In both aesthetics and information theory, the meaning of what is received depends as much on the consumer (receiver) as on the producer (sender). This dependency on the mental state of the receiver—as already informed or uninformed, literate or illiterate, interested or indifferent— is itself very different from the mass-produced commodity's relationship to its consumers. A ton of steel is a ton of steel, wherever, whenever, for whomever. Its nature has almost nothing to do with differences among consumers. What counts as art has everything to do with context, tradition, and the reception of specific receivers. And what counts as information has everything to do with what's news to specific hearers. What counts as information to one hearer will be redundancy to another who has already been informed.

This shift of emphasis from the producer to the consumer has profound implications for the conduct of business in a postmodern, millennial economy. Engineers were the heroes of the mass-manufacturing industrial economy. They increased productivity and lowered unit costs. In the knowledge economy, however, the niche marketing of differentiated products is the key to success. A niche marketing strategy calls for differences that make a difference in new product development, in packaging, in creating advertising messages that stand out from the clutter, and in choosing media that reach just the right segment of consumers. At each stage in the spectrum from producer to consumer, informed differentiation assures that the right messages about the right products reach the right consumers at the right time. This process of informed differentiation is the opposite of mass-manufacturing for a mass market.

Implicit in the shift from the mass market to niche markets is a shift from the modern to the millennial consumer. With each change in the structure of the macro-economy there is a corresponding shift in the micro-economics of the individual purchase decision. Rather than trying to keep up with the Joneses, rather than conforming to widely held fashions and assumptions about what it is to be (and look like) a successful human being, the postmodern, millennial consumer is more inclined to stand out rather than fit in.[3] The postmodern consumer is more of an individualist than the modern consumer.

Like the postmodern artist or architect, the millennial consumer re-gards the whole history of stylistic devices as fair game for contempo-rary expression. Rather than trying to keep up with what is most mod-ern, as if fashion were on some progressive trajectory worth following, the millennial consumer is more likely to mix and match bits and pieces from different eras or different ethnic traditions, just as a Robert Graves will adorn a building with a Doric column here, an art-deco gesture there, and a modern glass façade nearby. This eclecticism can extend from clothes to home furnishings to the construction of a life.

If there is a dark side to postmodernism, it lies in an inability to make commitments that are not tinged with irony. Postmodern man and woman are all dressed up with everywhere to go. They have costumes for every occasion, but no truly compelling reason to choose one occa-sion over another, one career over another, one life over another—and this, too, is what's wrong with taking "postmodern" as the last word about the mood of the millennium.

The postmodern self has lost touch with society. The social norms that bound the mass market into a semi-predictable whole have been loosened so that the individual is left to make it up as he or she goes along, or to conform to the norms of a subculture or cult. In reaction to the free fall of postmodernity, many timid souls latch onto premod-ern certainties. Fundamentalism is an entirely understandable reaction to postmodernism, more understandable than it looked in comparison to the sober and sensible Protestantism brought to us by the Reforma-tion and modernity.[4]

The popularity of evangelical Christianity serves as an index for an-other trend that is part and parcel of the information revolution: the growth of what can best be called *the experience industry*.[5] From the world of religion to the marketplace, it is clear that there is a growing thirst for vivid experiences—whatever makes the heart beat faster.

The appeal to gut experience is part of the information revolution. People don't go out shopping for bits and bytes. They purchase infor-mation, in part, in the form of vivid experiences. When consumers pay money for movies spiced with computer-created special effects, they don't really care that the monsters were produced on Pentium® chips. They just want a vivid experience at the movies.

The experience industry includes many of the fastest–growing parts of the millennial economy, from the travel and entertainment industries to an art-collecting scene that has witnessed phenomenal increases in prices for art. The experience industry has its dark side: addictions to vivid experiences from video games to narcotics. In each of its many manifestations, the growth of the experience industry represents a satiation with the stuff that the industrial revolution produced.

The quest for vivid experiences is part of the *sublimation of the economy*, part of the shift from the solid goods of the industrial economy to the intangibles known as information and services. But with this shift from goods to experiences, there is a corresponding shift in the appropriate mode of organization. Just as the decorum of the Catholic cathedrals and hierarchy has been challenged by the spread of gospel tents, so the organizational structure of the modern corporation is being challenged by new modes of organization in the information-intensive entrepreneurial start-ups.

IMPORT FOR ORGANIZATIONAL DESIGN

The shift from industrial mass production and mass marketing to niche marketing in an information and services economy calls for a corresponding shift in organizational structure. When the output changes from mass-manufactured goods to information and services, the fundamental production function changes from standardized repetition to innovation. If form is still to follow function, there must be a shift in organizational form from bureaucratic hierarchy to something else.

The shift away from hierarchy as the dominant organizational form is a systematic and pervasive feature of the new millennium. It is evident not only in individual companies, not only in the structure of the economy as a whole, but also in the character structure of the consumer.[6] While the modern consumer bought goods to adorn and express a more or less consistent and recognizable lifestyle, the millennial consumer plays with a mixed bag of goods and services in order to experience a series of oftentimes inconsistent identities.

The modern self was a hierarchy. As conceived and modeled by Freud, the modern self was structured and organized much like a modern corporation or a modern nation-state, with a single monarch—the ego—reigning over the rebellious desires and instincts of the id. The millennial self is less centralized. Rather than suffering an identity crisis on the way toward a single, stable identity, the millennial self is a series of rolling identity crises. Moving from job to job, career to career, marriage to marriage, the millennial self is less a stable substance than the node of shifting and changing relationships.

The shift from bureaucratic hierarchy—in the corporation, in the economy, and in the self—does not entail a decay into anarchy. The problem is not, as in anarchy, the absence of hierarchy, but rather, the proliferation of hierarchies. Following information theorist Warren McCulloch,[7] I like to call this proliferation of hierarchies a *heterarchy*. We each serve many masters. There is no single captain of the ship—not in the self, not in the corporation, not in society, not in the cosmos. Contrary to the fears of conspiracy theorists, *no one is in charge*.

Nietzsche once proclaimed that God is dead. By this statement he meant that European society was no longer organized according to the stable hierarchy of the Holy Roman Empire where the authority of the Pope symbolized a singular peak of a stable pyramid. The significance of Nietzsche's saying can now be extended from religion to politics and psychology: bureaucratic hierarchy is ailing if not altogether dead—in the Church, in the State, and in the structure of the millennial self.[8]

BEYOND THE NATION-STATE: FROM THE POLITICAL ERA TO THE ECONOMIC ERA

One of the crucial steps in the transition from the premodern to the modern world was the separation of Church and State. Along with the Reformation's restructuring of religious authority came a shift in the relationship between the religious and political orders. Religious leaders once occupied the driver's seat of history, but political leaders now assumed more control. While many of the basic functions of society—health, education, and welfare—had been in the hands of the Church in premodern times, modernity delegated these functions to the State.

With the transition from modernity to postmodernity, these same functions are moving out of the hands of the State toward the private sector. Corresponding to the separation of Church and State, we are now seeing a separation of state and corporation. The new reformation is called privatization. Like the Reformation and the separation of Church and State, the worldwide process of privatization represents a fundamental shift in the way societies allocate their scarce resources. Where the premodern church once dispensed scarce resources according to religious interpretations of divine grace and mercy, and the modern bureaucratic state dispensed resources according to varying weights of power and justice, the postmodern method for the allocation of scarce resources is the marketplace.

The history of transitions from the premodern to the modern to the postmodern eras can be described as a movement from a religious era to a political era, and from a political era to an economic era. This is not to say that the nation-state will disappear; indeed, the Church did not disappear in the transition from the religious era to the political era. I cannot over-emphasize that the shifts I'm describing—from a political logic toward an economic logic, from an industrial economy toward a knowledge economy, and so on—are not to be understood as radical discontinuities. Let's not overdramatize! I prefer the imagery of tectonic plates: deep, but slow–moving. Much of the old endures in the new. The Vatican still stands and the White House will endure. But the main arena for the allocation of resources has moved from the public sector to the private sector, just as it once moved from the altar to the throne.

These broad transitions help explain the spread of markets and privatization. The worldwide move toward privatization and the valorization of the marketplace represents much more than a periodic "swing to the Right" within the political arena. No pendulum will swing back toward the Left. Instead we are experiencing a long–term secular trend toward the gradual displacement of the political arena by the economic arena as the place where societies allocate their scarce resources. The political pendulum that swung from Left to Right is being replaced by the digital watch of an electronic economy.

One of the main reasons for the growth of the modern nation-state was the need for concentrations of military power as a means for mediating ideological differences and protecting scarce resources. For a variety of reasons, from the advent of nuclear weapons to changes in the nature of strategic resources from raw materials to information, the marketplace is replacing the military as a means of mediating differences and allocating scarce resources. This transition is part of the meaning of the movement from a predominantly political to a predominantly economic era.

Some people are disturbed by the rise of the almighty marketplace. In addition to obvious instances of crime and corruption, there is the feeling that values in general are shot to hell. They say there is a crisis of values, that the predominance of market mechanisms leaves us in a world where people know the price of everything and the value of nothing. Further, they say that the marketplace may be an efficient means for distributing private goods, but that it cannot handle public goods like national defense, the quality of the environment, consumer protection, drug enforcement, or social justice. They say that there are absolute values like the right to life, liberty, and the pursuit of happiness that we cannot afford to put on the block to the highest bidder.

These are serious challenges that go to the heart of several centuries of political philosophy. This is not the place to lay to rest each of these charges in detail. Nor is it clear that the marketplace can handle each and every public good. In the next chapter, I'll make a case for the limits of the marketplace and the abiding need for democratic institutions in the public sector. While it would be a glib and foolish piece of neo-conservative rhetoric to argue that the marketplace can and should handle each of these challenges, let me make a few points about the role and nature of the marketplace in the economic era.

First, to repeat, the nation-state will not disappear. It will simply take a back seat to the marketplace. Economic leaders, economic forces, economic institutions will, generally and for the most part, guide history, just as political leaders and institutions have guided it for the past several centuries, and religious leaders and institutions before that had the reigns. Just as religion has not disappeared from the face of the earth, neither will politics. While the economic era will surely privatize some social functions formerly handled by the public sector, the case being made for the economic era does not require that *all* such functions be privatized.

Second, there may be questions about markets in general that differ from particular questions about the marketplace's ability to handle some functions but not others. On this more general level, there are serious differences of understanding about whether the marketplace is an intrinsically ruthless arena where there must be at least one loser for every winner (and probably more losers than winners), or whether the marketplace is a positive–sum game where people don't complete trades unless all parties are able to come away from those trades feeling that they have more of what they want than when they entered the marketplace.

The simple fact that it takes *differences of preference* to make a market lies at the heart of the centrality of the marketplace in the information economy. The butcher comes to market to sell meat and buy bread; the baker comes to market to buy meat and sell bread. Rather than conceiving of the marketplace as a zero-sum game that mediates the redistribution of physical goods from one place to another, always leaving one person richer and another poorer, remember that different people have different preferences, and the marketplace is the most efficient means yet devised for real-time optimizing over an incredibly complex array of *different* preferences.

When the nation-state was first finding its footing in the political philosophies of William of Ockham, Hobbes, and Locke, there was a good deal of talk about the divine right of kings. Early on in the political era, religion seemed to be the only place to look for a source of legitimacy for political institutions. Religion was the main game. The Church set the rules, so if you wanted to start a new franchise you had to go to God and his representatives to get a license. Only later, after some very radical moves by Hobbes and Rousseau, did it become even thinkable that the State was more than a bureaucratic extension of the Church, that the creation of the State by civil society meant more than a new franchise in the old league, that the passage from the religious era to the political era meant the foundation of a new league where legitimation by divine right was replaced with legitimation by the consent of the governed.

Looking forward to the equally gradual but equally epochal transition from the political era to the economic era, we need to make some moves every bit as radical as those made by Hobbes and Rousseau. We need to relocate the ground of legitimacy. Just as the State was not an extension of the Church, and therefore required legitimation in its own political terms rather than by theology, so the marketplace is not an extension of the State.

The economic era represents another new league, not a new franchise in the old political league. We should not look to political philosophy to defend the legitimacy of business any more than Hobbes or Rousseau should have looked to theology to defend the legitimacy of the social contract underlying the modern state.

To emphasize the kind of argument I'm making for the economic era, note that it is essentially historical rather than theological, moral, or metaphysical. It reflects a fall from eternal verities into the contingencies of historical time. This argument makes no reference to some transcendent order of ultimate justification, no reference to absolute values that were, are, and ever shall be. Instead it relies heavily on the fall into time: that was then; this is now. In this sense the argument has come full circle and has returned to the first feature of postmodernity: the replacement of the idea of necessary progress by the idea of historical drift and the competition between different histories.

Now that industrial mass production is causing unintended side effects along with intended progress, now that the information and service sectors of the advanced economies are employing more than three times as many workers as the industrial sector, now that information is shrinking the globe and reducing the significance of national sovereignty, and now that the marketplace seems to be doing a better job of allocating resources than government bureaucracies did, it only makes sense to acknowledge the dawn of the information/economic era at this dawn of a new millennium.

Hedges on the dramatic claim for the emergence of the economic era plunge us back into the heart of the challenge to the legitimacy of business. For beneath the specifics about what functions can and cannot be privatized, or the question of whether there remains a role for a diminished State, there remains what can best be acknowledged as a feeling at the heart of the challenge, namely, that precisely in the modesty of its mission, the marketplace appears to be heartless and bloodless.

Perhaps the economic era will be a flatland of commerce devoid of passion. Postmodernism has no place for patriotic fervor, religious faith, or the ideals that move men with inspiration.[9] This feeling about postmodernism is well captured in Todd Gitlin's claim that postmodernism "neither embraces nor criticizes, but beholds the world blankly with a knowingness that dissolves feeling and commitment into irony. It pulls the rug out from under itself, displaying an acute self-consciousness about the work's constructed nature. It takes pleasure in the play of surfaces, and derides the search for depth as mere nostalgia." The affect of postmodernism is, in short, flat. No peaks and valleys of elation and despair. No nineteenth–century dramas of heroism in the face of evil.

To see how the apparently passionless affect of postmodernism is more than just exhaustion, it will help to relate the primacy of the marketplace in the economic era to several other features of millennial consciousness. I already noted the detachment from the idea of progress. As for the supplanting of scientific theory by modes of inquiry that are more empathic, intuitive, narrative, and holistic, it should be clear that there is more room for emotion in this millennial worldview than there was in the truly bloodless objectivity of the scientific worldview.

That is not to say that a millennial worldview will plunge us back into premodern religious faith, or that intuition can everywhere substitute for science any more than the marketplace can everywhere substitute for the State. But a millennial worldview can overcome some of the contradictions built into the modern worldview—as between mind and body, or subject and object—and by doing so can pump some of the life back into the cold and distant view of scientism.

Likewise, the sublimation of mass manufacturing in an industrial economy to a knowledge economy of information, services, and experiences may pump more emotion into the marketplace than the getting and spending for material goods ever allowed. The experience industry brings to market whatever makes the heart beat faster.

Of course there will be those who object to the commoditization of passion. But this is just the point: passion is so much safer when sublimated through the displacements of the marketplace than when it erupts through the sublimations of religion and politics. The unrestrained fervor of religious zeal, the unqualified love of country, right or wrong, can steer history into a lot of trouble. The absolute black–and–white, off/on, digital values of premodern traditionalism may need to be relativized into the shades of gray, trade–offs that an analog marketplace of marginal differences can provide.

In the millennial marketplace for information, services, and intense experiences, it's simply not true that values are absent or that passions have been commoditized. On the contrary, the marketplace provides a place where consenting adults can get together for safe passion, where millions of individuals can make billions of decisions to value one thing relatively more than another, the better over the worse, without fighting in the name of the One True Best.

To borrow for just a moment some leftover language from the political era, the moment–to–moment hum of relative valuations in the marketplace is a much more *democratic* process than the totalitarian hold of absolute values. Millions and billions of relative valuations in the give and take of the marketplace may not add up to the glories of religious salvation or the grandeur of empire, but so much the better for that.

As for the transition from hierarchy to heterarchy, once again we are dealing with a process of leveling that produces a nostalgia for heights and a yearning for depths. But here again a closer look reveals the difference between heterarchy and anarchy.

Heterarchy, whether in institutions or in selves, does not entail an anarchistic flattening of all values, all commitments. In heterarchical structures the problem is not that there are no hierarchies, no preferences, no valuations of one thing over another; the problem is that there are too many. Priorities overlap and compete, just as they do in the marketplace: For the butcher, bread over lamb; for the baker, lamb over bread. If the consciousness that can deal with conflicting hierarchies seems to be cool and ironic when compared with the hot-blooded servant of a single, unambiguous hierarchy, so be it.

Granted, there is a calculating, penny-pinching approach that is all too familiar among those who frequent the marketplace most. The economic era cannot evolve toward stable equilibrium if it is perpetually destabilized by excessive greed.[10] Each era has its characteristic version of excess. In the religious era it was the pious self-righteousness that produced crusades and inquisitions. In the political era it was the pride of empire that led to the excesses of colonialism. In the economic era, excesses of greed can muck up the marketplace just as surely as piety toppled the Pope and the pride of empire spawned revolution in the colonies.

In the next chapter, I want to take a look at how this transition from the modern-industrial-political era to a millennial-information-economic era changes the way we think about justifying our lives; how the rationales we use to give meaning to our lives have shifted beyond the religious beliefs that defined the parameters of meaning in premodern times, through the political ideologies of Right and Left that fired the passions of the modern, political era, to the economic motivations that move people in the new millennium. Does the marketplace demote our values from the higher passions of previous eras? Or is the hankering after the halo of religious belief and the passion of political ideology a species of nostalgia we can well do without? I want to make a case for finding meaning and passion in the new millennium.

CHAPTER THREE

THE LIMITS OF THE MARKETPLACE

The last chapter made a case for describing the turn of the millennium in terms of a transition from a political to an economic era. It was filled with broad historical descriptions and their interpretation based on certain facts about changing technologies. But what about values? Is the shift to the economic era a good thing?

This is the wrong way to frame the question. The shift to the economic era is inevitable for the reasons I've mentioned. The proper question to ask is, What is the right way to live one's life in light of the fact that we are shifting from a political to an economic era? And this question brings us to the issue of better futures and normative scenarios.

It's important to choose carefully where one puts one's shoulder to the wheel. Nice people can end up doing bad things. This was Hannah Arendt's point about "the banality of evil." In *Eichmann and Jerusalem* her real target was not Eichmann, but the good Germans, the functionaries who cooperated, the railroad switchmen who shunted cars from one track to another without questioning the fact that the contents of the cars were human beings headed for extermination.[1] The example is extreme, but the point is familiar: we don't want to associate ourselves with institutions whose achievements are evil or corrupt. Hence the question of the legitimacy of business. Can you go to work in the morning while holding commitments to social justice and compassion?

The point of taking the long view of history is to relocate the question of legitimacy. Rather than assuming a political framework of rights and responsibilities as the framework within which questions of legitimacy must be raised, I'm suggesting that the question of legitimacy needs a broader historical sweep. The question of legitimacy is too large for a purely political context to encompass. After all, political legitimacy was once defended on religious grounds. Prior to the granting of legitimacy by virtue of the consent of the governed—the idea we call democracy—there were claims made for the *divine* right of kingship.

If legitimacy was based on religious principles in the agricultural era, and political principles in the industrial era, so may it follow that legitimacy must be sought in economic principles in the information era—from prayers to votes to dollars as the tokens that confer legitimacy. A purchase resembles a vote in the sense that both votes and purchases reflect patterns of preference. We give a vote of confidence to a business every time we purchase one of its products. The corporation remains legitimate as long as it satisfies its consumers and meets its payroll.

Surely there is more to legitimacy than staying in business, you protest. What about the role of the corporation as a good citizen of the community? What about obligations to the environment and to future generations?

I do not deny the importance of these obligations, but I ask: what is the *source* of the obligation? Where is the *locus of legitimacy*? On what basis can one speak of duty? If we no longer appeal to divine right, then we may likewise leave behind the consent of the governed as a rationale. Less and less do we consent to be governed by the government. From draft resistance in the sixties to the tax revolt of the seventies to the trend toward deregulation in the eighties to the self-destruction of the White House and the paralysis of a gridlocked Congress, all signs point toward a withdrawal of legitimacy from the government.

When asked whether they trust the government in Washington to do what is right most of the time, three–quarters of the American people said yes in 1964. In recent years, depending on which poll you read, only a quarter to a third of the people have expressed the same confidence in our federal government.[2] This dramatic erosion of confidence in the government constitutes a massive crisis of legitimacy in the public sector.

The private sector inspires more confidence these days, even if big business is a favorite target of movies from *The China Syndrome* to *Erin Brokovich*. Of course there are corporations that are corrupt, just as there were corrupt priests and corrupt politicians. This defense of corporate legitimacy by virtue of the dawning of the economic era cannot justify *all* corporations any more than a defense of the concept of the state could justify *all* governments and their activities. Further, it would be as foolish to valorize all business now as it was foolish to condemn all business in the sixties. Life is not that simple. Distinctions must be drawn.

My concern is with the basis on which we draw distinctions. Do we base our claims to legitimacy on what seems fair in the eyes of the Lord? Or do we base our claims on what seems fair in the eyes of our elected representatives? Or do we base our claims on what seems fair to buyers and sellers who meet in the marketplace?

If we can now see the succession of the political order by an economic order as a kind of Second Reformation . . . now it is time to consider the issue of *counterreformation.* Are there some things that the marketplace is not that good at? Just as we have discovered some things that the Church is not that good at, and just as we continue to discover some things that government is not that good at, so likewise is it not time to ask, in this post-Reagan-Thatcher era, if there are not things that the marketplace is not particularly good at? Like health, education, the environment, or telecommunications policy?

Maybe there is an abiding role for government after all. Maybe we can't throw the bums out just yet. So what jobs will we entrust to them, just to keep their hands off other more important things like the economy? What tasks fall more legitimately to government than to the marketplace? Such a simple question. You'd think someone would have answered it by now. But no. You have to go back to *The Federalist Papers* to get any good discussion of this question. It's as if we all thought that the founding fathers answered that question once and for all. But things have changed, in ways not so dissimilar to the way things changed before and after the printing press, Luther, the Reformation, and the passage of power from Church to State. Now that things have changed on that scale, there's a chance that parts of *The Federalist Papers* could use some tweaking.

WHAT MARKETS CANNOT DO

Individuals can purchase in the marketplace a range of goods that become their private property: real estate, clothing, toys, home appliances—a whole range of durables and consummables. But who will pay for public goods like our infrastructure of roads and highways, our communications system, and national security? And what about those lumpy items, like hospitals, that make it possible for consumers to purchase health care services?

The funding issue—who will pay?—comes up similarly and differ-

ently in several arenas. As for the crisis in government itself, there are
those who insist that the political process is infected with inequities introduced by our current system of campaign finance. In the health care
arena, among the most frequently heard complaints is that the system
of third-party payment drives up costs. Consumers have little incentive
to hold down costs; doctors, traumatized by the threat of malpractice
suits, have every incentive for prescribing tests and procedures that drive
up costs. Meanwhile hospitals are singing the Bessy Smith classic,
"Empty Bed Blues," as the trend from inpatient toward outpatient care
continues.

Another arena in which government and capitalism are being tested
for their abilities to come up with efficient solutions is telecommunications policy. Margaret Thatcher privatized British Telecom, but the German Bundespost is still in government hands. In the United States we
broke up the monopoly held by Ma Bell. But each of the Baby Bells—
the regional Bell operating companies (RBOCs)—operated for over a
decade with near–monopoly control in their own regions. Their monopolies are coming to an end. The pressure of technological change,
and competition from long–distance carriers, cable companies, and cellular companies is breaking their monopoly over the local loop. If they
no longer enjoy monopoly privilege, the RBOCs argue, then they no
longer deserve regulation. Should we free the Baby Bells to compete on
a level playing field in an open marketplace? Or do we risk hopeless
confusion among competing technologies and wastefully parallel
networks?

To summarize: in health care, education, and telecommunications, the
battle between public administration and private competition is playing
out in ways that are both similar and different. In none of these industries are there simple answers. The elegance of ideology will not help us.
Instead we need to work inductively, up from the details, in order to
find slightly more general answers about the fate of capitalism.

It's not hard to find people critical of government these days. Hardly
anyone expects the public sector to solve any of the major problems facing society today. From the economy—and criticisms of heavy–handed
industrial policy—to health care, hardly anyone has any faith in the government's ability to improve things. To the contrary, government is
viewed as part of the problem, not part of the solution.

Take education. Government regulations cause colleges and local
school boards to increase the number of administrators, which takes
money from instruction and thereby damages the learning environment.

Test scores decline, teachers get blamed, and governments add regulations calling for more adminstrators to handle them. Rather than improving education, government intervention accelerates the vicious
downward spiral. What is the favored remedy? It is to take a leaf from
the private sector and introduce market mechanisms through a voucher
system that gives greater choice to education's consumers, thereby introducing an element of competition among schools? From a purely ideological point of view that favors privatization and marketplace mechanisms over public bureaucracies, school choice via vouchers sounds like
a good idea. However, when you look at the details of voucher initiatives and at research on systems for school choice around the country,
what looks good in theory does not work out so well in actual practice.[3]
Maybe there are limits to the effectiveness of marketplace mechanisms
in the provision of education.

Take drugs and crime. Government intervention through the war on
drugs has been shown to have been counterproductive. By trying to de-
crease the flow of drugs across our southern border, the Drug Enforcement Agency actually increased the profit margin on cocaine, thereby
increasing the incentive for dealers, which then increased the amount of
drugs from Mexico and Colombia reaching the streets of the United
States. Had the government left well enough alone, we would arguably
see less crack and less crack-associated crime. But are we ready to let
the government get out of crime control altogether? Do we want to privatize our prisons, or legalize cocaine? The answers are not as obvious
as an ideological approach might suggest.

Take health. Here the challenge lies in curbing costs while offering
greater access to the health care system to those who currently lack adequate insurance coverage, particularly the young or the old and poor.
Can the government do it? Some advocate an adaptation of Canada's
health care system, which would greatly reduce administrative costs by
replacing our complex industry of third-party payers with a single system run by the government and paid for through taxes. This might work.
But others note delays for treatment in Canada. They worry about so-
cialized medicine and insist on the same need for individual choice that
educational reformers are calling for to improve education. We've already got "choice" in health care: our highly privatized health care system. Why give it up now? Can we find ways of making the market more
efficient rather than getting rid of market mechanisms?

If an increasing role for government is problematic in areas of industrial policy, health care, education, and illegal drugs, does experience

in those industries dictate the preservation of a predominantly private health care system? Or are there good arguments for making distinctions among different industries as far as the relative appropriateness of a strong role for government? Rather than argue the proper balance between business and government on the high ground of ideological abstractions, maybe it makes sense to attend to the valleys where paths cross in messy contention. It could be that there is not one big ideological answer that will work across the board, but that there are good reasons for striking the balance between business and government differently in different industries.

Let's replace ideological debates over the political legitimacy of government intervention with industry–specific analyses of the optimum balance of public and private activity. Neither national security nor information infrastructure nor the atmosphere are easy to manage effectively by simply aggregating individual preferences in the marketplace. National security, standards on the Internet, and the maintenance of the environment require a degree of centralized planning for the allocation of vast resources over long lead times. These "lumpy" items—in the language of the economists—are not easy to accommodate in the sort of literal marketplace where consumers shop on a Saturday afternoon.

We may want to acknowledge that the historical action is passing from the public sector to the private sector, much as it previously passed from the Church to the State. Nonetheless, in at least some industries the rush to privatization will induce calls for a return to regulation. In some industries the fashionable rush to privatization will prove inappropriate. We will discover *what markets cannot do*.

The following sections treat education, health care, and communications in turn. The intention is to garner insights from each industry on its own, and then return to each industry after making some slightly more general conclusions. By looking at all three industries and not just one, there is a slightly greater likelihood of recognizing some more general historical trends that span all of the industries.

To anticipate a principal finding: in each of these industries there is a locus of debate and attention that turns out to play a similar role, despite differences among the specifics. The debate over standards in education, the debate over managed care, and the race toward the computerized, smart set–top box in telecommunications, though radically different on one level, turn out to be similar in that each is trying to come up with a surrogate or substitute for the adequately informed consumer.

The rationale for markets as the best means of allocating scarce resources relies on *informed consumers* who can make judgments about the difference between a better product and a worse product. Markets need knowledgeable consumers who know what they want. If the market is to be expected to help us deliver the goods, if the market is to be expected to deliver better futures, then consumers need to be able to make those distinctions between better and worse. In these industries, however, marketplace mechanisms do not work very well because the requirement for adequately informed consumers is not met. Students wouldn't be students if they already knew what they need to learn. Patients haven't been to medical school. Customers of communications systems are unlikely to know much about the differences between TDMA, CDMA, and GSM standards for cellular telephony.

However, just because market mechanisms do not function very well in these industries does not mean that government intervention is the only answer. It may be that social inventions like regulated managed care, hardware inventions like the smart set-top box, or educational assessment inventions like a better system of standards can substitute for the informed consumers who are, for a fact, missing from each of these industries.

So this is the gist of this chapter: government is not the only alternative to the unfettered operation of the marketplace. There are other institutions and technologies as yet undreamt by our political philosophers, other alternatives to the heavy hand of government regulation. For an articulation of those alternatives, we must get down into the valleys and look at the issues in greater detail.

FUNDING PUBLIC EDUCATION

In education, the funding issue is assuming critical importance. Public education is facing financial crisis, both at the K-12 level and in higher education. At the K-12 level there are the added problems of inequities in the funding of urban schools as compared to wealthier suburban schools. In order to introduce innovation and competition into the public school system, some policy makers are contemplating various systems of alternative funding, from vouchers to tax deductions to means-tested scholarships and student loans.

We would like to think that choice will make for increased competition, innovation, and productivity as eager and discerning consumers force providers toward perpetual improvements in their offerings. But when parents are offered tax-funded vouchers worth several thousands of dollars to allow them to send their children to private schools, the gift of choice does not of itself create demand for better education. As Ernest Boyer, a leading educational researcher, found when he studied the utilization of a range of school–choice programs, "In statewide programs, where participation is optional, we found that fewer than 2 percent of the parents in any state have exercised their right to switch." Further, "the push for school choice appears to be coming more from theoreticians and politicians than from parents . . . most parents who do decide to send their children to another school appear to do so for nonacademic reasons."[4]

The parents of inner-city youths are not informed consumers of education. Many of them failed to complete high school themselves. So how can marketplace mechanisms encourage good schools while pushing incompetent educators from the marketplace for lack of "customers"? Most public school teachers are tenured. They cannot be fired. How can marketplace mechanisms work on "services" that cannot be refused?

If consumers cannot be trusted to discern among better and worse service offerings, then no amount of school choice will improve the schools. This is only one of the arguments against voucher systems. A second problem is that not everyone has enough money to take their children out of a free public school and send them to private school. In an inadequate effort to satisfy the marketplace requirement of consumers' ability to pay, most voucher initiatives offer no more than two to three thousand dollars per year for each child; some offer as little as one thousand. If a parent wants to send a child to a private school, that voucher can be applied toward the tuition charged by the private school.

How will this plan work out in practice? Poor families will not have enough money to supplement the voucher to pay hefty private–school tuition bills. Rich families who are already sending their children to private schools will receive an immediate transfer of wealth. Meanwhile this transfer of wealth will remove money from the public–school budget, leaving a system of public schools even worse than we now have. In the name of "school choice" and marketplace mechanisms, we will witness a government–initiated redistribution of wealth that will do nothing to improve the public school system. This is not exactly a triumph of innovation through competition in the marketplace, but more like slow death by financial strangulation at the hands of political intervention in the educational process. Most voucher initiatives turn out to be a redistributive wolf masquerading in the sheep's clothing of the free–market rhetoric of free choice. The inner–city poor will not have any choice about the further decline of their school budgets. The transfer of wealth from the poor to the rich will take place way over their heads in the hallways of state capitals. This is why Rudi Crew, the much–admired superintendent of New York City's public school system, threatened to resign if Rudi Giuliani pushed through an experiment with $1,500 vouchers in New York's schools. Even a limited experiment with vouchers would amount to allowing the camel's nose under the tent, the beginning of the end of public education.

Is there any way of ensuring that the quality of education in inner–city schools can be improved if school choice in a free market won't do the trick? One way of substituting for informed consumers of education is the development and application of *standards*. Ever since the administration of Bush the elder called for standardized national testing, there has been a raging debate on the subject. It is not a simple matter. Once again ideological lines get blurred, and strange ironies appear. Some of the very people you would expect to be in favor of standardized tests oppose them, and those who are in favor sometimes invoke arguments you would not expect. A brief review of some of the pros and cons reveals themes that will reappear when we take a closer look at the debates over health care reform and the deregulation of telecommunications.

THE DEBATE OVER EDUCATIONAL STANDARDS

In favor: the first argument in favor of standards comes from *the need for benchmarking* so that gross failures and inequities can be identified and addressed with remedial measures that will shore up some of our failing schools.

Opposed: yes, but . . . standardization is an industrial-era concept for producing millions of the mass-manufactured same, same, same. Now we live in the information age when the paradigm has shifted to an appreciation for differences that make a difference. In opposition to educational standardization, you get an odd alliance of right–wing, states' rights conservatives in league with information–age advocates of differentiation, and multiculturalists pleading in defense of diversity.

So once again in favor: although *standardization* in the information age is obsolete, there is still a need for *higher standards* to give students a reason to try harder. Expect more of them and they will achieve more.

Higher standards may sound more appealing than *standardization,* but who's to decide which standards are higher? How can you honor diversity, local autonomy, decentralization of authority, self-determination, and school–based management if each community must live with standards that come from outside of the community?

Advocates for traditional values have an answer. Whether the standards come from outside or inside the community, there is a need for a *core curriculum* to provide a common vocabulary for all of the citizens of a democracy. E. D. Hirsch argues that without a consensus as to the body of facts that every child needs to learn, we run the risk of exposing our students to an incoherent smorgasbord of courses in each school, and the balkanization of cultures among our many schools.[5]

From black separatists to Latino advocates of bilingual education comes the response that a national core curriculum would carry a bias toward European ethnocentrism—a not-so-subtle form of racism. In his persuasive and moderately argued book, *The Disuniting of America,* Arthur Schlesinger, Jr., argues, "The ethnic upsurge . . . began as a gesture of protest against the Anglocentric culture. It became a cult, and today it threatens to become a counter–revolution against the original theory of America as 'one people,' a common culture, a single nation."[6]

Apart from issues of race and ethnocentrism, there are other arguments for honoring diversity. Consider Howard Gardner's research into different kinds of intelligence. Won't a core curriculum based on national standards run the risk of favoring one type of intelligence to the detriment of others?[7]

The debate has only just begun. To summarize its most salient points, note that the arguments for diversity are themselves diverse: from right-wing advocacy for local liberty from federal control, through ethnic pride, to a social-psychological argument for community involvement in decision making, and a cognitive psychologist's case for different kinds of intelligence. These are not arguments that fit neatly on a Right/Left spectrum of purely ideological debate. Yet these arguments are relevant to the merits of the case for national standards in education.

The arguments in favor of standards are equally diverse, from the need for benchmarking to address inequities to the motivational benefits of higher aspirations to the need for a common culture and a coherent curriculum. Not all of these arguments are political or ideological, but the case for school choice draws much of its support from a kind of knee-jerk conservatism that feeds off the global trend away from government control toward the privatization of formerly public services.

The diversity of arguments, both for and against standards, reflects an evolutionary logic of proliferation of species in diverse niches. According to Gregory Bateson, the logic of learning is essentially the same as the logic of evolution.[8] The process of biological evolution is best understood as the education of a species. Adaptation is a learning process. A species learns about its environment and embodies that learning in progressive modifications that allow it to adapt ever more successfully to its environmental niche. Those species that fail to learn, that fail to adapt, perish. Only the "educated" survive. Only those species that "learn" to adapt will procreate and prosper.

Now consider this logical equivalence of learning and evolution from the opposite direction. In order to understand what learning is all about, it is best to think of it as a process of trial and error—perpetual (if miniscule) modifications or mutations of behavior that either pay off or don't. Those mutations that succeed are repeated until they become habitual. Learning is the evolution of ever more adaptive behavior. Behaviors that are rewarded by your environment become embedded in your repertoire of tricks. Only by experimenting with your behavior can you discover more successful behaviors. Thus, learning is less about the ingestion of facts and more about an ongoing interaction between self and environment. The fittest behaviors survive. Their programs are known as knowledge, or at least as know–how.

Now consider the impact of this insight on our ideas about education. The evolutionary model of learning, as John Dewey saw long ago, is less cerebral and more pragmatic. Many approaches to education imagine it to be about packing the brain with facts and truths. For evolution, however, experiments are essential to improvement. You have to try things, and mutate in ways that may be random as well as planned. You have to break the chain of sameness and come up with something not only different, but—ever so occasionally—better than the current model.

If experimentation, mutation, and random modification are essential to the logic of evolutionary learning, then much of the current talk about the importance of educational standards may be fundamentally misguided. To listen to the proponents of national standards, it would appear that we are trying to mold our nation's students into a single species of androids: clones all driven by knowledge genes that are as close to identical as we can make them. If we have learned anything from evolutionary theory, it is that a rich, healthy ecology requires diversity. This principle has been codified as Ashby's law of requisite variety: the more varied a given gene pool, the less vulnerable it is to blight; the more uniform a gene pool, the closer to a monoculture, the more vulnerable it is to changes in its environment.

Evolution is divergent, not convergent. Evolution is not aimed toward some single goal of the best species. To the contrary, the evolutionary record is a story of the proliferation of ever more varieties, species, and subspecies. It is a tale of differentiation, not standardization, or, difference rather than identity. Let a thousand flowers bloom, and let the strongest propagate most. This is the logic of evolution, but it is not the logic endorsed by the current fashion in educational reform in which the preoccupation with standards has dominated the debate of the 1990s.

How could we have gotten it so wrong? The reasons aren't hard to divine. First and foremost, it makes sense to call for more accountability in education. What makes one lesson better than another? How do we know one student has learned more than another? How can we tell which education works and which doesn't without testing the results? How can we interpret the results of the test unless everybody is subjected to the same test?

While these sound like rhetorical questions that assume the need for standardized tests, there is an alternative more consistent with an evolutionary approach. Yes, accountability is important, but what accounting could be more definitive than the difference between survival and extinction? Education is literally a life–and–death matter. This harsh reality remains uniform, but the "tests" that our respective environments offer up are by no means uniform. We each have to adapt to a distinct niche. What the Inuit child needs to know is not in every respect the same as what the Arab child needs to know. One needs to know a lot about snow, the other a lot about sand. Likewise, survival skills in the inner city needn't be part of the core curriculum in the suburbs.

This pluralistic approach to reality testing is embedded in the wisdom of the Constitution, which leaves the shaping of education in the hands of states and localities. Only with the establishment of the federal Department of Education in 1962 did we begin to violate the pluralistic, evolutionary approach to education with a more industrial model that seemed intent on molding all students into a single ideal, measured by a single set of standards.

Once again, the wish for accountability is understandable. We cannot keep pushing students through the pipeline of successive grades without knowing something about what they know and don't know. But standardized tests are not the only route to accountability. Adaptability to a local niche can provide a definitive test for whether learning has taken place, and these tests may actually be far more appropriate and useful than a one-test-fits-all approach.

The best alternative to standardization is not to discard standards. The best alternative to nationally standardized tests is adaptability to one's local niche. Surely there are different sizes of niches—town, county, state, region. The sand surrounding an ostrich's submerged head is far too local a niche to provide an education adequate for survival. But the shortcomings of extreme localization do not make a good argument for the nation's being the minimal unit of curricular scope. We need to acknowledge the wisdom of diversity that evolution teaches. What works for educational reformers in New York City may not be appropriate to reformers in Iowa; what works in Texas may be a mutation for the worse in the cultural ecology of Seattle.

WHO IS THE CHOOSER OF HEALTH CARE?

Educational reform talks of vouchers, choice, and standards; the debate over health care reform covers very similar issues with a slightly different vocabulary. In place of standards we hear talk of outcomes research. In place of vouchers there is talk of third-party payers. And in health care reform, as in educational reform, choice is an issue that is clouded by ignorance.

The debate over health care reform reveals several different surrogates for the well-informed or knowledgeable consumer. First, there is the role of the primary care physician as gatekeeper at the front end of managed care organizations. Lacking knowledge about which specialist can provide the most appropriate care, the patient must be referred by a general practitioner acting as diagnostician.

Second, in the design for health care reform put forward by Alain Enthoven, the leading influence on Hillary Clinton's reform team, state agencies were envisaged as "public sponsors" that would represent all of the currently uninsured in bargaining with health care providers. Because the currently uninsured do not enjoy the benefit of membership in pools of employees, they find themselves in a weak bargaining position if they go to shop for insurance or medical care. To address this, public sponsors would pick up the currently uninsured, offer them the strength of collective bargaining to help them to negotiate on price, and perhaps most important of all provide the knowledge necessary for informed choice among health care providers.

Third, part of the information for informed choices—by public sponsors as well as by the currently insured—will be outcomes research on the quality of care offered by different providers. In the debate over health care reform, it has come as a revelation that some hospitals offer lower prices and better performance on the same procedures than other hospitals. Just as there is a call for standards that would benchmark schools, so there are now calls for outcomes research that will measure the quality of care provided by different hospitals. You would think that this was an elementary requirement for choice to be meaningful, but up until fairly recently this elementary requirement for a working marketplace has not been available in health care.

While public sponsors and primary care physicians as gatekeepers for HMOs sound different from the educational rhetoric of national standards, other parts of the debates over health care and education sound remarkably the same: outcomes research, access, and choice are all parts of the marketplace vocabulary. But, as in the educational debate; so also in the health care reform debate; the specifics involved in allowing choice and permitting access are not the sorts of specifics that economists and political theorists have in mind when they engage in ideological debates over the merits of free markets versus command economies. Having "access" to health care by virtue of insurance is very different from having access to the mall. Making a "choice" among different HMOs is very different from choosing which car to buy, or which piece of clothing. It's very hard to see just what you're buying when you choose an HMO and, in a medical emergency situation, buyers of health care are unlikely to be capable of making rational choices.

Like education, health care carries an imperative to universal access—and this is the principal reason for getting government into the act. The same rationale was used for telecommunications. Ma Bell had to be a regulated utility because a communications system must link *everyone,* whether or not they have the ability to pay. Health care, education, and communications all share this imperative to universal service—an imperative to *access.* In this respect these three industries differ from the markets for contemporary art, fine wine, or high-heeled shoes. Many items purchased in the marketplace are matters of want, not need. But education, health care, and communications are not just objects of desire; they are necessities for existence in modern society.

The dividing line between objects of desire and necessities is fuzzy and alterable over time. A car is a necessity in Los Angeles in a way that it is not in New York City. There are those who will argue that a high school diploma was once the certificate of entry to decent employment, but that a college diploma is as necessary now as a high school diploma once was.

WHAT ARE OUR CHOICES IN TELECOMMUNICATIONS?

Now we turn from health care and education to telecommunications. Here we find that the locus of attention is the smart set-top box. Entertainment, computing, and communications are all converging in the box that will allow Joe and Jane six-pack to sort through a cornucopia of offerings. Whether as a result of wireless technology plus data compression, or as a result of fiber-optic, broadband communications, the consumer will soon be besieged by 500 channels of entertainment and communications. As John Perry Barlow, former songwriter for the Grateful Dead and one of our GBN network members, puts it, people will be "free-basing television." People will need help. They will risk addiction in the realm of a super-enriched experience economy. So the smart set-top will be there to help the overwhelmed consumer. Once again, an information-intensive industry is finding a way to make up for the lack of an adequately informed consumer. The smart set-top will help the consumer of entertainment determine which of many offerings will satisfy his or her unique needs, wants, and desires.

Another piece of information technology that jumps out as a paradigm case of the broad phenomenon I'm describing here is the Internet browser. No wonder we've heard so much about the battle between Netscape and Microsoft. Their fight over the means of navigating the Internet is one of the foremost skirmishes in the larger war over consumer choice. Microsoft's battle with the government over whether Bill Gates is abusing monopoly powers is paradigmatic of the very latest stage of the contest between the public and the private sectors.

Like the primary care physician at the front end of an HMO, or a school board sifting among the results of outcomes research to see how well different schools measure up to national standards, or the smart set-top box, an Internet browsing engine is there to help the consumer sort the wheat from the chaff and find a path through the millions of Web pages to just those gems of information that will satisfy this particular consumer with these particular needs at precisely this moment in time: a tall order in a complex world.

What we find in all three of these industries—education, health care, and telecommunications—are arenas of life where marketplace mecha-

nisms alone are not sufficient. Where there is an imperative to universal
service, the market won't work because the market—even if it is a positive-
sum game—is bound to produce relative winners and losers, and this we
cannot afford. As a society, we cannot afford illiterates. We don't want
sick neighbors. We don't want a communications system that connects
just a few people to a few other people.

But what we are learning as we move from the political to the economic era is that, even when we are dealing with an imperative to universal service, the best answer to providing that universal service is not
necessarily a government–owned service. Yes, there is a public domain
that transcends private interests. Yes, there is a public sphere that is larger
than our private lives. But the nation-state, as many have said, is too big
for the small problems and too small for the big problems. Too big to
respect local differences in educational standards; too small to care for
the oceans or CO_2 levels in the atmosphere.

I want to make a case for the social philosophy of *some*—limited communities of interest defined by geography or by profession or by any
of a range of other criteria. Such communities are larger than the individual and impose moral restraints that transcend the individual will. Yet
they are smaller than the whole human race or most nations. I can't put
a precise number on *some*. That is precisely the beauty of the concept.
Not one, not all, but some. The point is that these communities cut the
difference between the shortcomings of both individualism and collectivism. They duck under the totalitarian terror of collectivist ideologies
and rise above the narcissism and subjective relativism of extreme individualism.

Chapter 6 makes the case for such communities as the agents for better futures. The next chapter addresses the issue of *representation*, both as
it arises in politics, and as we are learning to think about it in the theory
of knowledge and perception. The point is to see how what we're learning about representation in the theory of knowledge—as through the appreciation of paradigms and worldviews—can inform the way we think
about representation in politics. Rethinking representation in politics sets
the context for the journey through Chapters 6–10 in which I'll be assembling the new tools for building better futures: first, the *group process*
called scenario planning; second, the concepts that characterize a relational
worldview. While most of those concepts show up first in the context of
epistemology—the theory of knowledge and perception—in Part Five I'll
return to the question of representation in politics.

CHAPTER FOUR

RETHINKING REPRESENTATIVE GOVERNMENT

If markets can't do all of the things we want them to do, but governments are a relic of the political era we're leaving behind as we enter the economic era, then how are we going to solve the problems that markets can't solve? If markets create winners and losers, then a market in education will produce geniuses and illiterates. But we all suffer if we have too many illiterates, so how can we compensate for the market's tendency to produce losers in education? If a market in health care leaves losers to suffer sickness, and no one wants to suffer the risk of sick neighbors, how will we compensate for the market's tendency to produce losers in health care? If a market in communications produces competing and incompatible networks, how can we compensate for this failure to deliver what ought to be a universal service? The problem could be posed in similar form for some other services that government has traditionally provided or regulated, services that are increasingly being privatized—security, prisons, garbage collection, transportation—but the structure of the problem will be clear enough, and hard enough, if we tackle just health, education, and telecommunications.

It's a question of governance: how will we steer our major institutions? This question hits close to home for strategic planners, the people who are responsible for steering large corporations. It also has some import for leaders in the public sector. Where are we going, and why? Further, how? The question of governance involves more than just setting a goal. There's also the question of how you get others in an organization to embrace that same goal. It's one thing to know where you want to steer an organization; it's another thing to get the organization to move in that direction.

I want to address these questions here because the way we answer them has a lot to do with how we create better futures. As I remarked in the very opening pages, utopians can cause trouble. Idealized portraits of the best future can function as ends that justify any means, and that way lies madness. Rather than painting some idealized portrait of a utopian future, I am eager to present scenario planning and normative scenarios, not as a new ideology preaching a new world order, but as a *method of steering toward a range of better futures.* Scenario planning is a *method for creating a range of better futures, not a blueprint for a particular future.* We can see the need for the method by examining the practice of traditional strategic planning and contrasting it with the practice of governmental industrial policy.

STRATEGIC PLANNING AND INDUSTRIAL POLICY

The issue of steering large organizations arises in both the public and private sectors, and in a way that produces some surprises. Creating a strategic plan for a large corporation is in some ways very much like creating an industrial policy for a nation. Both efforts threaten to become matters of picking winners, something that governments are notoriously poor at doing, notwithstanding temporary appearances to the contrary in Japan. What many writers in the 1980s revered as the farsighted coordination of Japanese industry by the Ministry of International Trade and Industry was reviled in the 1990s as crony capitalism.

The challenge of strategic planning is similar to the challenge of industrial policy. In both cases there is the same presumption that a few clever masterminds at the top/center of a large organization can anticipate conditions and allocate resources in a way that will achieve maximum growth for their organizations. Both strategic planning and industrial policy presuppose a rationalist philosophy of the way things work. In the corporate world, as Kees van der Heijden notes, this rationalist philosophy takes the form of imagining that a few clever individuals can "get it right," "find the one right answer," and develop a plan for others to follow.[1]

In the world of nation–states this rationalist philosophy takes the form of industrial policy. Taken to its extreme in the form of Communist central planning in the USSR and China, this rationalist philosophy supposed that a few smart minds in Moscow or Beijing could calculate the best way to run an economy. Those of us who know that the complexity of the universe will forever elude complete knowledge know better than to embrace such extreme forms of rationalism. It may be a measure of wisdom to acknowledge the reality of mystery, whether at the edges of the sacred or at least in the psyche. And managers must manage those psyches. When making the transition from the industrial era to the information era, managers must change their mental maps from the cogwheel imagery of *Modern Times* (where things might have worked "like clockwork") to the managing of the hearts and minds of knowledge workers. And in those hearts and minds, things don't work like clockwork, no matter what a few rationalists might have thought.

I'll develop these ideas about how we think and talk about the psyche by drawing the several components of a relational worldview from several different disciplines, such as psychology, sociology, and anthropology. For now, I want to explore the idea that *strategic planning* is structurally similar to *industrial policy* in confronting the limits of conscious rationality. I want to pursue this exploration on the back of this analogy: that the structural similarity between strategic planning and industrial policy is similar to the likeness, explored in Chapter 3, between the logic of *learning* and the logic of *evolution*.

THE LIKENESS BETWEEN LEARNING AND EVOLUTION

This likeness between learning and evolution lurks among the several essays of Gregory Bateson's anthology, *Steps to an Ecology of Mind,* a mixed bag of essays that follows Bateson's eclectic career from evolutionary biology through systems theory and epistemology to his theory of schizophrenia. Because *Steps* is an anthology, the underlying structural similarity between Bateson's solutions to problems in these different areas is rarely explicit. But in *Mind and Nature,* completed with the help of his remarkable daughter Mary Catherine, the linkage between evolutionary theory and education becomes explicit: evolution *is* the learning of a species. Learning *is* a process of adaptation to one's environment, a process of trial and error, a process of perpetual innovation (metaphorical mutation) followed by the selection of what is most fitting to a particular environmental niche, a process of testing the affordances of different niches and differentially reproducing those innovations which the niche can best afford . . . and here the language of learning and evolution drifts ever closer to the economic language of the marketplace.

Getting smart—whether in education or in marketing—is a matter of learning what works. Species do it, kids do it, and so must corporations and communities. It is the job of strategic planners to facilitate this process of evolutionary learning through strategic conversations among many members of a corporation and between the corporation and its stakeholders in the community. By pressing the relationship between scenario planning and strategy, we learn that the language of this conversation needs to be better balanced: more biological, less exclusively mechanistic; more psychological than purely rationalist; more metaphorical, less literal; qualitative as well as quantitative; more ecological, less military.

Strategic planning can no longer be described the way it was described above, as a method to "anticipate conditions and allocate resources in a way that will achieve maximum growth for the organization." This language betrays its rationalist, as opposed to evolutionary, perspective by failing to stipulate: "maximum growth for the organization *and its environment.*" As Gregory Bateson told us, the minimum unit of survival in evolution is never simply an individual organism, nor even a species, but always species-plus-environment in dynamic equilibrium. Master the environment to the point of defeating and depleting the environment and you defeat yourself. Killing customers is not prudent business policy.

By identifying the deep structure underlying both the similarity between evolution and learning *and* the similarity between strategic planning and industrial policy, we might discover an approach to coping with the limits of the marketplace in the economic era. To the extent that competing forms of capitalism can be understood as competing ways of drawing the boundary between the public and private sectors, that debate can be framed in terms of the degree of central intelligence one is willing to attribute to the State. Asian capitalism of the kind we see from Singapore to Tokyo is a close second to communism in the degree to which it tries to steer an economy from the control tower of a rationalized central bureaucracy. European capitalism occupies a middle ground in giving the central state a job to do, not so much for the sake of growing the economy, but for the sake of preserving the social ecology. American laissez-faire capitalism at its extremes—what George Soros calls "market fundamentalism"—would leave everything to the marketplace, as if central intelligence were a contradiction in terms.

Just as we want to preserve some sort of role for strategic planners—not as the repository of central intelligence, or as imposers of a blueprint of utopia, but as the facilitators of an ongoing strategic conversation—so the advocates of strategic conversation must acknowledge the limitations of the marketplace and an abiding role for some sort of governance system responsible to the public. Marketplace mechanisms are adequate for the optimal evolution toward a climax ecology of certain goods and services. But market mechanisms are not entirely adequate to the allocation of services, such as health, education, and communication, to which a society has decided that universal access is a basic requirement. In areas in which there is an imperative to universal service, an argument *can* be made for natural monopoly. (This is a long but familiar argument, and I will not make it here. In brief, it has to do with the inefficiencies inherent in building parallel delivery systems for universal services.) But wherever there is a natural monopoly, there remains a role for regulation in the interests of protecting the people from inadequate service, insufficient innovation, or monopolistic rents.

Even as we move beyond the crudities of Soviet central planning and toward a global market economy, it is clear that we have not reached the end of history—if that dramatic phrase implies the complete triumph of market mechanisms over central control. To claim total victory for capitalism is as foolish as claiming total victory for a species over its environment. There are no total victories in ecology. Yes, there is growth; yes, there is dramatic growth; but hypergrowth is cancerous and tends to kill the host. The hypergrowth of one species, like locusts or rabbits, or, for that matter, Microsoft, will sooner or later look like a pestilence to other species.

Balance is the name of the game: dynamic equilibrium between state and corporation, between central intelligence and market mechanisms, between strategic planning and environmental adaptation, between a skilled guiding hand and the hidden hand of acute sensitivity to a market environment.

What about governance? How do these reflections on learning and evolution and strategy and industrial policy help us answer the initial quandary, namely, what do we do with the jobs that used to be performed by governments now that we're moving into the economic era? Now that power is shifting from the public sector to the private sector, what happens when we crash up against the limits of the marketplace? If markets produce winners and losers, but we don't want to have illiterates, ill neighbors, or people unconnected to our communications system . . . what will substitute for what the market cannot do and governments don't do well?

Here it's worth retreating to first principles: if the fundamental challenge is to provide universal access to certain services—health, education, and communications; and if history is telling us that neither marketplace mechanisms nor governments as we know them are up to the job; if, therefore, neither the private sector nor the public sector as we know them are adequate to the task . . . then maybe it's time to rethink some of the fundamentals of representative democracy. Maybe it's time to rethink the very idea of representation.

RETHINKING REPRESENTATION

The representational logic of the marketplace—one dollar, one vote— ends up shortchanging the public good by reneging on the mandate to universal service. But the representational logic of the ballot box—one person, one vote—is giving us democratic governments that don't seem to be able to mediate conflicting interests in a very skillful or intelligent way. Maybe it's time to find a different principle of representation, nei- ther "one person, one vote" at the ballot box, nor "one dollar, one vote" at the cash register.

Redrawing the principles of representation is not unprecedented. A large part of the work of our forefathers was devoted to working out principles of representation that were appropriate to the agricultural so- ciety of the late eighteenth century. The houses of Congress are organ- ized around the compromise between representation by states—two sen- ators per state—and a more populist representation of individual voters in the House of Representatives. Going back even further, the old House of Lords, as opposed to the House of Commons in the British parlia- mentary system, gave more weight to representing the power of ances- tral heritage. No wonder the Blair government, in looking ahead rather than looking to the past, found it necessary to introduce changes to the House of Lords. Representation is not simple, and its rules are not un- alterable. There are different systems for representing different interests in different ways. Perhaps it is time to rethink how we represent dif- ferent interests.

Certainly there have been enough complaints about "single interest" politics. Whether it's at the hands of the tobacco interests, the gun lobby, the Christian Right, or the American Association of Retired People . . . so-called representative democracy, Washington–style, has gotten tan- gled in a web of competing single interests such that no one, it seems, has time or attention for the public good. Representative democracy is in trouble because the mechanisms of representation are no longer ap- propriate to the information era. Yes, democracy is superior to monar- chy, tyranny, and communism. But we're working with a government whose system of democratic representation was worked out when agricultural land ownership was the main criterion for the right to vote. We need to revisit our principles of representation in order to tweak democracy in the new millennium.

I want to suggest a way of thinking about representation that might be more appropriate to the knowledge economy. It's based on another analogy. Let's think about representation in politics by analogy with the way we are learning to think about representation in perception and the theory of knowledge.

The old and inadequate way of thinking about representation in politics is *one X, one vote,* substituting one person, one dollar, or one special interest for X. This old and inadequate way bears similarity to an equally inadequate way of thinking about perception and knowledge, namely, a simple-minded empiricism that imagines a straightforward, one-to-one correspondence between facts in the world and ideas in the head. Volumes have been written and dead ends repeatedly reached in the attempt to make sense of a one-to-one correspondence between facts "out there" and knowledge "in here."

Call it the picture theory of knowledge. According to this theory, for every object outside my mind, knowledge (or true belief) requires a corresponding subjective impression inside my mind. Accurate perception is the means by which I imprint those objects inside my mind. If there are five apples on the table and I say, "There are five apples on the table," my statement is true because it accurately represents reality. I know that there are five apples on the table because my senses do not deceive me. My perceptions picture what is outside my mind and leave corresponding impressions inside my mind. Nice theory. Too bad it's wrong.

Representation is not so simple. In fact, it's unbelievably complex. For example, think of a picture of a heart, then think of an electrocardiogram of that same heart. Which is more "accurate"? Think of a picture of poorly lighted party at midnight taken with regular film; then think of a picture of that same party taken with infrared photography. Which is more "accurate"?

Think about the simple act of making a telephone call. Your distant friend says, "Hello, how are you?" If the line is clear, you hear just those words, and with an intonation you recognize as your friend's. But now think of the "shape" those words and that voice take when they are halfway between your friend and you. It's not as if your friend were shouting from the next room. Your friend's words have been transformed from analog sound waves into digital signals for transmission over wire or through the air by microwave transmission; they are then retranslated from digital into analog form at the receiving end. When they are in digital form, as bursts of bits between your friend and you, are they "accurate"? Do they accurately represent what your friend said and how he said it? Well, if the signal shows up at your end as "Hello, how are you?" with your friend's intonation, you have to believe that the transmission was, indeed, accurate. But the "picture" of the bits in mid-transmission bears little obvious similarity to the words as they emerged from your friend's mouth. They *represent* your friend's words, and, as your reception of them proves, they represent them in some sense "accurately". But the rules of representation are hardly simple or one-to-one.

Maps represent territory. But as Jean Starobinski is famous for observing, "The map is not the territory." And a good thing, too. If your map of California were exactly equivalent to the territory it represents, it would never fit into the glove compartment of your car.

Is your map of California inaccurate because it is smaller than the State of California? Of course not. Indeed, it contains in one corner a conversion bar, or legend, showing its rule of representation: one inch equals so many miles. This is a relatively simple rule of transformation, one that would seem to preserve a rule of one-to-one correspondence: one inch equals one stretch of so many miles. But show me the one-to-one rule between my friend's words and the bits of his phone call in mid-transmission.

Representation is actually an incredibly complex subject. It lies at the heart of the thorniest problems in linguistics and semantics. It is the number one headache in perception theory and consciousness research. So why should we take for granted the idea that representation should be simple when we think about representative democracy?

Lest you think I'm building this argument about representative democracy on a false analogy, let me introduce a concept that will drive home the degree to which representation in knowledge and perception really does map (albeit by analogy) representation in politics: the idea of *sampling*.

Opinion polls are often reported together with what is called their *sampling error*. If only 500 people have been polled, the so-called sampling error will be plus or minus 5 or 6 percent. If 3,000 people have been polled, the sampling error drops to plus or minus 2–3 percent. The more people you poll, the bigger sample of the whole population you take, the closer the result will be to polling everyone. If you ask everyone which candidate they want, the sampling error will be zero because then you will not have sampled at all.

There is a similar sampling phenomenon with recorded sound. I have a son who is an expert on technologies of recording sound. He got his first radio DJ's license when he was 13. In college, he majored in the physics of sound. He works as a recording engineer. To this day, he doesn't own a CD player. He listens to music at home by playing vinyl records, many of them from my old collection. Why? He doesn't like the way digital CDs sample the sound.

Another example: look at the difference between European and American television sets. More pixels to the inch in Europe. Clearer picture. Higher resolution. Likewise with digital photography. Lower-priced cameras, fewer pixels, fuzzier picture. The sampling rate is lower with cheap digital cameras than with analog silver halide film photography.

In perception and political opinion polling, a high sampling rate will give you better results than a low sampling rate. This is true. But will you ever be able to reach perfect equivalence? Sampling always uses a part to represent the whole. So the question is which part, and for what purposes? If you don't sample, if you take the territory instead of the map, you'll never have anything you can fit into your glove compartment, or your mind. But if you do sample, you're always sampling according to some rule or other. And the rules we use for sampling are usually not as simple as we assume them to be.

"One man, one vote," sounds so simple, but recall: it took an amendment to the Constitution to include women under that rule. And then it took a civil war and a civil rights movement to get African-Americans registered to vote. And, oh, by the way, you have to be at least 18 years old. Representative democracy is not *that* simple. Look at the record of disputes over the gerrymandering of election districts. Gerrymandering amounts to messing with the sampling rules. The political party in charge rigs the map of voting districts in such a way that the rules of representation will favor their party in the next election. Sure, one man, one vote; but the way the votes are aggregated will, after the map has been gerrymandered, send more of the dominant party's "representatives" to Congress in the next election.

You think your clear-eyed perception is not equally subject to alterations in the rules of sampling? Try the dentist's nitrous oxide or the surgeon's anaesthetic for an experience in the "gerrymandering" of perception. Granted, examples that demonstrate the operation of sampling rules precisely by their distortion—anaesthetics and gerrymandering—might make it seem that there is such a thing as perfectly undistorted representation. Hence we speak of "sampling error" or "hallucination." The philosophy of empiricism amounts to the claim that perceptions enter the mind as if through a clear pane of glass, as if there were no sampling and no complex rules of sampling. But this is a mistake. This is why Starobinski's statement, as simple as it sounds, is so important. The map is never the territory. Any time you take a part for the whole, you do so according to some rule or other. So the question is not whether or not there are rules of sampling. The question is whether one set of rules is better than another set, and in what sense. The old House of Lords sampled to give weight to the voice of ancestral nobility. The U.S. Senate samples to give each state equal representation. The House of Representatives samples to give each congressional district of approximately 600,000 voters (however its lines are drawn) equal representation.

One-to-one representation? But what are the units of measurement? Who are the players? Nobles, states, congressional districts, individuals, dollars, pixels . . . What is the principle of individuation? What makes a voter? What is an individual such that it deserves a vote?

Lest you think that these issues are arcane, or too philosophical and abstract to deserve urgent attention, let me relate them to the day's headlines. The issue of campaign finance reform turns on precisely this issue of representative sampling. One man, one vote, you say? This is the principle of representative democracy, as opposed to rule by the almighty dollar? But in today's world of politics through the media and paid ads on television, no politician can win a state or national election without spending millions on TV advertising. Where will those millions come from? How can a candidate finance his or her campaign? If we don't have rules that prevent the oversampling of monied interests, then our elections will sample for dollars rather than the aggregated and undistorted preferences of individual voters. Those who have the dollars will be able to influence votes by the amount of money they have to buy TV ads promoting their views as opposed to their opponents' views. Campaign finance reform is about changing the sampling rules for "representative" democracy.

Both the civil rights movement and the women's movement are, as already suggested, all about representation. And the argument can be extended to the environmental movement. As the title of a famous book by philosopher Peter Singer asks, *Do Trees Have Standing?* And what about endangered species? Or unborn fetuses? What is an individual such that it deserves a vote?

Many of the major issues of our public and private lives revolve around these issues of sampling, representation, and individuation. Building better futures depends, in large part, on getting a better understanding of these issues: an understanding that is both conceptually coherent and appropriate to our particular moment in history.

Before finishing with this extended analogy between representation in politics and representation in perception and knowledge, let me be clear about what I am *not* claiming. First, I am not claiming that the analogy is perfect. Here, as elsewhere, the map is not the territory. Issues of representation in politics do not perfectly map issues of representation in epistemology, or vice versa.

Second, neither in the realm of politics, nor in the realm of epistemology, will I leap to skeptical conclusions. An amazing amount of nonsense has been spoken and written by people upon their first discovery that the systems of representation that they thought were simple turned out, on further examination, to be fraught with distortion. A large part of the history of philosophy is a long ride on the discovery that our senses can deceive us. Generations of philosophers have taken flight from the evidence of their senses and have argued to generations of eager students that what we know is never things in themselves, but only our perceptions of things. Well . . . yes, but drop a bowling ball on your foot and your pain will tell you that your perception of the bowling ball is a pretty effective representative for the real bowling ball. However complex the sampling rules may be, there are real things and real people out there beyond my own private consciousness.

The point I'm making is pretty simple. There is a third way beyond two opposite and equally mistaken extremes. At the one extreme are the empiricists who believe there are no sampling rules, that our perceptions are undistorted, that we can gain easy access to objective facts. At the other extreme are the radical skeptics who think you'll never know anything with any degree of certainty. You're locked in the cell of your own mind, forever cut off from things in themselves and from other minds.

Happily, there is a way to accommodate the elements of the truth while avoiding the errors of these extremes. Distancing ourselves first from the empiricists, let's acknowledge that there are sampling rules, that the map is not the territory, that *how* we know is a function of the sampling rules we use to represent reality. Distancing ourselves from the skeptics, let's acknowledge that *what* we know are real things and real people, albeit through different sets of sampling rules depending on our time, culture, language, and perspective.

Still employing the analogy between political representation and the theory of knowledge, we move along this third path beyond equal and opposite nonsense about extreme forms of liberalism and conservativism. That last line about depending on our time, culture, language, and perspective might seem to be carrying us toward some untenable form of ethical relativism, some extreme and permissive interpretation of individual liberty and freedom that says, "Hey, it's a free country and I can do whatever I want. What's cool for me is cool for me. What's cool for you is cool for you. You like string beans? I like rape." This is not a viable political philosophy!

Nor, however, is the opposite extreme espoused by fundamentalists, whether Christian or Islamic, viable either. Those who believe that they have heard the word of the Lord, speaking in their language and in no uncertain terms, are dangerous. And they are wrong. Their error is directly analogous to the error of the empiricists who believe that reality has shown its face to them with no representative sampling. In both cases these proponents of the One True Path need reminders that *their* sampling rules are not *everyone's*. And further, that others come along to remind them about *different* sampling rules does not mean that those others are on a slippery slope that leads to skepticism or pernicious relativism.

Much of the criticism of postmodernism in America derives from a failure to make the distinctions and follow the third path I'm describing here. Postmodernism's critics see only the attack on the old absolutes. The creators and defenders of postmodernism, for their part, have not done a very good job of showing that morality and meaning can survive the absence of absolutes. We have what it takes to find morality and meaning in the absence of absolutes. The relational worldview, as distinct from the darker side of postmodernism, *can* support a genuinely ethical pluralism.

This third way is, alas, messier than the simplistic extremes, so it will take some pages to sort it out. In the next two chapters I want to find the third way through the issue of *individuation*. I want to find a way beyond the extremes of individualism and collectivism. I want to lay out the fundamentals of what I call the social philosophy of *some*. I'll argue that the fundamental unit of social and political philosophy is neither the solitary individual nor the universal collective. That Communism is dead does not mean that the debate between individualism and collectivism is over. If anything, the death of Communism puts us in increased danger of falling too hard for extreme individualism.

After I find the path beyond individualism and collectivism in the next chapter, I make a case in the following chapter for *communities* as the appropriate units of representation—the players—in representative democracy. While the next chapter is about rejecting the extremes of *one* and *all*, the concluding chapter of Part Two shows how *some* can function as an intelligent agency of social creativity. The community, the corporation, and the company are the subjects of social history, the creators of alternative scenarios, and the choosers of paths into better futures. Scenarios are the means that communities use to imagine and choose their futures.

We've had a taste of that new way of knowing in this chapter, in the extended analogies I've drawn (with Bateson's help) between learning and evolution; between industrial policy and strategic planning; and then between the two previous analogies and the issue with which this chapter was launched: How can we find a way to make up for the shortcomings of the marketplace if we've lost faith in the guiding hand of government?

For the reasons given in Chapter 2, power has shifted from the State to corporations. The game has shifted from politics to economics. We're no longer guiding our advanced economies by the political logic that prevailed in the industrial era. Now, with privatization separating the marketplace from the government (just as we earlier separated Church from State), the main principles of legitimacy are economic rather than political. But, just as the Church continued to function as the conscience of the State, so the State still has a job to do in functioning as the conscience of the economy—to compensate the losers that marketplace mechanisms are bound to produce.

We are all better off, and the public interest is better served, by a mandate to universal service for health care, education, and communications. If the marketplace cannot deliver on that mandate to universal service, then we need some form of governance that will compensate for those marketplace mechanisms. Our existing form of government is not doing the job very well because its sampling rules for representation date from the agricultural era. We need to change the sampling rules and our understanding of the principle of individuation that determine the units of representation. We need to take account of *new players* in the new game of the economic era.

I'm going to argue for a social philosophy of *some;* that limited collectives—communities, corporations, and companies of more than a few persons—are the best units of representation to accomplish a democratic, equitable, free, and just society. Part Two, *New Players,* explores the principles of individuation in political philosophy. What is an individual such that it deserves a vote?

Part Two
New Players

CHAPTER FIVE

BEYOND INDIVIDUALISM
AND COLLECTIVISM

In February 1997, just days before the death of Deng Xiao Ping, Global Business Network sponsored a conference in Hong Kong on the rather large subject of the future of China. In keeping with our belief that reading about a subject is not enough, we wanted to give our members a closer look by taking them on a learning journey from Hong Kong to mainland China. So we boarded two buses and traveled across the border, an experience that felt for all the world like tense moments at the Berlin Wall back in the sixties.

We made our way into China easily enough, but we were detained on the way out. It seemed that one of our members had been born in mainland China and was now traveling with a visa that stipulated that he would fly back to Canada. However, the plane ticket he was holding was for travel to the United States. A little thing, you might think, but not so little to the Chinese bureaucrats managing that border crossing. Not only would he be detained, but our entire party of 56 could not pass until the matter had been straightened out.

We sat in our buses while our guides argued with the border guards. We fumed. How unreasonable to detain us all while they sorted out this hassle over just one individual! Couldn't we return to Hong Kong and let him catch a cab? No, our papers said our party comprised 56 travelers. We could not proceed with just 55! The measure of the group had to be correct, and the freedom of the individual to travel as he wished would not be honored. It was odd: we 55 individuals felt a little like spoiled children in someone else's home. We wanted to be treated like the precious selves we were used to being—individuals free to travel as we wished, but we were being reminded that we were guests in a country in which the values of the collective are more important than the rights of the individual.

Eventually we worked it out. Hours later we were on our way back to Hong Kong. That night we gathered for cocktails and dinner. The incident at the border was the topic of conversation at most of our tables. At my table I was joined by Rory Mongovern, head of Amnesty International in Asia. The conversation moved, not surprisingly, to human rights. After the events of the afternoon, I expected to find myself enthusiastically agreeing with Rory. Yet the longer we talked, the more I found myself in passionate disagreement, not over the goals of Amnesty International, which are altogether admirable, but over the language of "human rights."

The longer we talked, the more thoroughly I realized that this language is all wrong. "Human rights" presupposes an intellectual tradition of Western individualism, a tradition running from Socrates to the Magna Carta to the philosophy of John Locke. To those like Thomas Jefferson, who are steeped in that tradition, the dignity of the individual seems obvious. "We hold these truths to be self-evident" may sound good to others who share that Western tradition, but human rights are by no means self-evident to the Chinese, for whom the values of the collective come first.

"Rory," I found myself arguing, "I agree with your goals, but you're using the wrong means. The language is all wrong. Go straight at cruelty and human suffering. Don't take the detour through the language of human rights. That language is simply offensive. It presupposes the dignity of the individual, which is part of our tradition, but not theirs. It's as if you're waving a red, white, and blue flag in their face when you talk about human rights. Human suffering they can understand. Human rights, they can't. Talking about 'human rights' to the Chinese is like talking about the classless society to Americans. Plays well back home in Beijing, but you'd be waving a red flag at the folks in Peoria. We can all agree that human suffering is a bad thing, but you won't get the Chinese to reduce human suffering by talking about human rights."

I was surprised at my own passion in that conversation. While just that afternoon I'd felt so offended to be treated as one of a crowd of 56 rather than as a free individual, the deeper we probed the differences between Western individualism and Chinese collectivism, the more it became clear that we could not assume our Western truths to be self-evident to a Chinese border guard. He was brought up in a tradition based on a different political theory, different sampling rules. More than that, he and I did not even share the same psychology.

In this chapter I would like to review some recent developments in psychology and political theory. Is such a goal overly ambitious? Of course it would be if I were claiming to *cover* these vast fields. But I am not seeking total coverage, only a very selective sampling in order to find that which is exemplary and illustrative of ways of thinking that are changing.

The point is to identify the new players in the new game of the economic era. We're looking for the new players with a new worldview, and we're trying to become more aware, more self-conscious, about the ways the old worldview has hampered our thinking. We're also looking for a legitimate source of moral purchase, a rock to stand on when we criticize the present in the name of better futures. We want to look at the relationship between self and the polity, but we need to question those Robinson Crusoe-like individuals, the solid selves that supposedly come together to negotiate the social contracts that political theorists talk about with expressions like, one man, one vote.

Self and society . . . Are there selves before there is society? Can you have a society that is not a society of selves? The last several centuries of Anglo-American political philosophy assume fully self-conscious individuals who then join together to make a society. A European tradition of thought that runs from Hegel to Marx to Nietzsche to Foucault takes a very different perspective on collectivism rather than individualism. For this European tradition, mankind arrives on the scene as a herd. The tribe precedes the individual. Individualism is not our natural condition, however self-evident it may have seemed to John Locke and Thomas Jefferson.

From the perspective of collectivism, our Anglo-American individualism is not a natural, original condition but the result of centuries of economic history that have alienated individuals from their more natural home in a community. Individualism, as seen through the lenses of the collectivist worldview, is a sickness called alienation. We weren't meant to be as solitary as Robinson Crusoe on a desert island. We just came to feel that way because the sociopolitical system that took shape in Western Europe caused us to think that way. Individualism, from the perspective of this collectivist worldview, is an illness induced by our particular social history, not an original state of nature from which we emerged to create societies.

This tension between the primacy of the individual and the primacy of the collective runs deep. It has not been settled by the fall of Communism. Despite the triumph of capitalism, most other cultures are more collectivist than individualist. Look at the priority of the interests of society over the interests of the individual in Japan.[1] Look at the primacy of the extended family in China. Our persistent calls for human rights in China fall on deaf ears because, in a collectivist tradition, bleating about the rights of the individual has much less force than talk of responsibilities to the collective. The conflict over human rights is a conflict of worldviews. The contestants do not really hear one another because they are talking from radically different perspectives, relating different stories about the human condition.

The best way to resolve a conflict of worldviews is to become aware of the fact that it *is* a conflict of worldviews: it is not a question of conflicting interests alone, or a question of different evidence. So before diving into texts that propose to study The Individual, and, following that, texts that propose to study The Collective, I would like to review the dynamic that pits individualism against collectivism. The point of this review, once again, is to demonstrate the worldview-dependent nature of the conflict. The point of *that* demonstration is to establish the immense significance of the *worldview shifts* taking place in both psychology and social theory—shifts that will then be described in greater detail once the frame for those shifts has been illuminated.

REFRAMING THE CONFLICT BETWEEN
INDIVIDUALISTS AND COLLECTIVISTS

The differences between individualists and collectivists will not be settled by some utilitarian calculus that could tally the greatest good for the greatest number at the end of two histories guided by individualist or collectivist ideologies. The differences between individualism and collectivism go beyond guesses about probable historical consequences of the two different approaches. The differences between individualists and collectivists are—as is often the case where worldviews collide—ontological

Ontology is a word we don't use every day, and a quick dictionary definition—"the logic of, or speech about, being"—is not quite sufficient to justify dragging in such an esoteric term. But drag it in I must because this issue of representation concerns our inventory of existence. *Are* there individuals? Or is the individual, as Michel Foucault claims, a modern invention? We don't let ghosts vote because there *are* no ghosts. We don't let corporations vote because we consider corporations to be legal fictions. When we ask, what is an individual such that it deserves a vote? we are asking not only about the boundaries of individuation—atomic, molecular, cellular, organic, personal, communal, royal, species, and so on—we are also asking what it is to *be* an individual, of whatever size.

Clearly there is something odd about this question. We know what it is to sit as opposed to walk, to walk as opposed to run. We can distinguish the ways we use our feet and our posture. But what can we say about what it is to *be* as opposed to not being? The mind fogs at such a level of abstraction. For the purposes of this discussion about individualism and collectivism, we don't need to plumb the subtleties of the two greatest texts on ontology—Aristotle's *Metaphysics* and Heidegger's *Being and Time*—but it is worth noting, without exhaustively reviewing, these speeches *(logoi)* about being *(ontos)*. Why? Because they tell us about what we take for granted. They render explicit what is usually left implicit.

Just shy of this ultimate abstraction, Being, we can be explicit about our inventory of physical elements. Once upon a time the Greeks thought that the four elements—earth, air, water, and fire—in various combinations, were sufficient to account for everything else. Our modern table of elements contains more than a hundred elements, from hydrogen through iridium and beyond. Contemporary physics lists a smaller number of subatomic particles that make up the so-called elements: protons, electrons, quarks, etc. None of these things are observable to the naked eye. They all require definitions that verify existence according to the operations of atom smashers, cloud chambers, and electron microscopes. Can we draw an analogy with the table of elements in physics and find comparable operational definitions that would tell us about the fundamental elements, the fundamental units, the players of political analysis?

In the individualist tradition, the individual is the fundamental unit, the alpha and omega of social philosophy. Society supposedly begins with the coming together of individuals whose being as individuals is already assumed. The social contract theories of Locke, Hobbes, and Rousseau assume the existence of already constituted individuals who come together to form society. Without the benefits of civil society, these man-as-an-island individuals would run the danger of retreating to the jungle; they would fall back into that "state of nature" famously described by Hobbes as a hostile environment where life is "nasty, brutish, and short."

Rather than submit to the war of each against all, these already constituted individuals supposedly enter into a social compact. Civil society and the mechanisms of the State are then constructed as means to protect the ends of individual rights. In the individualist creation myth, the earth was not without form and void prior to the emergence of the State. Instead, there were individuals already present on the first day of creation. They shape the State as a means toward satisfying their own ends. So, on the last day of creation, it is the interests of individuals— their liberties and their rights—that define the final purposes and measure the success of the State apparatus. Individuals stand at the beginning and at the end of this creation and destiny myth.

In the collectivist tradition, the story, the ontological myth, is precisely reversed. For Marx, as for Hegel before him, the individual is not the concrete beginning point but an abstraction from the whole interconnected web of existence. Both Hegel and Marx saw the individual as a product of alienation from that prior whole. Mankind is first social, at however primitive a level, and only after certain social dynamics have been played out do individuals emerge as a social product. Individuation is accomplished, not primordial and given. Both Hegel and Marx see history as the progressive overcoming of alienation. Individuality is a kind of necessary and inevitable mistake that the collective must make if it is to develop from an undifferentiated herd on the first day of creation to a well-functioning, classless society on the last—that seventh day after the revolution when the alienation of the individual from the collective shall be overcome. Nice story.

Just as the individual is the alpha and omega of the individualist creation myth, so is society the beginning and the end of the collectivist creation myth. Just as society served as a means to the end of individual gratification, so the stages of individual alienation appear like the labors of Hercules on an odyssey which the collective human spirit must traverse before the individual can return to his true home at the bosom of the collective.

There, then, are the ontological creation myths at the heart of the conflict of worldviews between the individualist and collectivist traditions. It is important to appreciate the depth of the difference, the degree to which each ontology can be cogently interpreted as delusional within the context of the opposing worldview. Like the therapist who can interpret a patient's resistance to therapy as part of the problem to

be overcome, the proponents of each worldview can interpret the resistances of their opponents as founded on fundamental errors that will
be overcome in the course of history—what the Marxists call *false consciousness.* Collectivists can hope that individualists will overcome their
regrettable alienation from society. Individualists can hope that collectivists will someday see the merits of liberating individuals from the un-
fortunate, unnecessary, and therefore temporary, yoke of the State.

Each tradition becomes a regrettable if necessary chapter in the longer,
more comprehensive story that the other tradition has to tell. Each tradition consistently rejects the story told by the other, not because the
other story is heard and understood, and its calculus of benefits is computed differently; rather, the calculations are fundamentally incommen-
surable because the units of measure—the players—differ at an ontological level. Their sampling rules are different because their principles
of individuation are different. Social benefits that are seen as the goal of
the collectivist creation myth are mere means to the gratification of individuals in the individualist creation myth. Individual self-realization
that is the goal of the individualist creation myth is seen as a mere means
to bringing about a healthy society in the collectivist creation myth.

Given the symmetry of these opposed approaches to means and ends,
there is little hope of these two paths converging at a point at which the
trade-offs between individualism and collectivism would balance or, better yet, achieve a synergistic or symbiotic relationship. Because the two
myths are so different in their appraisals of both the beginnings and the
endings of their respective stories, there is little likelihood that their
tellers could ever agree on what counts as a happy ending.

So much for social ontology and its expression in creation myths. The
point of elaborating these myths is not to choose between them but to
grasp the symmetry of their opposition and the consequent improba-
bility of either side convincing the other in a purely ideological debate.
As long as each side sees its world through the lenses of its own worldview, the argument of the other side can be deflected as the product of
a delusional process, and each side has a fully cogent account for how
and why its opponents have become so deluded. Until both sides appreciate the character of their opposition, that is, until both sides appreciate the fact that their arguments will be reinterpreted through the
eyes of a different worldview with different principles of individuation
and different sampling rules, neither side will be truly heard by the other.
Misinterpretation will persist, not because Americans and Chinese are
so different, but because the principles of individuation of individual-

ism and collectivism describe different worlds. In the worldview of the collectivist, society or the whole is the fundamental unit of social existence. In the worldview of the individualist, the individual is the fundamental ontological unit.

It is as if collectivists see the individual as the intersection of two preexisting lines of relationship, and individualists see the lines of social relationship as coming after and connecting preexisting points. The axioms of their respective social geometries differ accordingly—and like two parallel lines in Euclidian geometry, never the twain shall meet.

Just as flies piece together an integrated picture from many images coming through the hundreds of facets on their spherical eyes, and frogs see a world where flies appear more prominently than the background, so individualists and collectivists alike tend to see worlds that nourish and support their own respective predispositions.

IN FAVOR OF INDIVIDUALISM

There is hope for a further revisioning of social relationships within and between East and West because the process has already begun. On both sides of the ideological divide, theorists have begun to question their own ontological creation myths. We are already in the midst of a process of demythologizing. In the West, several scholars have begun to question whether we haven't overdone individualism in the Western tradition. At the same time, the costs of collectivism and the merits of individualism have now been acknowledged in the Eastern Bloc, as the remarkable turns in Russia and Eastern Europe have demonstrated.

There can be little doubt that individualism is one of the cornerstones of the American tradition. The Founding Fathers of the Constitution were heavily influenced by individualist teachings in the philosophies of Locke and Rousseau. Early American philosophers and essayists added even more weight to the final authority of individual conscience as opposed to the laws of the State. "Why has every man a conscience, then?" asks Thoreau. "I think that we should be men first, and subjects afterward. It is not desirable to cultivate a respect for the law, so much as for the right. The only obligation which I have a right to assume is to do at any time what I think right."[2]

In his famous essay on "Self-Reliance," Emerson writes: "No law can be sacred to me but that of my nature. Good and bad are but names very readily transferable to that or this; the only right is what is after my constitution; the only wrong what is against it." In these and similar statements, the founders of American individualism make it perfectly clear that the individual's appeal to his own conscience provides a higher court than the law of the land or the general will of the collective. Individual conscience is the rock on which morality must rest.

Individualism as construed by Thoreau and Emerson allowed for lofty defenses of civil disobedience in situations where the State condones injustices like slavery. But the dangers of such strong appeals to individualism were already apparent to de Tocqueville: "Individualism is a calm and considered feeling which disposes each citizen to isolate himself from the mass of his fellows and withdraw into the circle of family and friends; with this little society formed to his taste, he gladly leaves the greater society to look after itself."[3] Not only is there danger to "the greater society" when individuals leave it to look after itself, there is also the psychological risk of implosion. "Each man is forever thrown back on himself alone, and there is danger that he may be shut up in the solitude of his own heart."[4]

Throughout most of the nineteenth and twentieth centuries, individualism has held the upper hand in the Anglo-American tradition. There are exceptions. Philosopher George Herbert Mead directly challenged the ontological priority of the individual self: "The process out of which the self arises is a social process which implies interaction of individuals in the group, implies the pre-existence of the group. . . . [T]he origin and foundations of the self, like those of thinking, are social."[5]

For the most part, however, claims for the primacy of society, the collective, or the group were met by authoritative statements like David Riesman's in his essay (and book by the same title) "Individualism Reconsidered" (1951): "We must give every encouragement to people to develop their private selves—to escape from groupism—while realizing that, in many cases, they will use their freedom in unattractive or 'idle' ways. . . . I am insisting that no ideology, however noble, can justify the sacrifice of an individual to the needs of the group."[6]

Riesman finds it necessary to reconsider individualism because he realizes that its form is changing. He observes that the process of modernization freed people from external restraints imposed by religion or hereditary aristocracy. But the individuals thus freed carried with them many of those same restraints, which they had *internalized*. "These men were bound by a character orientation I have termed 'inner-direction': they were guided by internalized goals and ideals which made them appear to be more individualistic than they actually were."[7] Only because one could assume that social restraints were still operative, in internal-

ized form, was it possible to praise and pursue the virtues of individualism. "In sum, it proved possible in the West in early modern times to
carry individualism to its limits of usefulness—and, in some cases, far
beyond these limits—because a fair amount of social cohesiveness was
taken for granted."[8]

It is precisely this assumption of social cohesiveness that has come
into question since the 1950s. Social cohesiveness can no longer be
taken for granted, in part because individualism has been pursued to
its limits and beyond, in part because *different* societies have become
intermingled in our increasingly multicultural world. Since the 1950s,
individualism has in fact increased in the United States. For the very
reason that it has increased in practice, the theoretical questioning of
its costs and benefits has also increased. Let me review some evidence
of the increase of individualism in practice. Then I'll discuss alternative theoretical interpretations of the evidence for the growth of
individualism.

TOO MUCH OF A GOOD THING?

In the Values and Lifestyles (VALS) Program at SRI International, a
number of us conducted empirical research on American values. Arnold
Mitchell developed a typology to describe and track different lifestyle
segments. Partly influenced by David Riesman, Mitchell chose as a fundamental dimension of differentiation the distinction between the
"Inner-Directed" and the "Outer-Directed." The Outer-Directed are
those who live their lives according to external restraints, overt or covert.
They want to "keep up with the Joneses." They want to fit into the
group by conforming to its norms. The Inner-Directed, on the other
hand, listen more closely to their inner voice for guidance.

Despite all the rhetoric in favor of individualism in America, most of
the American population is more Outer-Directed than Inner-Directed,
at least as these terms are operationally defined by responses to the VALS
questionnaire. Just as Riesman described the freed individuals of early
modernity, so also in the America of the 1950s, most so-called individualists had in fact internalized the norms of society. Given the choice—
which they were given by the rhetoric of individualistic free choice—
most Americans tended to choose freely the very same values that had
earlier been socially imposed. As Philip Slater put it in his trenchant critique of individualism, "Our society gives far more leeway to the individual to pursue his own ends, but, since *it* defines what is worthy and

desirable, everyone tends, independently but monotonously, to pursue the same things in the same way."[9]

Let me encapsulate what both Riesman and Slater are describing with the expression *conformist individualism*. This label threatens to be self-canceling—an oxymoron. Aren't individualists the most likely to be nonconformists? So it would seem. But Riesman's talk of internalization of external norms, and Slater's complaint that individuals abuse the leeway of individualism by choosing "independently but monotonously," are both intended to question the quick assumption that individualists will be non-conformists. They are both pointing to the fact that individualism, whether in early modern or late suburban forms, can be remarkably conformist in its actual expression.

The 1960s introduced a major break in the tradition of *conformist individualism*. In the 1960s there arose, as if by a dialectical turning over into its opposite, a new kind of *nonconformist collectivism*. In the 1960s the youth rebelled *en masse*. The youth movement of the sixties was nonconformist—witness the importance of long hair and styles of dress—but remarkably collectivist. Solidarity among members of the counterculture was manifested in mass demonstrations and in communal lifestyles. Even in their nonconformity to mainstream styles, the blue denim on political activists, the long hair, and the tie-dyed costumes of hippies were as instantly recognizable as military uniforms.

The longer–term effects of the 1960s were as complex and rich with ironies as the reversal from conformist individualism in the 1950s to nonconformist collectivism in the 1960s. By the 1970s the Vietnam War was winding down, inflation was ratcheting up, and unemployment increased as the baby boom youth of the sixties entered a labor market limited by oil-starved recessions. The rebelliousness of the 1960s had loosened the ties to old authorities. But the solidarity of "the Movement" disappeared as students graduated from college and each faced the job market alone. With neither loyalty to the old establishment nor solidarity with their peers, many baby boomers slipped into what Tom Wolfe dubbed "the Me Decade."

The 1970s were experienced by many as individualistic to the point of rampant selfishness. Psychoanalytic literature became preoccupied with narcissism. Important testaments of the times include Christopher Lasch's book, *The Culture of Narcissism* (1979), Heinz Kohut's *The Analysis of the Self* (1971), and Richard Sennett's *The Fall of Public Man* (1977). In each of these books you'll find a strong critique of the withdrawal of the individual into what de Tocqueville called "the solitude of his own heart." But more important, you'll find an acknowledgment of the historicity of that heart, its ability to be influenced by changing social and historical conditions.

Sennett is particularly attentive to the difference between the new notion of personality as unique, and the Enlightenment ideal of a universal human nature. Lacking the Enlightenment belief in natural character, we no longer pursue a universal science of the sympathies and humors yet "We need to understand this alien notion of a natural realm of the self because we continue today to believe in notions of human rights which arose because of it."[10] Recall my conversation in Hong Kong with Rory Mongovern of Amnesty International.

History has come full circle from Thoreau's call for individual civil disobedience against the State on behalf of the rights of slaves. What these modern critics are arguing is that the voice of individual conscience eventually defeats itself if that voice represents—samples—only one unique personality. If the voice of individual conscience has, as Riesman and Slater suggested, already internalized the rules of society, then that voice can be trusted not to deviate too radically from the collective will. If that voice of individual conscience speaks from the universal text of a fixed and timeless human nature, then all voices can be expected to speak as one. In either case, whether by internalization of social mores or by the assumption of a universal human nature, the defense of human rights can be justified by reference to a universally shared human condition. But once the social cohesion that had been taken for granted is shattered into shards of personalities whose uniqueness is more important than their commonality, then the defense of universal human rights is thrown into question. Suddenly it is every man for himself, and every woman for herself. Thus we entered the eighties.

During the late 1970s and the 1980s our SRI surveys tracked an increase among the Inner-Directed from about 15 percent of the adult American population up to 21 percent. Other indicators also suggest an increase in individualism since the 1960s. Dan Yankelovich summarizes years of survey research in his book *New Rules*. There he speaks of an increase in individual *self-expression* since the sixties. Other survey data from the National Opinion Research Center (NORC) at the University of Chicago show that between 1968 and 1976 the percentage of people willing to be bossed around on the job declined from 56 percent of the population to 36 percent. Each of these indicators—from SRI, from Yankelovich, and from NORC—suggests that individualism is on the increase *in fact,* even as the theorists I have quoted are becoming ever more critical of individualism *in theory.*

Since 1980 the most significant works on the factual spread as well as the theoretical critique of individualism have surely been those by Robert Bellah and his colleagues: *Habits of the Heart: Individualism and Commitment in American Life* and *The Good Society.* Bellah and his coworkers conducted in-depth interviews with hundreds of people. What they found is very consistent with the dangers described by de Tocqueville and Sennett: "[I]f selves are defined by their preferences, but those preferences are arbitrary, then each self constitutes its own moral universe, and there is finally no way to reconcile conflicting claims about what is good in itself."[11]

One of the interviewees, to whom they give the name Brian, tries to explain his commitments: "Why is integrity important and lying bad? I don't know. It just is. It's just so basic. I don't want to be bothered with challenging that. It's part of me. I don't know where it came from, but it's very important."[12] Brian doesn't know where to find the fulcrum for his morality. Bellah and his colleagues are sensitive to the loss of a shared moral vocabulary, as is evident in Brian's inability to defend or justify his values: "He lacks a language to explain what seem to be the real commitments that define his life, and to that extent the commitments themselves are precarious."[13]

Brian seems to have values, but he cannot explain how he got them or where they came from.

> 'Values' turn out to be the incomprehensible, rationally indefensible thing that the individual chooses when he or she has thrown off the last vestige of external influence and reached pure, contentless freedom. The ideal self in its absolute freedom is completely 'unencumbered' . . . The improvisational self chooses values to express itself; but it is not constituted by them as from a pre-existing source. This notion of an unencumbered self is derived not only from psychotherapy, but much more fundamentally from modern philosophy, from Descartes, Locke, and Hume, who affect us more than we imagine.[14]

Let me summarize this brief review of the debate over individualism in America as follows: There is no question that, from the writings of Emerson and Thoreau to the practices of people in the 1970s and 1980s, individualism is central to the American tradition. However, while the early theoretical critiques of individualism, from de Tocqueville to Mead, occurred against a backdrop of strong social cohesion, by the 1970s and 1980s one could presuppose neither the social cohesion of the pre-1950s that was described by Riesman, nor the social conformity that characterized the 1950s, nor the solidarity in nonconformity that characterized the 1960s. By the 1970s and 1980s individualism, both in theory and in practice, had devolved from a defense of the individual's moral conscience to diatribes against narcissism and self-indulgence.

Bellah and his colleagues find themselves forced to level the following indictment: "We believe that much of the thinking about the self of educated Americans, thinking that has become almost hegemonic in our universities and much of the middle class, is based on inadequate social science, impoverished philosophy, and vacuous theology."[15]

I believe that part of the "impoverished philosophy" that Bellah has in mind is the individualist creation myth. The notion of the unencumbered self—as inherited "from Descartes, Locke, and Hume, who affect us more than we imagine"—is precisely that alpha and omega, that always already fully formed individual who supposedly exists prior to and after all social and historical conditioning.

Writers like Philip Slater, Christopher Lasch, Richard Sennett, and Robert Bellah are actively engaged in demythologizing the individualist creation myth, even as opinion research and trends in popular culture suggest an increase in individualism in America. These writers are correct to criticize the individualist creation myth, but its stark, extreme alternative, the collectivist creation myth, lies in ruins following the fall of Communism. Can we find a less harsh alternative to collectivism in a social philosophy founded on community?

As long as the conflict between individualism and collectivism is conceived as a real conflict between two real opponents—The Individual versus The Collective—I see no hope of resolution given the self-justifying nature of the symmetrically opposed arguments. As long as both individualists and collectivists assume the ontological priority of either the individual or the collective, and are able to support that ontological priority with a corresponding worldview, then never the twain shall meet. There is no point of convergence that would constitute a happy ending for both individualists and collectivists because they *see* happiness as differently as the fly and the frog see the swamp.

The way out lies not with opting for one ontology or the other, but in rising above, looking down, and appreciating the character of the conflict. Once we appreciate the degree to which our worldviews support sampling rules that are incompatible, then we are thrown back to questioning those worldviews and their corresponding principles of individuation. Once that questioning has begun, there opens up an opportunity for completely reframing the conflict: Rather than seeing the individual and the collective as ontologically given and concrete, individuality and collectivity can be recast as equal and opposite abstractions or samplings from the concrete life of everyday communities. Not one, not all, but some are the real subjects of history—corporations, companies, communities.

No individual is ever completely isolated. And no actual community has ever extended its reach to the entire species. Both individuality and "species-being" are abstractions from the concrete, day–to–day reality of life in communities. The concrete starting point of social theory should be neither the solitary individual—as much a fiction as Robinson Crusoe—nor the all-inclusive collective, which has never been concretely experienced by anyone. The concrete starting point of social theory should be those limited collectives we call communities, those groups of face–to–face others usually numbering somewhere between 50 people and 50,000 people—*some*.

Once we reframe both individuality and collectivity as equal and opposite abstractions from concrete community, then both the individualist and the collectivist creation myths appear as instances of what Alfred North Whitehead called "the fallacy of misplaced concreteness."[16] To the naïve observer, unbiased by either the individualist or collectivist tradition, nothing could be more obvious than the fact that real life as lived by real people always involves exchanges and interchanges among finite groups that are individuated by language, commerce, work, and play.

It is only the very rare shepherd or lighthouse keeper who gets through a day without hearing a single word from another human. At the opposite extreme, it is only the rare astronaut or mystic who has had an opportunity to *experience* the human species as a single totality. The rest of us can speak the words *the human species,* and we can do our best to identify and empathize with people at great cultural and geographical distances, but the fact remains that the idea of all human beings remains an abstraction as compared with the concreteness of our face-to-face community.

You can argue that we *ought* to experience an immediate feeling of brotherhood with all human beings, that it is callous to be indifferent to the sufferings of others just because they happen to be halfway around the world rather than next door. Such arguments are worth making. It may well be the case that the measure of your psychological development lies in the degree to which you identify, as the Buddhists say, with all living creatures. Perhaps. But the point I'm making has nothing to do with moral exhortation. The point I'm making here is about worldviews rather than morals. I'm suggesting that the universalist ideal of embracing the entire human species, whether it ought or ought not to be *achieved* by dint of moral persuasion, is in any case not automatically *given*. Consequently, the concept of the universal collective is an abstraction, an idea reached by various steps of extrapolation from the concrete experience of what are always only limited collectives.

The same argument can and must be made against individualism. A long tradition from Emerson and Thoreau to Erik Erikson (originator of the concept of identity crisis) may well have something important to teach, namely, the need to become your own person, to be responsible, to think for yourself, to exercise a degree of subjectivity that is creative, to be more than a carbon copy of the influences that shaped you. All these exhortations can be put in ways that make a great deal of sense, even to the collectivist. How you, as an individual, *ought* to be is not at issue here. The point is that individual autonomy is *achieved*, not *given*. Consequently, the concept of the utterly isolated, self-sufficient individual is an abstraction, an idea reached by various steps of extrapolation from the concrete experience of life lived in a web of relationships with others.

Yes, there are individuals, some of whom are more autonomous, idiosyncratic, and creative than others. Yes, there are collectives, and some are larger and more embracing than others. But neither The Individual nor The Collective is ontologically given as a privileged starting point for social philosophy. Both individuality and collective solidarity are biographical and social achievements.

When individuality and collectivity are seen as possible achievements rather than as alternative ontological starting points, then the advantages of both individualism and collectivism appear as complementary rather than conflicting. The collective needs the spark of creativity and autonomy. The individual needs language, community, and all the rest of the benefits of society. The interests of liberty and creativity on the one hand, and social cohesion and tradition on the other, will always pull at the heart of each community. The point of this brief review of the individualist and collectivist traditions is hardly to resolve that tension once and for all, but to sustain that tension within the lives of all communities. Neither The Individual nor The Collective can win, because neither ever existed in the first place.

THE SHIFT OF WORLDVIEWS IN PSYCHOLOGY

Having framed the debate between individualism and collectivism as a difference of worldviews, I now want to look at the players inside that frame by looking at the way others look at the players inside that frame. I'm not making this stuff up. Psychologists have been seeing the individual turn from a substantive identity into a structure of relationships. This paradigm shift in psychology is part of a relational worldview that contributes to the social philosophy of *some*. Meanwhile social theorists have been seeing the collective dissolve into a pluralistic array of competing interests. This equal and opposite paradigm shift among sociologists approaches the social philosophy of *some* from the other direction, from the *all* rather than from the *one*. These disciplines are changing their sampling rules and their principles of individuation to identify new players for the new game in the economic era.

Contemporary psychology is in ferment. A range of competing schools have undermined the solidity of The Individual seen as a singular ego. *Ego* is a concept, an invention, the product of a kind of conspiracy-theory-of-the-self. We see all of those actions that a self performs, and we become convinced that there is some unified conspiracy *behind* the actions, some unified intender, some ghost in the machine. But as Nietzsche wrote some time ago, "No such agent exists; there is no 'being' behind the doing, acting, becoming; the 'doer' has simply been added to the deed by the imagination—the doing is everything."[17] Outer existence precedes or replaces inner essence.

I know this deconstruction of the ego sounds nihilistic—no Santa Claus, no God, no ego, nothing? But here's where Nietzsche actually helps us. He distinguishes two kinds of nihilism: one of weakness, one of strength. The first says, "God is dead. The self does not exist. O woe. We are doomed." The second says, "God is dead. Daddy's gone. Now we can play." This second, active, lyric nihilism animates a lighter mood. And it is this second, active, dancing nihilism that can animate communal creativity precisely to the extent that it liberates us from the looming presence of God or the superego telling us what we *ought* to be doing instead of playing.

The good news, the glad tidings of the relational worldview, tells us that we don't need a unified ego for creativity to be possible. Creative intentionality has been elevated "up" to collectivities larger than the individual, and it has been deconstructed "down" to a plurality of agents within the so-called individual (who turns out to look more like a community of diverse agencies).

The *substantial identity* of the self has become suspect. Descartes claimed to have discovered a unitary subject of thought in the *Cogito*, Latin for "I think," such that the mere fact of thought proved the identity of the thinker. But when David Hume inquired as to the causes of this sense of identity, he found only relations of resemblance among different parts of experience. "The identity which we ascribe to the mind of man is only a fictitious one."[18] Even the author of the term *identity crisis*, Erik Erikson, is appalled at the metaphorical free play the phrase has assumed when "the papers run a headline, 'The Identity Crisis of Africa,' or refer to the 'identity crisis' of the Pittsburgh glass industry . . . or if, finally, the Catholic students at Harvard announce that they will hold an 'Identity Crisis' on Thursday night at eight o'clock sharp."[19] Yet Erikson's own attempt to make the term more precise by tying it to its origins carries telltale quotation marks indicative of metaphor and fiction. In its original application it applied to a group of World War II veterans "impaired in that central control over themselves for which, in the psychoanalytic scheme, only the 'inner agency' of the ego could be held responsible."[20]

What is this "inner agency," and why must responsibility require singularity? Freud himself, in his attempts to delimit the meaning of ego, marshaled a whole series of metaphors to describe its relation to the id. The ego is like a rider who, "if he is not to be parted from his horse, is obliged to guide it where it wants to go."[21] The ego "behaves like the physician during an analytic treatment."[22] The ego is "like a politician who sees the truth but wants to keep his place in popular favor."[23] One more image that begins to slide toward the interior commune or body politic: "the ego's position is like that of a constitutional monarch, without whose sanction no law can be passed but who hesitates long before imposing his veto on any measure put forward by Parliament."[24]

In his attempts to find likenesses for understanding psychic phenomena, Freud sought out well-known examples of command, control, and negotiation. But just as constitutional monarchy is a culturally limited and historically specific instance of control, so is identity-based ego-psychology. Contemporary schools reach for new metaphors in developing a new map for the territory of human behavior.

Jungian psychologists engage in interpretations of symbols whose meanings are always overdetermined—too rich in several possible meanings to be reduced to one unambiguous interpretation of significance. For Jungians, the real subjects of history seem to be a set of archetypes that appear again and again in our dreams, are reflected in our actions, and assume roles in the stories of our lives. The sensational popularity of Thomas Moore's books about the soul testifies to the immense appeal of this way of looking at our lives.[25]

Moore's mentor is James Hillman, whose "polytheistic psychology" sees the "individual" as already a collective: "Rather than a field of forces, we are each a field of internal personal relationships, an interior commune, a body politic."[26] With Jung's help, Hillman opens up "a view of personality that is no longer single-centered but polycentric."[27] From time to time, the population changes. "New partial personalities spring up with feelings, opinions, needs. A sociologist might speak of subcultures; a political scientist of states' rights and grassroots government. Whatever the category, central command is losing control,"[28] but not to the anarchy of anomie. Heterarchy provides a better model for this polycentric personality.

Yet another contributor to the ferment in psychology, the object relations school—Melanie Klein, D. W. Winnicott, Ronald Fairbairn, and Harry Guntrip, to name a few of the principals—sees the self as a structure of evolving relationships, not as a substance or thing with clearly defined boundaries. Their theories and their therapies treat the development of personality as a succession of relationships beginning with the primary relationship between parent and infant. The object relations school no longer begins with the assumption of a self-contained, atomic ego, but regards the self as established—successfully or unsuccessfully—through its relationships.

This shift in emphasis—from *things* to *relationships*—is fundamental. Its significance extends from the abstractions of philosophical ontology—the discourse about Being, and what it is to exist or not—to concrete decisions about everyday life. In ancient philosophy, especially in the influential writings of Aristotle, to be is to be an individual, and to be an *individual* is to be a *substance*. Relations were regarded as secondary or derivative, as added on by the perceiving mind. If A is to the left of B, that relationship depends in turn on the relationship between A, B, *and an observer*. Substance, on the contrary, was defined as that which is self-sufficient.

This Aristotelian principle of individuation was rendered even more explicit by Spinoza, who defined substance as "that which is completely self-sufficient and needs no other in order to exist." It doesn't take a card-carrying feminist to identify the macho presuppositions underlying the priority of substance so defined. Nor does it take a degree in psychoanalysis to see the import of Spinoza's—and behaviorist psychology's—attempt to reduce human subjectivity to a set of observable behaviors and properties of physical substance. The reduction of subject to substance, and the privileging of self-sufficiency over relatedness, are part and parcel of a worldview that puts facts before values, objects before subjects, points before lines, and matter before mind.

Working within a nineteenth–century scientific worldview, "Freud did not start with the concept of the whole person. Psychoanalysis became obsessed with distinguishable aspects functioning as parts needing to be fitted together"[29] like so many elements or unchanging, replaceable parts of a machine. Working within the emergent, holistic, relational worldview, existential therapists, Jungian psychologists, and those in the object relations school stress the importance of seeing the whole person before reducing him or her to an assemblage of syndromes, neuroses, or elemental instincts.

Their holistic perspective carries over into their view of the relationship between psyche and soma, or mind and body. "It has been assumed hitherto that mind (that which enabled the scientist to create his science) is a kind of secretion, if anything, of the body. But now we have to think in terms of developing psyche as the vital stimulating factor evolving a body to meet is needs."[30]

Neither the body nor the so-called primitive instincts can be regarded as fixed elements always exerting the same pressures or constraints. The relational and existential perspectives in psychology object to the idea that archaic elements lie unchanged beneath newer layers of mental or cultural refinement. "The equation of 'mature' with 'up-to-date' and 'infantile' with 'archaic' is a misleading error perpetuated by the idea of evolutionary layers of the psychosomatic whole. It needs to be replaced by the concept of an evolutionary whole in which every constituent is appropriately different from what it would have been in a different kind of whole."[31]

This last sentence could be grafted directly to a description of the way scenarios of better futures should replace predictions. Scenarios are precisely those narrative wholes whose logics cast each part into a context different from what it would have been in a different kind of scenario. For example, the rapid diffusion of computing technology may contribute to social decentralization in one scenario or to the spread of invasive Big Brotherism in another scenario. Ripped out of context and viewed—artificially—as an isolated element, the rapid diffusion of information technology cannot carry its meaning or significance on its own face. Only by embedding that technology in a larger text or context—a set of scenarios—can its several possible meanings be explored.

Neither culture, psyche, nor mind is added on top of physical nature, body, or technology taken as unchanging elements. From a holistic perspective, in the evolved organism of psyche and society, matter is informed and altered by mind. There is no fixed foundation, no unchanging elements into which organisms can be analyzed and reduced for purposes of explanation and prediction. Worldviews contest one another all the way down.

This chapter has focused on The Individual in both the conflict between individualism and collectivism and in the fermenting discipline of psychology. The next chapter turns to social theory in order to focus on The Collective, whether in the form of the entire human species, or in the Enlightenment ideal of a universal human nature. While this chapter argued, in effect, "not *one*," the next chapter shows why "not *all*." It shows how *some* can be the subjects of voluntary histories for each and every community.

CHAPTER SIX

SOCIAL FORCES AND CREATIVITY

Do we trust a psychotic to offer his own best diagnosis? No, individual introspection is almost bound to be warped by the biases of self-deception. Too much is at stake for an individual subject to see herself clearly. Likewise, to the extent that sociology uses the cultural and intellectual artifacts of a society—a culturally bound set of categories—to understand that society, it is just as suspect as introspective psychology. Subjectivity in selective sampling is the original sin of sociology: Thou shalt not use one's own ethnic customs as the standard for judging one's own society, much less other societies.

As a consequence of their suspicious origins, the claims of sociologists are often subjected to close scrutiny for telltale signs of self-serving biases. For this reason, sociologists have often attempted to be utterly objective in their methods. Knowing that they are stained by the original sin of subjectively biased sampling, they have sought to be holier (that is, more objective) than the Pope (in this case, the natural sciences).

For the founders, Weber and Durkheim, sociology was supposed to be "value free" (*wertfrei*). Weber's studies on the relationship between religious beliefs and economics allowed a distance between the subjectivity of the sociologist and the object under study by using evidence drawn from a safe distance. Chinese Confucianism and Indian Hinduism could be correlated with economies and societies separated by centuries and miles from his own perspective. Durkheim's landmark study of suicide attempted to base its findings on cold statistics that had nothing to do with subjective variations among individual suicides. Behavior, not subjective intention, was the object of study. Hence there was less danger that the social scientist's own intentions would cloud his understanding of the object under study. Simply by seeking correlations between actual numbers of suicides and other objective measures like economic performance and demographics, the social scientist could seek out laws that might describe the past, predict its future, and explain the present.

By treating society as if it were an aggregate of atomic individuals whose contrary intentions average out under the law of large numbers, sociologists might discover certain valencies, certain tendencies to aggregate and divide, and certain iron laws that would unlock the secrets of social organization just as elegantly as the table of the elements unlocked the secrets of the atom. Humanity, though an aggregate of subjects, could be treated as an object after all. Subjective intentions, about which the sociologist could make no truly unbiased claims, could be canceled out as so much thermal noise or random perturbations at the microlevel of society. Even if society could not be treated like a clock or other complex machine, its movements might nevertheless reveal a determinism that makes a mockery of reasoned intentions at the helm of history.

Reasonable people tend to be offended by arguments that wrest their fates from their own hands. Consequently there has been no lack of critics of positivist sociology.[1] The romantic reaction against positivism—"Yes, we *can* choose our destiny! We *do* have free will!"—misses the point. Positivism need not deny the efficacy of intentions at the microlevel. The romantic reaction falls into a myth of subjectivism which, by its own one-sidedness, tends to keep objectivism alive—as such antitheses so often do. By missing the point, by confusing statistical with mechanical determinism, the romantics offered the positivists targets for legitimate criticism. As is the case in so many paradigm wars, the parties talked past one another, neither side satisfied that it had been heard, neither side convinced that it had been justifiably criticized. In their eager attempts to find each others' dirty linen, they ended up taking in each others' wash.

As long as the romantic reaction continued to distance itself from positivism's insights as well as its failings, the world studied by sociologists remained divided by a conceptual Maginot line that separated the two camps in the ongoing worldview war. As Richard Harvey Brown draws the lines in an essay entitled "Symbolic realism and sociological thought: Beyond the positivist-romantic debate:"[2]

On the side of science	*On the side of the subjective/romantic reaction*
truth	beauty
reality	symbols
things and events	feelings/meanings
"out there"	"in here"
objective	subjective
explanation	interpretation
proof	insight
determinism	freedom

Any sociology adequate to the task of comprehending a complex society will have to integrate these columns. During the last several decades, sociology has shown signs of moving beyond the old paradigm war toward a new synthesis that bears many of the marks of the relational worldview.

JÜRGEN HABERMAS AND REFLEXIVE SOCIOLOGY

One of the crucial players is Jürgen Habermas. Heir to the throne of the influential Frankfurt School of Critical Theory, Habermas has achieved a subtle synthesis of Marxism, psychology, and communications theory. He begins with a distinction between two kinds of human interest: theoretical and practical. Theoretical interests include elements in the left-hand column above; practical, the right-hand column. Human beings are not interested in just one or the other column, but both. Because our knowledge serves both sets of interests, an adequate social theory cannot exclude either set of interests.

The main point of distinguishing practical from theoretical interests is to acknowledge that we are (or at least can be) free to choose who we will be. Objective, theoretical science does not have the last word when it comes to humanity. We are (or can be) a bootstrap phenomenon. Always within the context of very real constraints, some historical, some biological, humanity can frame its own laws. This is a liberating lesson. It is central to this book. We have a practical interest in building better futures. Theoretical reason helps us know what is and what must be: the laws of science. But practical reason concerns what might be and ought to be: our hopes for the ways our futures might offer more of what we want than our past or present has.

Think, for example, of the difference between physical laws and traffic laws. We can choose—and different societies have chosen differently—whether to drive on the right side of the road or the left. We cannot choose to alter the value of Planck's constant or the force of gravity. We can choose the color coding of traffic lights. Despite the fact that the British do not break ranks with the rest of the world by choosing blue rather than red as the color of a stoplight, the universality of "red = stop" should not be confused with the universality of the laws of physics. "Red = stop" is conventional law; gravity is natural law.

Faced with universal conventions like "red = stop," it's easy to forget the difference between conventional law and natural law. To a religious mind–set, both seem equally "God–given." But conventions are human creations, and the history of human creativity is not finished, despite famous claims to the contrary. The power of Habermas' work, and the reason it's worth wading (at least part way) into the subtleties of his thinking, lies precisely in his grasp of the difference between natural law, which is the object of our theoretical interest, and conventional law, which is the *product*, not the *object*, of our practical interest.

An individual compelled by an obsession or compulsion to make certain "choices" is not a free individual. Likewise, a community driven by economic or technological imperatives is not a free society. Both in the case of the individual and in the case of society, deliberation among options is a characteristic of freedom.

However, social deliberation is no more free than the individual deliberation of a psychotic if social deliberation is compelled by some overriding, determining force. What the fetish is to the obsessed individual, some comparably unquestioned object of desire might be to a society. If a society forbids an exchange of ideas about some social goal—whether the eradication of AIDS or the achievement of racial equality—then the behavior of that society turns out to be just as compulsive, just as unfree, as the obsessed individual's.

I want to describe some of the dilemmas that critical theory fell into as a way of setting the context for scenario planning's achievements. I want to stand on the shoulders of the giants of social theory, even as I claim that those giants are crippled. They lift us up by virtue of the moral outrage that motivated their attacks against inequity, ugliness, and repression. But their noble motivations—their practical interests—remain hobbled by problems in their theory.

If these noble giants are crippled, why is it so important to sort through their works for bits and pieces to retrieve? Answer: because they've come closer than anyone else to seeing things whole. Habermas and his forefathers are the closest thing we have to an honorable ancestry for scenario planning. Unlike academic specialists, they looked at all aspects of the human condition, and they were not shy about their eagerness to make it better. Since the fall of the Berlin Wall and the demise of Communism, however, the entire tradition of Marxist scholarship is in danger of being forgotten like a bad dream. New generations of students in the human sciences are therefore in danger of inheriting a smug satisfaction with value-free social science. The theoretical interests of the bean counters will not so much refute as cause us to forget our practical interest in building better futures.

Marx made mistakes, and the Marxists did more to perpetuate than to correct them. But the demise of Marxism-Leninism should not be taken as grounds for abandoning the practical interests of theory. We must not be afraid to use our minds on behalf of our hearts. We must not abandon our practical interest in better futures simply because Marxism botched its theory.

It is important to disinter the body of Marxism and perform an autopsy. We need to understand where Marxism went wrong, both so we can salvage what was right about Marxism—its practical interest in a better future—*and* so we can avoid the theoretical mistakes that kept Marxists from a pluralistic appreciation of better futures. To leave Marxism buried and forgotten is to risk falling into an uncritical acceptance of whatever capitalism serves up in the global marketplace. But to listen to the Marxists alone is to fall into their errors. So let's listen for a moment to Marx and his heirs, and then let us ferret out the errors that led Marxists astray.

MARXISM'S PROBLEM

To listen to some Marxists, the juggernaut determinism of the dialectic unfolds with such force of necessity that there is nothing much for a mere individual to do but lie back and enjoy it. To imagine that any single individual can change the course of history is to fall into the mistake of bourgeois subjectivism. The *real* cause of historical change lies in objective conditions, not in the minds of individual subjects. While hoping to gain followers by promising alignment with the inevitable triumph of the proletariat, Marxists who stressed the inevitability of the revolution opened themselves to the following response: If the revolution is so inevitable, why should I, a mere subjective individual, lift a finger to help it along? The revolution will do just fine without me.

When apathetic individuals in a democracy try to rationalize their failure to cast their votes, it's easy enough to criticize their apathy while remaining consistent with the tenets of liberal democracy. In a system where the individual comes first, and the collective will is the sum of individual wills, each individual has a responsibility to register preferences that are collectively regarded as decisive. Apathy is harder to criticize in a tradition that argues the primacy of the collective and the determinism of objective conditions.

Unlike pursuits like mathematics or, for that matter, stamp collecting, Marxism purports to have a moral purpose: the expropriation of the expropriators on behalf of the oppressed. At the heart of the appeal of Marxism is its steal-from-the-rich-and-give-to-the-poor program. While appearing to be morally motivated, Marxism runs the risk of sawing off the branch it is sitting on when it attacks the usual foundations for morality: God and/or philosophy. Marx's atheism is well known. But God is not the only basis for morality. Certainly philosophy has offered other bases, from Plato to Kant and John Stuart Mill. Marx and critical theory dismiss these bases for morality. How then can Marxism claim moral authority if morality has no basis for its authority?

Among the noblest aspirations of Marxist theory was its attempt to overcome *alienation.* The literature on alienation is immense.[3] No wonder: the topic offered an outlet for every intellectual malcontent to express his dissatisfaction with the ways of the world in general, and capitalism in particular. Feel out of sorts, depressed, unhappy? It's not my/your fault, according to Marxist ideology. Private pain is the result of a capitalist system that has alienated each of us from our *essence.* Whether we know it or not, our private ills are the outcomes of public, social, and economic processes that pry each of us away from our own true nature. Psychological depression is the private expression of social and economic repression. Alienation is the name that critical theorists give to this sundering, this distancing that separates each of us from our essence.

This story about alienation is immensely appealing—and so addictive it became the opiate of many disaffected intellectuals. The literature on alienation played a particular role in the evolution of critical theory: it allowed Marxists to put a warmer face on cold economism. The tradition of Marxist humanism allowed those who were interested in the psychology of alienation to find a home within the Marxist tradition without surrendering to the ruthless repression of individual freedom so characteristic of Stalinism. By harking back to the discussion of alienation in the early Marxist literature—particularly *The Economic and Philosophic Manuscripts of 1844*—you could have your warmer humanism and scientific Marxism too.

Despite the cozy humanism at the heart of this salvation of subjectivity, it was doomed from the start, not only because the practical power of Stalinism was so strong but, just as important, because the theoretical foundations of Marxist humanism were so weak. The concept of alienation turns out to be theoretically incoherent. It presupposes a human essence from which human existence is alienated. Whether the existence in question is individual or collective, the concept of alienation presupposes some form of a fall from grace, some sundering of existence from Edenic essence. But Marxism cannot have historical self-development and eternal essence too. It won't do to preach out of one side of your mouth this self-making, historical nurturance of human progress while out of the other you condemn the deviation of history from some ahistorically given natural essence. But this is just what Marx and many Marxists after him have done. If the essence of man is not eternal but historically malleable, how can that essence be used as a stable standard against which alienation can be measured?

Why is this chink in the rusted armor of Marxism so important? Recall the objective: to find some moral leverage, a fulcrum for social criticism. Whatever its faults, at least critical theory *tried* to criticize the present for the sake of a better future. We could do worse than inherit from critical theory the mantle of moral critique. However, Marxist theory's dependence on the concept of alienation leaves it vulnerable itself to critique.

Collectivist traditions have a real problem identifying the role of the individual in history. Whether they identify the proletariat, vanguard intellectuals, the collective, or language as the real hero of the human drama—the lead player in the game called history—they fail to do justice to the fact that the rest of us are walking around with this common sense conviction that we are indeed the authors of our intentions, the agents of our actions, the subjects of our own biographies. What could be more obvious?

Critical theory failed to account for subjective agency in the face of all of those economic and historical forces that purportedly serve as the true subject of history. Critical theory needs to find a place for the living, breathing individual. Without wallowing in the romanticism described by Richard Harvey Brown, Marxism must find some place for some form of subjectivity that more or less corresponds to our intuitive sense of agency. We are not *entirely* the victims of forces larger than ourselves.

To their credit, Marxists were not content to leave the world as they found it. They were interested in more than simply describing, analyzing, and understanding. They wanted to change the existing order of things. Strategic planners can appreciate this activist bias. But who will provide a conscience for the mechanisms of the marketplace in the economic era? Neither individualism nor collectivism by itself can correctly identify the source of moral agency. Because morality is so often the search for the correct balance between the will of the individual and the requirements of the collective, it is a mistake to base moral theory— ethics—on the priority of one or the other. Neither existentialism nor Stalinism was adequate to the moral challenge of life in Europe between the two world wars, but these seemed to be the only philosophies available at the time. However powerful the effects of class consciousness, culture, language, or genes, we are not *entirely* bereft of individual autonomy. As Margaret Mead once put it, "Never underestimate the power of small groups of people to change the course of history; indeed, who else ever does?"

Having now exposed the shortcomings of taking the collective All as the ultimate player in the game of history, and having also acknowledged the perils of relying too heavily on the individualistic Ones as the ultimate players, I want to turn to the idea of Some—communities as creative agents. Let me be clear about the strategy of turning from One and All to Some. First, this is not a case for elitism. The argument is ontological, not ideological. I'm not claiming that elites should rule. I'm claiming that groups are a helpful unit of analysis for understanding where agency and creativity come from. If you want to understand how history happens, don't fall for either Marxist collectivism or radical individualism. Neither the collective All nor individual Ones give us enough players to understand the creation of conventions in social history. We need to appreciate another player: the communal Some.

One more caution about what I'm *not* claiming. I'm not saying that communities are the ultimate subjects of history. To Ken Kesey's question, "Whose movie is this anyway?" my answer is: there is no single star, not the entire collective cast, not a single individual hero, not some elite ensemble. Let's be done with the star system. Let's cease seeking any singular ultimate subject of history. The new players in the relational worldview include all of the above: individuals, communities, all human beings, *and* the natural ecosphere. Forget any of them at your peril. Remember all of them, and their systemic interaction, and there's a chance we can, together, build better futures.

As I've repeated perhaps too often and will remark yet again, I'm not making this stuff up. The name of the game and the names of the players are drawn from already existing theories and stories. If there is an innovative dimension to a new story I'm weaving from the old, it is an emphasis on the group, the community, the Some as a unit of analysis. Less simplistic than either individualism or collectivism, this social philosophy of Some finds in groups a useful synthesis of the creativity attributed to individuals and the power attributed to collectives. Now I want to make the case for communities as creative agents to complete the roster of players.

COMMUNITIES AS CREATIVE AGENTS

People make buildings and buildings shape people. People speak language, and then language shapes the forms and meanings that motivate people to become who they are. Novelty *can* emerge, in literature, music, or architecture. While the site of that novelty is usually a creative act signed (in the modern era) by an individual, the contribution of the relational worldview is to show that those transgressions of the old order toward the unprecedented can also be ascribed to a community that uses scenario–based planning to articulate its hopes, frame some alternative futures, and choose among them.

Yes, there is creativity. No, history is not the result of a juggernaut determinism following necessary laws of economics, physics, biology, or language. Yes, the creation of the unprecedented is always possible. But, no, the site of that creation, the site of creativity that we are used to locating only in the Cartesian Cogito, the autonomous subject, the ghost in the machine, the self-transparent, fully knowing, homunculus at the helm of the Self (that is in fact a social creation of the Enlightenment), can just as well be located in a community.

Let me be clear about what I do and do not want to invoke by using the word community. I do not want to invoke a nostalgic image of happy families cleaving to one another in some organic whole where there is no friction. I do not want to invoke some idyllic, utopian vision of unalienated social innocence. What I do want to invoke are everyday life practices: an existing language, actual buildings, traffic patterns, haircuts, and the physical manifestations of culture in artwork, songs, and rituals—those individual and social practices that are the concrete manifestations of culture. So perhaps I should just say culture rather than community. But, no, a particular community is a smaller unit of analysis than a culture. A community exists within a culture. A community can play a role that is subjective relative to the objective givenness of a culture. Thus, as the Cartesian subject stands to nature as object, so does a community stand to culture as passive recipient of what is already determinate, as well as active agent of the yet-to-be-determined.

Now that we are coming to the end of modernity, now that we are coming to see the limits of individualism and the limits of the marketplace in which individuals meet to exchange goods, we need more than a postmodernism that deconstructs the Subject; we need a relational worldview that looks ahead. We need a worldview that preserves the strengths of subjectivity—freedom and creativity—but locates those strengths in communities rather than in isolated, alienated individuals. We need a worldview that can compensate for the shortcomings of the marketplace with a public conscience that does not suffer from the sampling errors of our current forms of representative democracy. We need a worldview that appreciates the fact that we're moving from a political toward an economic era, but that as we travel, we can't forget the calls for social justice that some economists would abandon in the name of market fundamentalism.

Note how all these pieces are beginning to fit together: the historical transition to the economic era; the legitimacy of business, notwithstanding the limits of the marketplace; the role of the individual, notwithstanding the limits of individualism. We need a social philosophy of *some* that invests in communities the subjectivity and creativity to build better futures. Chapter 5 provided an analysis of the conflict between individualism and collectivism. This chapter picks up pieces from the paradigm shifts taking place in psychology and sociology to show how theorists are already moving from sampling the One of individualism and the All of collectivism to focus on Some, the community that provides a platform for creative subjectivity.

SOCIAL CREATIVITY

Scene One: A dozen of us are gathered in our living room back in the early 1970s viewing slides from one of the first trips into China after Nixon's ping-pong diplomacy opened up the People's Republic. One of my students, John Kao, a Chinese-American who made the journey, is showing living–color shots of teeming masses, happy comrades doing

T'ai Chi in the public square before bicycling off to work in the morning.

The slide that sticks with me most is that of a wall-sized dragon composed of tens of thousands of multicolored feathers pasted into place by dozens of Chinese "artists." The result is collectivist art that avoids the decadence of bourgeois subjectivism. Shades of socialist realism! Yes, it looks very like a dragon. And, yes, it is intricate and very colorful. But is this art? All those artisans had, in effect, painted by the numbers. Each and every one followed directions for which color feather was to go where. Is this communal creativity? Surely the act of creation was communal. And the dragon is surely an artifact. But if this is the model for communal creativity, I'll take mine solo, thanks.

Harvard psychologist Howard Gardner wrote a book about art education in China in which he contrasts the collectivist ideals of Chinese education and their emphasis on the one correct way to do things, with the more individualist approach to education in the United States. In his concluding remarks he writes:

> In China, education is considered a race. Students should begin as early as possible and should proceed as quickly as possible along the track which is known and available to all. The education system is judged successful when many individuals have made it to the finish line as soon as possible. In America, we recognize the race too, but we feel that the students should have a chance to wander or meander much more, even if in the end not all of them make it to the finish line. As a result of their wandering, some of the participants may have more to offer by the conclusion of the race.
>
> The advantage of the Chinese way is that more of your students become proficient and make it to the goal line. The disadvantage is that they may have less to say or to show once they get there. The disadvantage of the American way is that many students never make it to the end or even get close. The advantage is that some who do go "all the way" have very interesting and original things to say when they get there.[4]

Scene Two: It's now 1993. A bunch of us are gathered at a Global Business Network conference in London. In this particular workshop, Brian Eno, student of art history, rock musician, and producer of U2 albums, is talking about the difference between genius and "scenius." He's making the point that we in the individualistic West may need to modify our mythology about creativity springing only from the tortured soul of the individual genius. Just because the Chinese and Japanese are less individualistic than we are, it doesn't follow that they can't be creative. Maybe we need to decouple our concept of creativity from our idea of individual genius.

Eno's is a radical idea to many of us in the West, where an individualist approach to creativity prevails. This attitude is nowhere more unabashedly defended than by Harold Bloom in his magisterial book *The Western Canon:* "Social energies exist in every age, but they cannot compose plays, poems, and narratives. The power to originate is an individual gift, present in all eras but evidently greatly encouraged by particular contexts."[5]

Individualism may have its limits. Robert Reich may be right about America's need for myths that valorize *team creativity.* Most of our American mythology is so individualistic, so heroic, so libertarian as to plunge us into anarchy and narcissism. But if the alternative is painting by the numbers, then what happens to freedom, innovation, and the brute irreverence that have always been so near and dear to the entrepreneurial spirit at the heart of the American economy, to say nothing of the oedipal struggle that artists have always fought to escape the anxiety of influence?[6]

Here's the dilemma, the contradiction on which our concept of creativity may founder: on the one hand creativity calls for a break with the elders, innovation, something new under the sun, something that must erupt from the soul of the isolated individual because it is precisely this isolation that allows liberation from *that which has been,* the established, the traditional, the old. On the other hand, we in the West may have taken this individualism thing a little too far. We have valorized Horatio Alger and Thoreau's civil disobedience to such an extent that we've got people doing any damn thing in the name of rebellion, then expecting it to be honored as innovation. You can't run a company—or a school, or a family, or a community—if everyone feels entitled, even encouraged, to do any damn thing any damn time any damn place. Not all graffiti is art!

We need to find a locus for creativity—a creator—for building better futures. But the job must be done in a way that does not fall into the old trap of identifying extreme subjectivity as the only source of creative genius. Nor do I want to rely on some hidden objectivism that makes all creativity the work of culture, language, genes, or the technological means of production. Who chooses? What creates? If we are to take time and novelty as real, then something must choose in order to create. If we take the fall from eternity into history seriously, then it will not do to mumble one more time, "There is nothing new under the sun." But the old accounts of historical creativity served up by the individualist and collectivist traditions are no longer available once we've decided that not one, not all, but *some* are most often the agents of history. And at the end of the day, no matter how critical we may be toward extreme individualism, we must do better than critical theory when it comes to finding a role for the individual in history.

If communities are the agents of history, then how do communities (of individuals) create history?[7] The answer I'm developing is that *communities* create history by framing alternative scenarios, identifying a range of strategic options appropriate to those scenarios, and choosing among them. But that answer doesn't mean much in the abstract. I want to show just how communities come to do that, and what is involved in giving communities such a job.

COMMUNAL CREATIVITY IN PRACTICE

Let's see if we can get at communal creativity by ascending from the practice of living, breathing practitioners. In order to keep this concrete rather than abstract, I must exploit my own experience in making the move from academic theoretician to practicing scenario planner. I want to talk about the differences between life as a solitary professor of philosophy and life as a member of a network of people trying to create better futures. I've been to both extremes, done the solo trip and the team effort, and I'm here to say that communal creativity has its problems, even if Brian Eno is right about the need to move from genius to "scenius."

I'll begin with four very practical advantages of communal creativity, then address some very practical disadvantages. Following that, I'll discuss how to overcome the challenges of communal creativity and locate the agents—the new players—for building better futures.

So what's so good about communal creativity? First of all, it's fun. Working and playing with a group of people you like can be a lot more amusing than banging the keys in the solitude of your study. Second, communal creativity brings more resources to bear on a given creation than any single individual can muster. Whether or not the whole is greater or less than the sum of its parts, it's certainly greater than any one part. All of us are smarter than any of us. Different members of a team bring different resources to a team. We know different things. We have different strengths. We can make up for one another's weaknesses. In both quantity and quality of contributions to a task, a team has more to offer than any individual.

Third, if Arthur Koestler is correct to argue that creativity often springs from the unexpected juxtaposition of realms of thought not often combined,[8] then it is that much more likely that creativity will be found where different people with different realms of expertise find themselves thinking together. Koestler's insights into the Janus-faced logic of creativity argue persuasively against the organization of the modern research university with its departmental walls separating different specialties. Indeed, if one were to try to invent an organization whose structure encouraged the kind of creativity that Koestler describes, one could hardly do worse than the modern university. The scenario workshop, whose participants are selected precisely for the diversity of their expertise, offers a far richer medium for the cultivation of creative ideas in a social setting.

Fourth, teams can provide multiple sanity checks. It's no accident that in the tradition of European geniuses, there's a high degree of correlation between madness and creativity. Look at the tradition of mad or at least manic geniuses: Beethoven, Van Gogh, Wittgenstein, Wilhelm Reich. The tradition of genius glamorizes madness as the route to creativity, as if you had to be nutty in order to get free of the established way of doing things. Maybe you have to be mad to get in contact with some other-worldly wellspring of creativity. How romantic!

This mythology of the mad genius has something to it: weirdness is, almost by definition, nonconformist. And if the creative is, also by definition, out of the ordinary, then weirdness might provide a route to creativity. But what a license to self-indulgence! What an attractive rationale for being careless about the concerns of others! "Sorry for upsetting the apple cart. I was just trying to be creative." It may be tough to be a genius without seeming to be a little weird; but the converse does not hold. It's easy to be weird without being a genius.

Communal creativity has this advantage over the mad genius model: a team is less likely to be delusional than an individual. Simply by matching wits with one another, the members of a team have the advantage over an individual in that they reassure themselves that they are not losing touch with the rest of humanity. Consequently, the creations of a team are more likely to be of service, or at least of interest, to the rest of humanity. This then is a fourth advantage of communal creativity: it is more likely to be sane.

What are some of the disadvantages of communal creativity, practically speaking? One thinks of old saws like, "A camel is a horse designed by a committee" or: "Too many chefs spoil the broth." Clearly there are coordination costs. Say, for example, you're working on a project that calls for different people to contribute different skills in sequence. The report has to get to the client next Tuesday. Tom writes his section on Thursday, Mary adds hers on Friday, and Edward the editor has to have both of their contributions in front of him on Monday if he is to work his magic before Tuesday. Tom cannot wait around for inspiration to strike, or he'll never make the handoff to Mary in time for her to add her section before Monday.

This all-too-familiar dynamic of teamwork calls for *management*. But the "management of creativity" strikes many of us as oxymoronic. This is why we romanticize the renegade, the outlaw, the lone ranger who can break away from the pack and solve the problem on his own. Forget about going through channels! In the East it's a little different. But does that mean that the Japanese and Chinese cannot be creative? That they can only copy or, at best, make incremental improvements but no breakthroughs?

Look at the linkages between different concepts and practices: the genius myth goes with the valorization of the individual over the collective. And it also fits with the Christian concept of creation as *creatio ex nihilo*—creation from nothing. The God of Abraham didn't pick up where some earlier God left off. He started from scratch. So, likewise, the solitary genius is not supposed to settle for mere modifications on the work of prior masters. The solitary genius—on the American model that praises the garage inventor over the corporate functionary—would rather do it all by himself. See the linkages that make a worldview: individual heroics, Christian monotheism, creation *ex nihilo*. Conversely, Oriental culture's emphasis on conforming to social norms fits with Hindu polytheism and an approach to creativity that does not start from scratch but works by incremental improvements and line extensions that respect the value of tradition, what has gone before.

The trouble with the oriental model—and this is the downside of communal creativity—is that sometimes you need a break with the past, a breakthrough to a novel future. Sometimes respect for the tradition and social norms will lead to a groupthink that cannot see its way clear of shared delusion. Sometimes, as for example in Japan at the turn of the millennium, there's a need for the sort of existential "leap" that existentialist philosopher Sören Kierkegaard wished upon individuals. But how can a whole society leap together? The best approach to this question that I've been able to find is not in the revolutionary ideology of Marxism but in existential sociology.

Let's return to the work of Richard Harvey Brown and his colleagues in order to pick up a few more bits and pieces of the relational worldview to which they contribute. Once again, we already have many of the pieces of the puzzles that we need to solve to create better futures. We need only review them, appreciate them, and later synthesize them into normative scenarios of better futures.

In a series of books, a group that includes Jack Douglas, John Johnson, Richard Brown, and Stanford Lyman has developed an approach that has all the marks of a new school held together and reinforced by a common worldview. Like Habermas, they confess their values and their interest in practical uses to which their research may be put. The paradigm case that best illustrates the impossibility of the researcher maintaining a disinterested distance from the subject under study is the book by Jack Douglas and Paul Rasmussen, *Nude Beaches*. Imagine the value-free social scientist strolling out onto the southern California sand clad in the white coat of the laboratory technician, clip-board in hand. The phenomena under study would escape him.

Brown and Lyman pull together many of the elements of the relational worldview in a virtual manifesto issued as an invitation. "Symbolic realism and cognitive aesthetics: An invitation" is the essay with which they introduce a paradigm-defining anthology of essays by the school of existential sociologists. Their essay not only offers rich *evidence* of an emergent worldview; just as important, it serves as an eloquent and original statement *defining* the relational worldview.[9]

Lyman and Brown not only acknowledge the importance of worldviews and their construction; they also see the inevitability of conflicts of worldviews—the struggles between rival worldviews and the debate over whose map provides the best guide to the territory we inhabit together. These paradigm wars are no mere academic quibbles. To the extent that their outcomes determine the very meaning of human and social behavior, they amount to titanic struggles over the future of humanity.

The practice of sociology ceases to be disinterested. Instead it becomes a poetizing of human purposes: Whither humanity? Shall we, as the cybernetic, systems-theoretical map would have it, become more like machines?

[T]he spokesmen for cybernetic systems theory argue that society is (or is like) a great computer, with its input and output, its feedback loops, and its programs; this machine—society—is in turn guided by a servo-mechanism—the techno-administrative elite. To see this imagery as a metaphor, however, is to reject it as a literal description, to unmask it as a legitimating ideology, and to provide a basis for criticizing its rhetorics. By doing a close textual analysis, it becomes clear that in the rhetoric of social cybernetics, there is an atrophy of the very vocabularies of citizenship, moral responsibility, and political community. In place of these, the machinery of governance, initially conceived as serving human values, becomes a closed system generating its own self-maintaining ends. The polity—the arena for the institutional enactment of moral choices—dissolves upward into the cybernetic state, or downward into the alienated individual, whose intentionality is now wholly privatized and whose actions, uprooted from their institutional context, are bereft of social consequence and deprived of moral meaning.[10]

Their final sentence caps it off: "Our recognition that social order is a construction invites us to actively reconstruct our worlds."[11] This is the invitation to which scenario planning provides a response. Scenario planning is a way to "actively reconstruct our worlds" to create better futures. Scenario planning solves the dilemmas of critical theory without ever having set out to do so. Scenario planning is a crucial tool for playing this biggest game in town, the shaping of human history. It's a megalomaniacal job, but somebody's got to do it. Far better that the agents of invention be social and community-based rather than left to the private fantasies of a few individual experts.

Scenario planning solves the theory problem by finding a moral fulcrum for social criticism without relying on a theory of human essence. Scenario planning resolves the practice problem by involving concrete communities (not just scholars) in the effort to build their futures. Finally, scenario planning offers roles to different individuals to contribute their unique perspectives to the shaping of communal creativity. There *is* a role for individuals in the communal practice of scenario planning. Scenario planning provides a medium for sorting our hopes and fears, and hence, a medium for investing our plans with our values. Because scenario planning allows groups of people to deliberate collectively over the possible consequences of their collective choices, scenario planning turns out to be a medium for collectively choosing courses toward *better* futures.

If different cultures have different values, how do the members of one culture come to know another, and what *are* values such that they can transcend and oblige the individual without being universal? What does better *mean?*

In the following chapters I'll pull together more pieces of the relational worldview from the writings of anthropologists, philosophers, and literary critics. We need, and can find, the pieces of a new relational worldview in the works we have at hand. But first I want to clarify just what I mean by the term *worldview*. I'll do so in the next chapter by differentiating it from the overused but ill-understood term *paradigm*.

Part Three
New Lenses

CHAPTER SEVEN

FROM WORLDVIEWS TO BETTER WORLDS

In 1996 a young physicist named Alan Sokal rocked the academic world by pulling off a delicious literary hoax. He published a paper entitled "Transgressing the Boundaries: Toward a Transformative Hermeneutics of Quantum Gravity" in a journal called *Social Text*. The hoax was worded in the obscure language of deconstructionism, an intellectual import from Paris.

Jacques Derrida, the philosopher behind deconstructionism, takes delight in turning upside down and inside out virtually every tenet of common sense. Which came first, speech or writing? Obviously cavemen talked before they learned to write, but Derrida would have us believe that there is a sense, a deep sense, a sense far more profound than callow Americans could possibly understand, in which speech is unintelligible, and therefore not speech but babble, unless it is preceded by an *arche*-writing, a foundational writing, a presupposed writing in terms of which speech can make sense . . . and many of Derrida's sentences are at least this long.

Within weeks *The New York Times* and other major newspapers ran stories about the incident. At first blush—and there were many flushed faces—the joke was on the deconstructionists. Clearly, it seemed, if the editors of *Social Text* could not distinguish send–up from sense, then they had a very weak grasp on reality.

The story did not end with blushing deconstructionists, however. The battle continued in the letters section of *The New York Review of Books*. Those who thought that Sokal's hoax was enough to dismiss those damned deconstructionists forever had another think coming, and as long as deconstructionists hold tenured chairs, as many do, you can bet the battle will go on for some time to come.

What we've got here is a new skirmish in a very old worldview war—between the objectivists, who think that truth is a pretty simple matter of matching statements against facts, and the subjectivists, who think that what count as "facts" depend on who you are, where you are, and when you are. As well-deserved as Sokal's hoax was—and the French fashion of obscurity cried out for a send–up—I'm prepared to tip my hat to the French at the end of the day, despite their damnably obscure ways of putting things.

So that's what this chapter is about: blowing holes in Anglo-American empiricism. Empiricism is a philosophy that says complex ideas are built up out of simple ideas, and simple ideas come to us through our senses as undistorted as light through a clear pane of glass. No sampling, no sampling errors, just a one-to-one transfer from objective facts to subjective impressions. According to empiricists, we can be confident in our knowledge of objective truth, because nothing in our subjective ways of knowing does that much to distort what comes to us from objective reality.

Europeans know better. Perhaps it is the result of their geography. Because they've spent centuries rubbing up against one another in different languages with different intellectual traditions, they have more experience dealing with people who see things differently. The French *know* that they see things differently from the Germans just across the Rhine. The Germans on the other hand, know they are different from those hot-blooded Italians. Whereas we Americans, at least for most of our history, have occupied most of a continent, sea to shining sea.

You have to appreciate at least this much history, this much context, to understand why all the talk about paradigms over the past couple of decades has gone the way it has gone. How has it gone, and where is the delicious irony? It's more like a persistent case of mistaken identity: we Americans have a hard time with this idea about ways of seeing because our way of seeing says that there's really nothing to this concern about ways of seeing. Once you unpack these Chinese boxes, you find something, but the something you find is not as simple as what you thought you were looking for.

Because this idea about paradigms is so slippery—if you think you've got it in clear, simple, objective terms, then you haven't got it at all—the next section on the history of the idea will be followed not by a clear definition of a paradigm, but instead by a section on what paradigms are *like*. The oblique view turns out to be the more appropriate view.

Why is it so important to be careful about how we approach paradigms and worldviews? Because this book hangs on the question of whether what we see in the future is just in our heads or is there to be predicted on the basis of the facts. It's important to see how and why neither conclusion is on the mark. Thinking something doesn't make it so. Feel–good faith in the inevitability of progress toward the New Age will not bring it about. Nor can scientific analysis of the way things *are* determine the way they *must be* in the future.

There is a margin for human choice. The choices we make will depend in part on the way we see the present, and in part on what we want for our future. Getting the right balance between what *is* and the way we *want* things to be is a large part of what building better futures is all about. A colleague, Stewart Brand, is fond of quoting Bernal's line, "Desire always misreads fate." I persistently disagree. Desire, or a vivid sense of hope, can create what comes to be called fate. To think otherwise is to resign oneself to a predetermined future. Play up fate and you play down planning. Planning presupposes freedom and refutes the very idea of destiny.

Simply to be a human being is to be a planner of sorts. For human freedom is largely a matter of imagining alternative plans and then choosing among them. To be a *good* planner, you must at least aspire to being a good human being. You must care about the welfare of others. Your visions of the future must be informed by more than the science of what *is* or an imagination for what *might be*; your visions of the future should also be informed by a sense of what *ought* to be.

In order to enhance our ability to build better futures, we need to rethink the very nature of future studies in the larger context of disciplined inquiry. If there is such a thing as futurology—a disciplined *logos* or discourse about the future—is it an art, a science, or, as many suspect, nothing more than hopes and fears dressed up as science? To put the question very concretely: If futures research is a legitimate field of disciplined inquiry, then why are there so few courses or departments of future studies in our major universities? Why is futures research not recognized by academics as one among the many *disciplines*?

Faced with the slimness of our academic portfolio, we find ourselves on the defensive. We turn to our computers and our databases; we develop models; we debate methodology as if we were building the foundations for a science. We refine our polling procedures, brandish our statistical techniques, and do our very best to make our trend analyses and technology forecasts look as thoroughly engineered as the technologies we are forecasting. In our anxiety about our academic credentials we strive to become more scientific than the scientists, more rigorous than mathematicians. In such a mood, the last thing we want to hear about is normative scenarios. We want *facts*, not values. We want well-founded theory, not well-meaning morality.

There is, consequently, a constant danger of bad faith in the work of most futurists. Eager to escape the charge of subjective bias, of claiming that what we *want* to happen will *in fact* happen, we do everything we can to make sure that our scenarios of what *will* happen have been scourged of every relic of what we ourselves might *want* to happen. I call this bad faith, but not because I think we are unsuccessful in scourging our hopes. I call it bad faith to the extent that we *are* successful. To the extent that we mimic scientists in claiming value-free objectivity in our view of the future, we deny the very thing that makes us good human beings and good futurists. We deny that we *care*. But we *must* care.[1] If we do not, we are doomed to a dreadful future.

One approach to establishing the legitimacy of future studies would be to argue, from accepted ideas about what constitutes a science, that futures research is indeed scientific, but because we are good caring people, we will use this science for the betterment of humankind by developing *better* futures. We might place future studies on the firm foundations of accepted science and then make the further argument that a good science must be an ethical science. This is precisely *not* the strategy I will follow.

Rather than defensively placing future studies on the firm foundations of science, I want to pursue an offensive strategy. I want to show how very infirm the so-called foundations of science have become. Rather than dragging future studies over into the camp of the sciences, I want to show how the so-called human sciences are moving in the direction of future studies.

We futurists (including all human beings trying to shape their own futures) don't have to learn how to play *their* game of objective, value-free science; *they* are learning to play *ours*. The human sciences are moving through a paradigm shift that makes them much more amenable to the work of the futurist and far less pretentious about their place at the academic high table with the hard sciences.

The burden of this book is to *show* this movement among the human sciences. It is not enough simply to *say* that the paradigm shift is here. There is no brief way to demonstrate in detail the very real movement taking place in the fields of anthropology, psychology, literary criticism, philosophy, political theory, and sociology. All it takes is a passing glance at recent trends in these disciplines to show that the human sciences are moving toward a widespread recognition of the need for value-laden better futures. These disciplines are adopting normative scenarios as an essential feature of their own new ways of seeing the facts. What a sad irony it would be if, just as these reinforcements from the human sciences arrived to support futures research, futurists themselves had decamped in the direction of the hard sciences!

A review of recent developments in the human sciences reveals new tools not available in the hard sciences. Rather than trying to found their own legitimacy on mimicking the hard sciences with their solid methodologies and confident access to objectivity, the human sciences are accepting their irreducibly interpretive, literary, storytelling status. They are acknowledging their lack of foundations in hard facts and accepting their dependence on revisable interpretations. They are therefore waking up to their *interest*. They are coming alive to the absurdity of claiming that sociology and social philosophy can conduct their inquiries in a wholly disinterested manner. We must *care*. If we don't, then all is lost. But if we do, then we are hardly disinterested.

Thus do these several strategies and objectives come together: the first, making a justification for normative scenarios; the second, placing future studies in the context of the human sciences; the third, affirming our own values in shaping our visions of the future. These three strategies support one another. Having justified normative scenarios, it is easier to stop ignoring one's own values in the name of objectivity. The claim to objectivity turns out to be compromised in any case, if reports from the other human sciences are to be believed.

KUHN'S CONTRIBUTION

Science, it turns out, does not always march steadily forward by piling fact upon theory upon fact. Instead there are, from time to time, sharp breaks, revolutions in place of evolution. This revolutionary view of scientific progress was developed in an important and frequently cited book by Thomas Kuhn entitled *The Structure of Scientific Revolutions*. According to what had been the conventional wisdom prior to Kuhn, science consisted in the gathering of ever more data under the ever wider umbrella of ever more comprehensive theories. Each successive theory represents a refinement and/or extension of those that preceded it. So, for example, Newton's laws are supposed to represent a special case under the wider and more comprehensive umbrella of Einstein's relativity theory.

Kuhn revolutionized the common understanding of scientific progress by pointing out an important distinction between what he called *normal science*, which grows by gradual additions to our fund of knowledge, and *revolutionary science*. Normal science proceeds by more or less continuous additions to the fund of knowledge. Kuhn describes normal science as a kind of puzzle solving. People fill in blanks of ignorance by applying well–known techniques to well–recognized problems. Normal science depends on the shared acceptance of a given paradigm among a community of scientists. That shared paradigm is the set of shared beliefs and practices that graduate students learn in order to be accepted into the community of scientists.

But every so often normal science reaches the end of its tether. Most of the holes seem to be filled in, except for a few odd pieces that won't fit into the almost completed puzzle. These odd pieces are known as *anomalies*. Socrates picked at the anomalies in Athenian morality. It got him into trouble. Galileo picked at the anomalies in the Ptolemaic map of the universe. It got *him* into trouble. Einstein picked at the anomalies in Newton's map of the universe. It got him famous. Sometimes the revolutionaries win, but the stakes are always high: it's glory or execution.

Revolutionary science, as Kuhn coined the term, is different from normal science in creating discontinuities in the history of science rather than continuous accretions of knowledge. That's why the stakes are so high and the outcomes—glory or death—so unpredictable. Revolutionary science upsets the whole apple cart and rearranges all the intellectual and cultural apples. Life isn't the same afterwards, even though it may take a long time for some people to notice. But how could they fail to notice?

The remarkable thing about paradigm shifts is that the reordering—the shifting—takes place at such a fundamental level that it changes almost everything, and for that very reason is very nearly invisible. This is odd. On the one hand one would think that something so important would be very evident. On the other hand, if paradigm shifts really are invisible, then they can't be very important, can they?

If someone changes the arrangement of the furniture in your living room, you notice it immediately. If, while you are sleeping, however, someone somehow shifts the foundations of your dwelling to a different part of town, you won't be able to tell the difference by looking at the furniture in your living room. It will seem, until you go outside, that all the furniture is still in the same place.

A paradigm shift is like this transplanting of foundations. All the parts of life get moved together. The art, science, politics, religion, and economics of a society are all equally touched by a paradigm shift. But you can't "go outside" of history to check the difference the way you can go out of your house to check the neighborhood. The best you can do is look inside history for different configurations in disciplines that are very distant from your own. So Kuhn, a historian of science, showed how Newton upset the apple cart of Ptolemaic astronomy.

Kuhn's own use of *paradigm* is, as he later acknowledged, ambiguous. On the one hand, the word means exemplary experiment, or a set of procedures that every member of the scientific community learns to accept as the hard core of scientific method. On the other hand, *paradigm* has a much broader use associated with entire belief systems or maps of reality—the lenses, as it were, through which a people sees its entire environment, and itself.

In the first definition, a paradigm shift can mean an alteration in the set of exemplary experiments that define the curriculum for budding scientists. In the second definition, a paradigm shift is closer to remapping the shared consciousness of a culture. Clearly, the two meanings are related, for a given set of exemplary experiments contributes to our general sense and understanding of the orderliness of our universe. Depending on our general belief system, we may accept the fulcrum and lever or the voodoo doll as the proper experimental equipment for teaching and understanding how to make things happen.

KUHN'S CONTRIBUTION IN CONTEXT

Though Kuhn has given currency to the concept of paradigms and paradigm shifts, the basic insights have been around for about two centuries. Why, if they are so important, were they not noticed? The question is worth asking, not just for the sake of scholarly fastidiousness. The case of Thomas Kuhn is a fascinating study in the very phenomenon he tried to tell us about. There are reasons why these ideas, evident in Europe in the late eighteenth century, went unnoticed for two centuries in England and America: they didn't fit the dominant Anglo-American paradigm!

Kuhn's insights made big news on these shores only by virtue of our ignorance and the persistence of an anti-paradigm empiricist paradigm . . . which persists, as we see in the crowing over Sokal's send–up. Because empiricism persists, it will not work to go back thousands of years to

Athens, or hundreds of years to German idealism for an alternative theory of knowledge. After all, maybe the reason we now think differently from the way they thought then is simply that they were *wrong* and we now know better. This is the arrogance of modernism that is finally being undercut by postmodernism.

Because most of us are so used to thinking of experience as a direct copy of a given world, the very idea of a paradigm seems strange. Surely we would know if there were some mechanism distorting our perceptions. Like rain on the windshield, paradigms should be evident to the senses. And once seen, they would be swept away by some internal version of windshield wipers.

The eighteenth-century Enlightenment claimed to be just such a set of cognitive windshield wipers sweeping away the distorting influences of superstition and bogus authority. Science was the weapon of intellect against the biases of provincialism and the prejudices of outmoded beliefs. With the aid of the experimental method and mathematical calculations, humankind could banish once and for all the limitations of particular perspectives. The One True World would emerge from behind the curtains of inherited errors . . . At least that is how the empiricist paradigm has it.

But paradigms are not like drops on the windshield. They cannot be seen in front of the eye, for they are more like the eye itself. For other ways to get at what these shifts in our basic belief systems are *like* we should reach toward more pervasive influences on cognition and perception: moods, myths, and metaphors.

WHAT PARADIGMS ARE LIKE

Paradigms are in some ways like moods. When you are depressed, everything is depressing. No evidence is sufficient to remove the mood of depression, for every piece of evidence can be reinterpreted to confirm the view that life is not worth the trouble. Happy people must be deluded. They just don't know any better. They appear to the depressed as incurably insipid.

A similar certainty characterizes moods that are the opposite of depression. Elation is its own proof. People in love find that all the world loves a lover. Moods, whether high or low, color everything we see and do. In this way they are like paradigms. But in other ways moods are unlike paradigms. Moods are emotional. Paradigms are more intellectual. Paradigms are to the life of the mind what moods are to the life of the heart.

Paradigms are like metaphors to the extent that metaphors, too, shape our understanding. If someone says, "I need a cup of coffee in the morning to get my brain in gear," he is using a metaphor—the mind as a machine. There are no gears or cogwheels in the brain, but the expression is understood because the brain is often thought of as if it were an information processing machine.

Like moods, metaphors often exercise influence altogether unconsciously. When we think we are describing things as they really are without any dependence on likenesses or mere similarities, both our language and our thought processes are often in the grip of unacknowledged metaphors. For example, what does it mean for our thought processes to be "in the grip" of unacknowledged metaphors? Do metaphors have hands? Are thought processes the sort of things that can be gripped? A phrase like "in the grip of" may subtly suggest that our language and our thought processes are like physical things that can be grasped with the hand.

"The essence of metaphor," write George Lakoff and Mark Johnson, "is understanding and experiencing one kind of thing in terms of another."[2] This statement could apply as well to paradigms. In asking what paradigms are *like*, this chapter seeks metaphors that will illuminate the nature of paradigms. Moods, myths, and metaphor itself each serve as *metaphors for paradigms.* One kind of thing, paradigms, can be understood and experienced in terms of these several other kinds of thing.

Like metaphor, properly understood, paradigms recast the concept of truth. Truth with a capital *T* turns out to be more than we need. Humble truths like whether or not the car is in the garage are quite sufficient, and the commitment to paradigms does nothing to undermine the status of such truths. Just as *food* can be quite enough to eat and satisfy our hunger, without The Food (after which we would never need to eat again), so *truths* will be quite enough to nourish our taste for reality (without reliance on The Truth as some great blueprint in the sky).

It is possible to talk about paradigm shifts without facing certain implications. Some talk, for instance, as if it were only a question of a new method for approaching closer to The Truth. It is as if Kuhn's distinction between normal science and revolutionary science—between the continuous and the discontinuous—were a merely methodological distinction between baby steps and giant steps on the path toward The Truth. But the implications of Kuhn's thesis are much more radical. The point is not only that we make breakthroughs in our representations of reality, but that there are fundamental alterations in what counts as "reality."

Once we have several times altered the criteria for what counts as reality, the old connotations of the term *reality* must fall away. We can no longer think of reality as something that remains what it is no matter what people think about it. A rose by any other name is still a rose, but an atom by another name may not be what people used to think they were naming by *atom*, that is, an indivisible particle. We can no longer think of reality as utterly independent of human cognition.

The study of different cultures and their different realities—anthropology—is a good place to continue our tour of several different disciplines to see how our understanding of understanding is changing. The next section shows how anthropology has shifted from laws-and-causes scientific explanation to an interpretive study of *meaning*. Consistent with the idea that paradigms or worldviews span different disciplines, the case for a new worldview must span more than one discipline. To fill out our understanding of the new anthropology, I'll join it with philosophy and literary criticism, the discipline of interpreting the meaning of literary texts.

So to come back to Sokal and his hoax, yes, the French deconstructionists and their American epigones (deconstructionists like to use such words) were due for a send–up. Their language, their taste for obscurity, their cliquish, clubby, in-group humor was ripe for a roasting. But at the end of the day they are actually on to something that Americans need to hear.

Subjective relativism is clearly nonsense. That I believe something does not make it so; but some degree of cultural relativism is not nonsense. Different languages cast their worlds in different categories. Different cultures live in different worlds. Let us turn to the study of different cultures—anthropology—and see how anthropologists have come to see how different cultures see quite differently.

ANTHROPOLOGY: FROM EXPLANATION BY
LAW TO THE INTERPRETATION OF MEANING

Once upon a time, anthropology was a pursuit of the origins of humanity and the laws of basic human interactions. Grubbing about among the bones and broken crockery of ancient civilizations, anthropologists sought clues from which to reconstruct the social habits of prehistoric human beings.

Among more than a few students of anthropology, this quest after origins was also a quest after *essence*: if only we knew more about the advent of civilization, then perhaps we would better understand the deepest mysteries in the contemporary human heart. Perhaps the riddle of human nature, and the endless debate over the priority of nature or nurture, could be unlocked if we knew more about the first humans. Were they noble savages? Were they social beings or Robinson Crusoe-like loners? Loving or aggressive? Matriarchal or patriarchal?

These questions were pursued as if their answers could tell us something important about contemporary society, such as the fate of feminism or the plausibility of a politics based on the perfectibility of the human heart. From Karl Marx to Margaret Mead, arguments based on anthropology made claims about human nature that were based on anthropology's access to the first terms in the "language" of human culture. Call it the Adam–and–Eve school of anthropology.

Then so-called structural anthropology achieved a breakthrough from a preoccupation with individual *terms*—first or last—to an articulation of structures of *relations*. And not just relations among terms, but relations among relations among relations—whole structures, like the family structures known as kinship systems.

Structural anthropology, as developed by Lévi-Strauss, made the move from atomic terms to "molecular" relationships. But Lévi-Strauss tended to think of some relationships as fundamental, even universal. However varied and arbitrary the vocabularies of different myth systems, for example, "The vocabulary matters less than the structure." Further:

> If we add that these structures are not only the same for everyone and for all areas to which the function applies, but that they are few in number, we shall understand why the world of symbolism is infinitely varied in content, but always limited in its laws. There are many languages, but very few structural laws which are valid for all languages. A compilation of known tales and myths would fill an imposing number of volumes. But they can be reduced to a small number of simple types if we abstract from among the diversity of characters a few elementary functions.[3]

Lévi-Strauss moved anthropology away from the atomism of an original, essential human nature that could biologically dictate the structure of human society. But the molecular structures of relationships with

which he replaced elementary atoms came to play a role in anthropo-
logical theory that was not so very different from the role of
Adam–and–Eve terms. Call them Adam–and–Eve structures. To reach
these unchanging essences—relational though they may be—all we have
to do is "abstract from among the diversity of characters a few elementary functions."

More recently anthropology has moved beyond the quest for universals of the sort that might be evident in first terms or first relationships. Clifford Geertz's contributions to anthropology manifest several
aspects of a paradigm shift. Not only does he accept the move from primary terms to structures of relationships—"In short, we need to look
for systematic relationships among diverse phenomena, not for substantive identities among similar ones"[4]—but he further argues that these
systematic relationships, once revealed, have a status very different from
the laws of human nature that anthropologists once sought. Geertz re-
gards anthropology as "not an experimental science in search of law, but
an interpretive one in search of meaning."[5] The difference is immense.

The difference between the quest for law and the quest for meaning
has implications that extend far beyond anthropology. The distinction
extends throughout the human sciences to psychology, sociology, and
history. At stake in this distinction is nothing less than the nature of human freedom.

Geertz calls his concept of culture "essentially semiotic." Semiotics
is the theory of signs, of how they signify and mean what they mean.
In regarding culture as semiotic, Geertz is treating the artifacts of culture like a language. The great advantage of the semiotic approach to
culture is the light it sheds on the role of symbols in constituting the
human condition. According to an older view, symbols, sign systems,
language, and literature come only very late in the human story. First,
it was thought, we had to deal with nature. Only later could we afford to dabble in culture. It is humankind, after all, that manufactures
symbols.

Symbols manufacture us as well. This is what the existential sociologists mean by *symbolic realism*. We *are* our marriages, our wars fought
beneath flying banners, our oaths cast in blood and language. We *are*
the results of our dedications to our symbols. Human beings are unique
among animals for this self-making evolutionary creativity that takes
place alongside strictly biological evolution. "What this means is that
culture, rather than being added on, so to speak, to a finished or virtually finished animal, was ingredient, and centrally ingredient, in the pro-

duction of that animal himself."[6] Our physical and cultural evolution is thus a kind of mutual bootstrap operation in which nature and culture are woven into the web of meaning.

To get a sense of just how radical this view of culture really is, it's worth a minor detour to a similarly paradigm-breaking breakthrough in geology—the Gaia hypothesis. James Lovelock and Lynn Margulies stunned their colleagues in the earth sciences by suggesting that the earth's atmosphere was not something that was "added on, so to speak, to a finished or virtually finished" planet, but "was ingredient, and centrally ingredient, in the production of that" planet itself. Even more radical, the evolution of organic life forms plays a role in the supposedly inorganic chemistry of the earth's surface. We are part of the nitrogen cycle that is part of the earth that is part of our origin. It's hard to get to the bottom of systems that mutually self-organize this way.

One hope of social science—to know the nature of the human species so well that optimal living arrangements could be correctly computed—is a naïve hope, if Geertz is right. If cultures are objects for interpretation rather than explanation under natural laws, then the study of culture is endless. There is no hope of a definitive answer to the nature of human culture. It is always and forever up for grabs, ever subject to new creation through reinterpretation of what has become old.

The import of this idea for bioethics is profound. Should we allow genetic engineering of the human genome just because we are now capable of making "improvements"? While most debates on this issue are cast in a language that makes it sound as if one side is right and the other side simply wrong, if Geertz is right, then the debaters on both sides are wrong. They are both mistaken in believing that they can prove their points by reference to some intrinsic, eternal human nature that can be read by science. If Geertz is right, then so-called human nature is a work in progress. We are making it up as we go along. We are creating ourselves through our interpretations not only of what we have been and are, but of who we want to be.

So it now appears for the human sciences, with anthropology among them: *interpretations all the way down and all the way out.* "The fact is that to commit oneself to a semiotic concept of culture and an interpretive approach to the study of it is to commit oneself to a view of ethnographic assertion as, to borrow W. B. Gallie's by now famous phrase, 'essentially contestable.'"[7]

Will we discover that collectivism, as opposed to individualism, is the most natural, and therefore essentially correct ideology for the optimal

arrangement of human cultures? No. Nor will we discover that individualism is the "right" answer. To say that these interpretations are *essentially contestable* is just to say that there is no foundational essence
or nonarbitrary human culture that is incontestable. On this and other
issues, rival interpretations will continue to contest the reading of whatever evidence is brought to bear.

This point is a central plank in the platform for ethical pluralism. The
rivalries among different interpretations of *reality* are tied up with rivalries among different interpretations of *morality*. There are different
interpretations of the rivalry among interpretations of morality. One interpretation says there should be no such rivalry. The Good is good for
everyone everywhere forever. Another interpretation says no, morality
is not a science. Its rules are not universal. But just because there is no
universal code of ethics for everyone everywhere, it does not follow that
we have to submit to a subjective relativism that says anything goes. The
slope is slippery, but we can stop short at *cultural* (not subjective) relativism. The unit of moral integrity is not one (the individual subject),
not all (everyone everywhere forever), but *some* (a corporation, a company, a community, a culture). By stopping on the slope from all to one
at *some*, we can find all the obligation we need.

Well–meaning attempts to lift morality ever higher up that slippery
slope toward the pinnacle of universal reach have a nasty way of back-
firing. People who think they have the answers for everyone everywhere
are dangerous. They impose their utopian visions on others. They think
they know the One Best future. To make the case for better futures is
to renounce the universal reach of an absolute morality, but without
sliding down the slope toward no morality altogether. We *can* have better futures without the One Best future, and we *can* defend the better-
ness of those several futures with an approach to ethics that is genuinely
pluralistic.

The way rival interpretations work, the progress of inquiry in the
symbolic realm does not guarantee that they will converge on some goal
that could therefore be considered a fixed Reality. Scientific measurements in the physical realm tend to converge as our instruments get better. What were once only approximations of the distance from the Earth
to the Sun became "more accurate" with improvements in our instruments. But where meaning is concerned, it is not a matter of getting
closer to the "truth." Where meaning is involved, alternative contexts
can determine widely divergent significances for the same physical sign,
whether it be a bone or a pun. And what finally stymies the positivist

is the fact that the divergent contexts are determined in turn *not* by some secure and single basis, but by other interpretations which are the symbolic products of an unpredictable human creativity. Turtles and interpretations, all the way down.

In his work since *Interpreting Cultures*, from which the previous quotations are taken, Geertz has become even more explicit about the semiotic, sign-interpreting nature of anthropology, and about the contagious spread of semiotic methods across the whole range of social sciences. Further, he has become more self-conscious about the significance of this movement *as a movement*, as a change of approach (or paradigm shift) reflecting a broadly recognized failure of earlier, more mechanical approaches that tried to mimic the hard sciences.

> Ten years ago, the proposal that cultural phenomena should be treated as significative systems posing expositive questions was a much more alarming one for social scientists—allergic, as they tend to be, to anything literary or inexact—than it is now. In part, it is a result of the growing recognition that the established approach to treating such phenomena, laws-and-causes social physics, was not producing the triumphs of *prediction, control,* and *testability* that had for so long been promised in its name.[8]

Futurists, strategic planners, industrial policy analysts, and utopians take note: prediction and control are well beyond the reach of so-called social science.

While the shift of method in anthropology is in part a function of the failure of the older laws-and-causes approach, it is in part also a function of a new blurring of disciplinary boundaries. Once upon a time, the articulation of different academic disciplines—mathematics, English, anthropology, sociology, and so on—was thought to represent much more than arbitrary conveniences erected for purposes of university administrators. The different disciplines were thought to represent the different branches of a naturalistic tree of knowledge whose joints were determined by nature and not by mind. The differences between the disciplines rested, it seemed, on real differences in the world, like the differences between sheep and goats, or the organic and the inorganic.

In recent years, these lines between the disciplines have come to seem increasingly arbitrary, and it is this phenomenon within the working lives of researchers that is the subject of Geertz's opening essay in *Local Knowledge*, "Blurred Genres: The Refiguration of Social Thought."

It is a phenomenon general enough and distinctive enough to suggest that what we are seeing is not just another redrawing of the cultural map—the moving of a few disputed borders, the marking of some more picturesque mountain lakes—but an alteration of the principles of mapping. Something is happening to the way we think about the way we think.[9]

IMPORT FOR SCENARIO PLANNING

These recent movements in anthropology—Lévi-Strauss's structuralist turn, Geertz's semiotic or interpretive turn—suggest similar moves on the part of planners. Forget about the laws-and-causes approach toward a predictive science. Focus instead on multiple interpretations of the present. This, after all, is what a set of scenarios amounts to: alternative interpretations of the present as the first chapter of several very different futures. Today's decisions and events take on different *meanings* depending on the different tomorrows that are their possible contexts or consequences. What is the meaning of today's hike in the prime rate? Is it a move to protect pensioners from inflation? Or is it an unnecessary curb on the economy that will cost many workers their jobs? Scenarios can paint these different consequences in rich, narrative detail.

Contemporary anthropology has made the shift from emulating the hard sciences toward a more literary, narrative approach—what Geertz calls *thick description:* a storytelling approach that stresses not general laws or universal principles, but the narrative relationships among specific details. This is precisely what scenarios accomplish: a narrative synthesis of many details into a story about the future that makes sense of the present. There are always several such stories for any given present, several different possible meanings of the present as interpretable from the perspectives of different future scenarios.

As anthropologists and futurists alike make the move from a laws-and-causes positivism toward a more literary interpretive approach, both would do well to turn their attention from the methods of the hard sciences toward the methods—or is it madness?—of literary critics. For it is the literary critics who are the experts at reading and interpreting texts.

So how do literary critics read texts these days? In reaching from the physical sciences to literary criticism to find a better model for the anthropologist's (and, by turns, the futurist's) task, Geertz can only find more turtles, for the foundations of literary theory are no firmer today than the foundations of anthropology.

LITERARY CRITICISM AND THE LEGACY OF EXISTENTIALISM

If it weren't for the fact that Geertz's inquiries steered us in this direction, literary criticism would qualify on its own for inclusion among contemporary disciplines turning up new tools from the human sciences. In recent years, a paradigm war has been raging in the upper stories of that vast academic mansion known on lower floors simply as The English Department. Some of the generals in this titanic battle of paradigms are actually from departments of French or Comparative Literature. The labels over the door don't much matter, though careers may be made or lost depending on whether the main heat of the battle moves from one flank to another. The major point of importance, whether your battalion speaks French or English, is that the rules of the contest are changing. The reading of texts isn't what it used to be. This is important to us because, after the symbolic turn we saw in anthropology, *interpretive reading* is the skill we need in order to make sense of our increasingly symbol-laden environments.

Surely there have always been fashionable -*isms* to complicate the unselfconscious act of reading a good novel. From Russian formalism to the New Criticism (now quite old), professors have earned their keep by telling us how the text was *really* working in ways far removed from our naïve following of the yarn. But in recent years, particularly since the 1970s, the cries from the attic have become particularly raucous. From the floors below, the esoteric squabbles often sound like the unintelligible babble of people who have read too much European philosophy. But one ignores these squabbles at one's peril, especially when words with ominous connotations, like "deconstruction," drift down. The literary critics have ganged up in an intellectual wrecking crew.

Deconstructive criticism works like a corrosive against all pretenses at systematic explanation. The corrosion works at both the foundation and at the upper stories of theoretical abstraction. At the foundation, deconstructive criticism shows that the simple elements that make up a text are not that simple after all. Each sentence, each phrase, each word is packed with complexities introduced by the several different contexts: social, economic, political, psychological, to say nothing of literary and historical contexts. Deconstructionists are blurrers of genres, to use Geertz's phrase. If the reader should want to take a foothold in any one of those genres or contexts, such as by taking the political context as basic and primary, then the deconstruction operation moves to the upper stories where the status of, say, Marxism as a theory will come under

attack. Deconstruction challenges the very idea of seeing the world as
neatly displayed beneath the gabled eaves of theoretical hierarchies with
their unifying abstractions at the peak of the roof. The word *deconstruction*, does not refer to the process of taking something apart or
watching it disintegrate. Rather, it refers to the analytic technique of
showing that what is deconstructed was never all that unified and solid
to begin with; it never had the integrity that its name suggested.

The corrosive force of deconstruction came into play against the calmly
assumed categories of earlier critics. Categories like author, reader, and
text were grand enough to assume a solidity in need of deconstruction.
Not quite content with deconstructing the unifying abstractions of theory and the unitary atoms at an elementary level of analysis, deconstruc-
tionist literary critics also challenge the unity of the author of the text. In
what seems at first more a bad pun than an argument, literary critic Edward Said deconstructs the *authority* of the author: "authority is nomadic:
it is never in the same place, it is never always at the center . . ."[10] Said
contrasts the situation of the contemporary critic with that of a critic like
Leo Spitzer, who was among the last of those to draw on an orally received training in a canonical tradition of world literature and languages
studied in the original. The "dynastic tradition" of interpretation could
tell you where and how to begin; but the dynastic tradition has ended. So
the contemporary critic is set adrift in a sea of competing schools—new
criticism, feminist criticism, reception theory, etc.—where none lays claim
to the legitimacy of one who learned in the old dynasty. The foundations
are lost along with essences and origins.

This way of thinking is important to scenario planners because it
shows how other categories that we might take for granted—like power,
leadership, property, consumer, health, and education—might call for
deconstruction. Terms we took for granted might take on very different meanings in the different contexts of different scenarios.

Said distinguishes between *origin*, a kind of passive if solid foundation, and *beginning*, something both more ambiguous and more active,
much like the free choice of the existential individual. There is a sense
in which we do not know where to begin, but must instead find out
what we meant to say by seeing, later down the line, what we have already said. As Roland Barthes describes his process of creation, "I begin producing by reproducing the person I want to be."[11] So, for Said,
"Beginnings, therefore, are for me opposed to originalities, or to those
ideal Presences whose ideal originality Yeats called 'self-born mockers
of man's enterprise.'"[12]

Let me unpack this compact passage as follows: Lacking a clear sense of origin or destiny—whether in a dynastic tradition, in a sense of personal essence, or in Bernal'/Brand's line about desire misreading fate—we must be enterprising! Those purported origins were self-born in the sense that, unlike beginnings, they were not born by free individuals. Instead, they mocked our enterprise by denying us the opportunity to create ourselves and our futures by our own enterprise. Origins of the sort that anthropologists once sought would have launched us on histories over which we had no influence—fates which, as Bernal and Brand believe, would only be misread by our desires. Those fateful histories could have been explained by laws-and-causes science, but we would have ceased to have any say about our fates or destinies, which would have been fixed and scientifically predictable.

In his discussion of Michel Foucault (among those genre–blurrers mentioned by Geertz), Said remarks that, for Foucault, "the novelistic model of successive continuity is rejected as somehow inappropriate to the reality of contemporary knowledge and experience."[13] Life these days doesn't always move resolutely forward in a plot that makes as much sense as Thomas Berry's Old Story (see Chapter 1, p. 8). Consequently, an author like Foucault is necessarily concerned with relationships of "adjacency, complementarity, and correlation, which are not the same as the linear relationships of succession and integrity."[14]

Said is nonetheless hopeful. He grants the perpetual possibility of beginnings, however infirm our foundational origins. His stance is radically opposed to the nihilism that he finds in authors like Paul deMan. This charge of nihilism is worth addressing for it touches the most sensitive chord of resistance to deconstruction. Is it true that, without a firm foundation, the entire edifice of human enterprise must crumble to the ground leaving us with nothing? *Nihil?*

After citing Nietzsche's oft-quoted lines on truth—"Truths are illusions about which one has forgotten that this is what they are"[15]—Said defends Nietzsche against the charge of nihilism. "This stance is relativistic, yes, but it is not the kind of manic hopelessness it is often taken to be. Nietzsche must not be interpreted, here or elsewhere, as a puerile, nay-saying nihilist."[16]

If it's nay-saying nihilism you want, you'll find it in the literary critic, Paul deMan, the favorite whipping boy of the enemies of deconstruction. DeMan's major work, *Blindness and Insight*, begins with an epigraph from Proust: "This perpetual error that is, precisely, life" and continues with lines like: "The human mind will go through amazing feats of distortion to avoid facing 'the nothingness of human matters.'"[17]

DeMan's rhetoric betrays the certainty of the nihilist, the calm despair that *knows* futility. How does Derrida, who is no nihilist, avoid deMan's trap? The answer lies in the distinction Nietzsche draws between two forms of nihilism: first, the nihilism of the weak, for whom the devaluation of all values then becomes an excuse for decadence; second, the nihilism of the strong, for whom the devaluation of values is a prelude to a playful, energetic *revaluation* that takes the risk of creativity.[18] This playful and creative revaluation is the work of creating better futures that are based not on some universal ethics, nor on a capricious, arbitrary, anything-goes spontaneity, but on *beginnings* that reflect the shared hopes of a community.

Derrida speaks of "the joyous affirmation of the freeplay of the world without truth, without origin, offered to an active interpretation . . . *This affirmation then determines the non-center otherwise than as loss of the center.*"[19] Lose the center altogether and you have nothing. Split the center into several centers and decentering renders a polycentric something—neither a hierarchy with *one* peak, nor anarchy with *no* peaks, but a heterarchy with *some* peaks. One minus one equals zero, nothing, *nihil.* But one divided by a playful decentering equals a polycentric subject with *some* centers, not none, not one.

This affirmation of "the non-center otherwise than as loss of the center" is crucial to ethical pluralism, the social philosophy of some, and the role of alternative scenarios in interpreting the present. If the "loss of the center" were bound to plunge us into nihilism and anarchy, as suggested by Yeats's famous line—"Things fall apart, the center cannot hold"—then the failure of the old dynastic traditions exemplified by critics like Leo Spitzer would mean real trouble. We'd have nothing on which to base our values, our aspirations, our hopes for better futures. But if the "loss of the center" is understood instead as a liberation from old strictures, old dynasties, such that new centers can be erected, then this kind of decentering can enable opportunities for new value creation.

What more can we learn from literary critics about how such a constructive (rather than deconstructive) decentering might work? This determination of "the non-center otherwise than as loss of the center" has exemplars in the works of Roland Barthes. For Barthes, the point is not that the modern protagonist loses his center altogether but that his character becomes disseminated, decentered, pluralized. Like the modern au-

thor, the modern hero loses control, but not by an intentional act of ab-
dication. Authorial command and the unity of the self do not succumb
to nothingness. In place of a subtraction (one minus one leaves nothing), division and multiplication breed a profusion of contrary intentions and desires yielding a fragmented but still articulate structure.

Roland Barthes by Roland Barthes might promise to be a celebration
of ego. Instead, both in its aphoristic form and in its content, it constitutes a sustained spoof on pretensions to centered integrity. "To write
by fragments: the fragments are then so many stones on the perimeter
of a circle: I spread myself around: my whole little universe in crumbs;
at the center, what?"[20] So uncertain is the point of origin, the voice of
the text shifts back and forth from first person—I—to third person—
he. "Liking to find, to write *beginnings,* he tends to multiply this pleasure: that is why he writes fragments: so many fragments, so many beginnings, so many pleasures (but he doesn't like the ends: the risk of
rhetorical closure is too great: the fear of not being able to resist the *last
word).*"[21] So likewise, in scenario planning we don't utter the *last word*
in the form of a single utopian future. Instead we create the fragments
of several different futures.

Is Barthes a confident authority who knows just where he is going
when he sits down to write? Hardly. "I begin producing by reproducing the person I want to be."[22] This production, or reproduction, is not
guided by some singular, authoritative captain of the ship, nor by anything we could call a strategic plan. So likewise, in scenario planning we
begin producing by reproducing the future we want to inhabit.

THE IMPORT OF RECENT LITERARY
CRITICISM FOR SCENARIO PLANNING

What Said and Barthes have done for literary criticism has direct import
for scenario planning in several respects. Once upon a time literary criticism sought to ground the "correct" reading of a text by tying it to the
original intentions of the author, who was considered a kind of all-
knowing and all-powerful God in relationship to the text. A second
phase, New Criticism, placed more emphasis on the creation, the text,
rather than the intentions of the creator. Part of the force of deconstructionism has been to demonstrate that the text is no less ambiguous
in its meaning than the intentions of an original author. Consequently,
contemporary criticism now finds itself stressing neither the author nor
the text, but the reader.

As the fog of French deconstructionism begins to clear, one of the healthiest survivors on the literary critical horizon appears to be Reception Theory, a school of criticism that reframes the goal of criticism by emphasizing neither the author nor the text, but the role of the reader.[23] An instructive parallel to these stages in the history of literary criticism can be found in three comparable stages in the history of future studies. Once upon a time the study of the future was literally an attempt to uncover God's intentions. With the advent of secular science, accounts of God's design gave way to scientific attempts to trace causal chains in the manifest text of physical reality. If the plot of the present could not be told by reference to God-given purpose, then the plot of the present could be completed by predictions of the future; for example, today's struggle could be justified by dialectical materialism's "scientific proof" of what life would be like after the revolution—an end that would justify the sufferings imposed by today's means.

However, predictability in the social sciences now lies in the same dustbin with aspirations to validity of interpretation via text-based New Criticism. In place of prediction, future studies might borrow a leaf from literary criticism and develop its own kind of Reception Theory. Scenarios developed at the grass roots by those who will actually live those scenarios have certain advantages over predictions concocted by experts: most importantly there is a level of buy–in that comes with "receiving" a future that one has had a hand in creating. As Manuel Castells puts it, "there is no sense of history other than the history we sense,"[24] meaning that the story people tell themselves about their past, present, and future is bound to be a better interpretation of their history than any destiny foisted on them by master theorists who claim to have divined the direction of history.

Just as a text finds its multiple meanings in the multiple readings of its readers, so the present has a range of possible meanings. These are not to be interpreted solely by reference to the will of a creator God, nor by reference to a single future that could be predicted by a deterministic social science. Instead, the meaning of the present is a function of the future, yet the future that in fact unfolds will be very much a function of human choices based on several different "readings" of the present. Both the interpretability of the present and the multiplicity of future goals and values introduce uncertainty into the process of history. It is precisely this real uncertainty, this "textual" ambiguity, this objective indeterminacy, that opens a window to human will. Multiple scenarios can reflect both the descriptive and evaluative dimensions of uncertainty. Like Reception Theory in literary criticism, multiple scenarios locate the leverage for describing the future where it belongs: with the human beings who will "receive" a future they hopefully created by themselves and for themselves.

Just as Roland Barthes begins creating by recreating the person he wants to be, so the participants in a scenario planning process begin planning by reproducing—in several scenarios—the community they want to inhabit. By rehearsing several futures, they find at least one that will represent an improvement over their present condition. Thus do they build better futures.

By what values do they deem a future to be *better*? The desire for it? Why do they want it? Because it is better. But in what sense better? Because it accords with the will of God? Because it is consistent with some universal ethical dogma? Or is that future deemed better simply because they want it?

Evaluating different futures and choosing among them pushes us inexorably beyond the purely theoretical interests of the hard sciences and out onto the slippery ice of the practical interests inherent in the human sciences. We can't avoid the leap from the measurement and calculation of facts to the affirming and contesting of values. What are the rules by which we will live our lives? The next chapter contains a summary of the new tools—the features of the relational worldview. Part Four, *New Rules, New Tools*, then applies those tools to the shaping of new rules.

CHAPTER EIGHT

THE FEATURES OF THE RELATIONAL WORLDVIEW

Having hurtled through several of the human sciences in sequence, and having lain down their linear movements on the loom of the last several chapters, I would like to cross this warp with the woof of a few cross-disciplinary comparisons. This weaving maneuver will identify five features of a relational worldview by following their woof across the warp of the disciplines already visited. Second, I want to introduce two further features of the relational worldview woof-wise by simply stating what those features are, then serving up instances and examples from various disciplines. Third, I will use several of the seven features of the relational worldview to clarify what might be meant by *normative* scenarios in an era when the very idea of norms seems suspect or, at best, weakened by cultural relativism. The point of this exercise is to guide the argument toward normative scenarios that cash in on recent achievements in the human sciences rather than trying to emulate the hard sciences.

Since each of the first five features of the relational worldview has already been discussed several times and at some length in the several contexts of the disciplines that make up the warp, their review on the woof will be brief. The point is to pull the threads of the warp together by weaving this woof across the different disciplines so that a set of conceptual tools will be available for describing a new worldview. But the application of these tools is not simple or obvious. As I'll suggest, there is a danger of using these new tools in old ways. That is why, before they are applied to the fashioning of normative scenarios, there must be an intervening section on norms and values. Like our understanding of the theoretical structures for relating facts to one another, our understanding of values is also subject to change.

Here, then, is a short list of features of a new paradigm emerging from the human sciences, together with some hypotheses about how these features might apply to normative scenarios.

1. FROM THINGS TO SYMBOLS: THE SEMIOTIC TURN

First let's pick up the thread in the four disciplines of anthropology, philosophy, psychology, and sociology. Geertz described anthropology as a semiotic discipline in search of meaning, not a science in search of laws and explanations. Philosophers, particularly Richard Rorty, speak of the linguistic turn in characterizing the significance of Wittgenstein and Heidegger. But Roland Barthes and Michel Foucault apply the tools of linguistic analysis to a wider domain of signs than words alone. Likewise psychologists have liberated themselves from Freud's ego-psychology to give full weight to Freud's real contribution: his emphasis on the power of symbols in his greatest work, *The Interpretation of Dreams*. Finally, existential sociology embraces a "symbolic realism" that accords ontological weight and power to symbols. In each of the disciplines reviewed we see a turn away from a stolid materialism that would reduce symbols to the role of pale reflections of physical things. In each of these disciplines there is an acknowledgment of the way symbols can motivate action without relying on a reduction to physical causes to account for their efficacy.

Let me warn of a temptation toward misapplication of this concept. The simple but wrong application of the semiotic turn to normative scenarios might run as follows: as opposed to a reduction of norms to mere conventions of speech, we can now depend on norms that are resistant to reduction. We can identify symbols of values that transcend mere conventions. We can locate standards for the Good, the True, and the Beautiful in a semiotic order that replaces Platonic universals as the source of normative standards.

Just as I earlier declined the temptation to build the edifice of future studies out of towering stalagmites based on the purportedly firm foundations of the hard sciences, so I now hesitate to hang better futures on a series of normative stalactites reaching down from the lofty heights of some transcendent order. Recent studies in semiotics show that we have no independent access to a transcendent signified beyond the signifiers. Instead, the distinction between signified and signifiers is a "floating" distinction. Each signified becomes a signifier of some further signified. The distinction between signifier and signified is real and useful in particular cases, but when you press for an ultimate signified, it's signifiers all the way out. So the Semiotic Turn should not be used in the service of some new idealism that would substitute language for Platonic Ideas.

2. DIFFERENCE OVER IDENTITY: FROM AN EMPHASIS ON THINGS TO AN EMPHASIS ON RELATIONSHIPS

Geertz invites us "to look for systematic relationships among diverse phenomena, not for substantive identities among similar ones." He is less interested in what we all share than in how we differ. Likewise linguists are less interested in the identities that abide through the evolutionary changes traced by etymologies than in the differences that define the structure of a language at a particular point in time. Words mean what they mean, not by virtue of some one-to-one link between self-identical symbol and self-identical thing. Rather, words mean what they mean by virtue of the usage-place they maintain in a structure of differences, the latticework of an entire language.

In Guntrip's review of the object relations school of psychologists, he criticized Freud's preoccupation with universals. Instead he focused on the differences that make each individual unique. Finally, in the symbolic realist view of existential sociology, "there are multiple realities, including those of social scientists, and none has absolute priority over others."

Physical things impress us with their self–contained identity. Apples, rocks, chairs, tables—all the furniture of the physical world—come in clearly contained bundles with easily definable borders, what Geertz called "substantive identities." Identity is easy for physical things, and to the extent that we are preoccupied with physical things, we take identity as a tacit criterion of existence. To be is to be a clearly identifiable individual. When it comes to symbols, however, identity—and therefore ontological status—is less obvious. What about the number *3*? Or Beethoven's Fifth Symphony? Or the gross national product? Or the cause of the Civil War? Philosophers wax scholastic about such things because categories like identity, borrowed from a common sense schooled on the physical, turn out to be inappropriate and hopelessly clumsy when applied to such symbolically mediated "entities."

There may be a nontrivial relationship between this second feature of the relational worldview and the first feature—the symbolic turn. A preoccupation with the physical will lead one to focus on identities; preoccupation with the semiotic order of symbols demands that one focus on differences. To know a physical thing is (among other things) to know its shape and what is inside its boundaries: what it is made of, its material. To know a symbol is (among other things) to know how it relates to what is outside: its grammatical and syntactic relationships, the place it maintains in a logical space, what it is *not.* As the linguist Ferdinand de Saussure discovered with his insight into "the arbitrariness of the sign," it matters not at all what a printed word is made of, its letters, the ink on the page, the sound of the syllables. What matters is the pattern of relationships that differentiate the usage of that word from all other words.

This preoccupation with difference rather than identity in the symbolic order might also be prematurely elevated into a Platonic ideal for application to normative scenarios. We might rush off in praise of the organic and unique as opposed to the mechanical and the standardized. We might insist on schooling that treated every student as completely unlike every other. We might demand health care that treated every patient differently. We might oppose every attempt at bureaucratic standardization as an obsolete holdover from an industrial order that achieved economies of scale by mass–manufacturing sameness with the machine tools of Middle America.

There is something important to be gleaned from correlating the metaphysics of identity with the industrial era, and the metaphysics of difference with the information era. But an overly hasty idealization of difference will get us into just as much trouble as a habitual preoccupation with identity. There *are* things we have in common (such as our cohabitation of this planet's ecosphere), and a sensitivity to our commonalities will be crucial to the development of a global ethic.

3. FROM EXPLANATION TO NARRATION: THE IMPORTANCE OF STORIES

In each of the disciplines reviewed one finds increased attention to *story* as the form of redescription most appropriate to the human sciences. Whether it is Clifford Geertz giving thick descriptions of the plots that make sense of the rituals of different cultures, psychologists referring to archetypal myths, or sociologists seeking the meaning of social behavior in the contexts of stories with beginnings, middles, and ends, the importance of story, plot, and narration is now recognized well beyond the boundaries of literary criticism where it was always acknowledged. Among philosophers, Paul Ricouer, author of the monumental three–

volume *Time and Narrativity,* has probably done the most to show how narration does a better job of capturing the meaning of human actions than explanations that would reduce those actions to the interactions of simpler elements described by the hard sciences.

The implication of narrativity for normative scenarios is obvious: scenarios are stories with beginnings, middles, and ends. Narrativity distinguishes scenarios from predictions, which merely give a forecast of conditions at a single moment in the future. The narrativity of scenarios isn't something that will be added after an appreciation of new developments in the human sciences. Narrativity is essential to scenarios. To the extent that the human sciences embrace narrativity, they are emulating those futurists who use scenarios. Here we would have a clear instance of the potential irony, if futurists were to decamp in the direction of the explanatory hard sciences just as reinforcements were arriving from the human sciences bearing justifications for storytelling.

4. THE FALL INTO TIME

Once upon a time there was no sense of historical time. Aristotle, writing long before Darwin, regarded the number of species as fixed for all eternity. Neither Platonic Forms nor Aristotelian species were subject to change and evolution. The very idea of historical progress was an invention of thinkers like Vico, Herder, and Hegel. Still the hard sciences followed the paradigm of mathematics: just as two plus two always and everywhere equals four, so the truths discovered by physics and chemistry should be true for all time.

Hegel, Nietzsche, Heidegger, Wittgenstein, Foucault, and T. S. Kuhn transport us *from* a world where we could plant our feet firmly on the foundations of scientific materialism, then draw our gaze upward toward the fixed stars of timeless values . . . *to* a world where we float or fall (in relativistic space it's hard to tell the difference) and never come to rest on firm foundations. Things change. Nations crumble. Ideologies that had been likened to religions lose credibility overnight.

Hegel awakened us to history. Nietzsche and Heidegger worked out the significance of history for the individual: a certain amount of despair and confusion at the transitoriness of things and their lack of a clear direction. Wittgenstein and Foucault offer different but equally unsettling perspectives on the semiotic turn: the realization that almost all of our distinctively human experience is mediated by symbols, almost never raw or immediate, always culturally and linguistically tinged.

These lessons of the last century or so of philosophy—about time and history and the gradual displacement of the solid by the symbolic— leave us today just a little tentative about our commitments. We know better than to believe that we can gain universal acceptance for a compelling table of values by catching a quick express called the Absolute. We know that the best we can expect is a local ride on the relative. The Absolute left the station long ago. Further, we know that we are likely to switch trains a few times before we get to wherever it is we think we are going.

Rather than suggesting new norms, the Fall into Time seems to undermine the very idea of the normative—at least to the extent that norms are thought to transcend mere fashions. The Fall Into Time and the next feature of the relational worldview, the Democratization of Meaning, both threaten a Platonic commitment to timeless norms. These two features of the relational worldview therefore make a transition to, and compel us to entertain, an alternative to the Platonic interpretation of norms as transcending the realm of becoming.

5. THE DEMOCRATIZATION OF MEANING

From Reception Theory in literary criticism to communicative ethics in philosophy and sociology, the logic of legitimation is shifting from a dependence on transcendent norms to the immanent process of dialogue among writers, readers, and speakers of the language. The *real* meaning of love, happiness, or justice is not there to be discovered like diamonds or oil, trapped beneath layers of sediment just waiting for someone with enough intelligence and resources to find it. To a significant extent we are making it up as we go along. If we accept, as I think we should, Wittgenstein's insight that the meaning of a word is its *use* and not some timeless, Platonic meaning that is a transcendent signified above and beyond all the signifiers; second, if we grant that the use of a word will change through history, then we must acknowledge that what *love* meant in sixteenth–century London is not the same as what *love* means today in California. Popular usage changes, not by design or intention, but change it does.

Human virtues are renewable resources. They are created and sustained by practices. Reception Theory locates the ultimate authority for interpreting the meaning of a text neither with the author, nor in an autonomous text, but in a community of readers. Likewise scenario planners might draw a lesson from Reception Theory by locating authority over the future neither with God, nor with policy makers, nor with scientific futurists. Scenario planning cedes authority over the future to the citizens of today who "vote" for the shape of tomorrow through a range of symbolic transactions. A scenario workshop consists of words whose meanings are renewed—or not—by the way people use those words and behave in accordance with them in their practices.

This prospect of democratization raises a problem, the same problem democracy has always posed: What if the people are wrong? What if, to take an important example, a given group prefers racism to equality of opportunity? There is an abiding and intrinsic tension between the process of democracy and the concept of transcendent norms. To the extent that we surrender arbitration of norms to the will of the people, then there will always be some aristocratic voices who protest a descent to "the lowest common denominator." Ever since Socrates debated Thrasymachus (who said that justice was the will of the stronger), ever since Thomas Jefferson defended the need for more direct representation against Alexander Hamilton's support for a more aristocratic Senate, the old debate between transcendent norms and the immanent will of the people has been with us under one rubric or another: the ideal versus the real, high standards versus popular opinion, norms (as ideals) versus the normal (taken as median or average). See how our language reflects this dialectical ambivalence in the tension between *normative* (designating what we *ought* to do) and *normal* (designating the average of what *is*).

The next chapter is largely devoted to building a fire wall between a relational worldview that embraces the democratization of meaning and a relativism that says anything goes. I'll argue for pluralism, but not for subjective relativism. Unlike an amoral relativism, pluralism can be genuinely ethical if we can find solid support for norms that transcend mere whims. The shared hopes of a community, as articulated in normative scenarios, provide standards for distinguishing better from worse. But before taking a new look at norms and a fresh look at values, I want to introduce two more features of the relational worldview, Ambiguity and Heterarchy.

6. AMBIGUITY

Ambiguity lies at the very heart of scenario planning. A given event or headline can mean completely differently things depending on the context in which you read it. How does the difference of context affect the meaning of that event? How does the unfolding logic of one scenario cast the very same event in a completely different light? In order to answer this question, you need to spin out just enough of each scenario to demonstrate the different logics.

Ambiguity is not just a characteristic of man-made languages that exhibit linguistic imprecision. Ambiguity is not simply a bunch of confusions over the correct interpretation of terms with multiple meanings. Ambiguity extends right out through our signifiers and into the signified—on beyond our means of representation and right down through the physical structure of what is being represented. Because Ambiguity is ingredient in nature, not just in culture, it takes on greater importance than it would if it were one more rhetorical trope like metaphor or irony.

A great method for representing Ambiguity in visual terms is to use Escher's etchings and woodcuts. Before dismissing Escher as a mere graphic illustrator rather than an artist, think about the profundity of his central trope, visual ambiguity—up becoming down, inside becoming outside, figure becoming ground, and ground becoming figure. In discovering that Escher has something to tell us about Ambiguity—and by implication, the scenaric way of seeing—we open a door into the labrynthine maze of a book by Douglas Hofstadter, *Gödel, Escher, Bach*, and its sequel, *Meta-Mathematical Themas*; also, Hillel Schwartz's treasure trove, *Culture of the Copy*, in which he tells us everything we ever wanted to know about twins, parrots, mannequins, and several other existence proofs for a copycat ontology. Open up these depths and there is no end of ambiguous images for a scenaric way of seeing.

Because it is a matter of seeing, talk about paradigms is relevant. As Marcel Proust wrote, "The real voyage of discovery consists not in seeking new lands, but in seeking with new eyes." I came across this quotation on a pad of Post-it™ notes put together by my hosts at the Civil Service College of Singapore where we collaborated on a scenario planning training workshop. At the bottom of every Post-it™ note, this quotation alternated with another from Arie de Geus: "Planning means changing minds, not making plans." The point of these two quotations in context is simply this: scenario planning has less to do with stringing different events together in different sequences composing different possible predictions than it has to do with interpreting the same events in the present in quite different ways.

The rapid growth and acceptance of computer–assisted communications, for example, can lead in one scenario to pervasive surveillance and

Big Brotherism and in another scenario to greater humanization through increased customization of services. In the first scenario we worry about credit card companies using the information they have about our purchases to create consumer profiles that fall into the hands of the police, the FBI, and consumer credit–rating agencies. In the second scenario the same data is used to liberate us from broadcast advertising and assist us with product data on all and only those products and services that interest each of us individually. I don't receive the J. C. Penney catalogue that sells standardized goods for everyone. Nor do I get the more specialized catalogues of mail-order houses selling high–end fishing equipment. I receive the J. A. Ogilvy catalogue that contains all and only the things that interest me. This catalogue has been assembled on the basis of sophisticated, computer–driven data–mining techniques that map my purchasing patterns against a wide range of available goods.

So what is the *real meaning* of the growth of vast databases containing consumer–purchasing patterns? Precisely as Wittgenstein would have it, the meaning depends on the use, and only time will tell which use wins out. In order to interpret present meaning, we need to spin out alternative scenarios of future use. As only part of a snapshot of the present, today's data is ambiguous. Many scenarios are necessary to interpret the several possible meanings of these signs.

7. HETERARCHY

Non-hierarchical maps of organizational structure are emerging across a range of disciplines, a range sufficiently broad to justify talk of a new paradigm. The rest of this section reviews a selection of such maps drawn from the cognitive sciences, political theory, and psychology.

Habitual insistence that there *must be* a superhierarchy is the work of the hierarchical paradigm and is not always justified by the evidence. When Warren McCulloch and Walter Pitts began their investigations of the nervous system, they probably expected to find the sorts of hierarchical trees, with afferent and efferent branches, that you would expect in a central nervous system. Instead they often found strange loops in which neuron *A* stimulated *B*, *B* stimulated *C*, and *C* stimulated *A*. McCulloch was quick to see broader implications. In a fascinating paper entitled, "A Heterarchy of Values Determined by the Topology of Nervous Nets," McCulloch wrote: "An organism possessed of this [heterarchical] nervous system . . . is sufficiently endowed to be unpredictable from any theory founded on a scale of values. It has a heterarchy of values and is thus interconnectively too rich to submit to a *summmum bonum*[1]—or single, highest good. The problem is not too few hierarchies, too few values, too few principles of order. The problem is too many!

The argument is not that nothing is good, but that too many things are good, and that is why it is difficult to name one highest good or *summmum bonum*. Here we have a rigorous definition of the problem of overchoice, the bane of a busy life in the modern world. The problem comes close to the kind of crisis described by Tom Wolfe in his portraits of the splintering of American culture into many different "statuspheres." Wolfe is a master at bringing to life the different worlds of art collectors, motorcycle gangs, New York literati, and acid heads. These are not several layers in a single pyramid of Old Society. "Of course, with so many statuspheres now in operation, and so many shortcuts available, there is a chronic chaos in Society. People are now reaching the top without quite knowing what on earth they have reached the top of. They don't know whether they have reached *The* Top or whether they just had a wonderful fast ride up the service elevator."[2] This is heterarchy. And it is eminently characteristic of our contemporary condition.

You can complain about this condition. You can call for strong leadership to save us from the threat of confusion. Or you can try to understand and appreciate heterarchy as distinct from anarchy or hierarchy. The danger of the first path is not only that the strong leader may turn out to be one more tyrant, but also that the problems and issues to be addressed will not yield to a straightforward hierarchical control system. Complex problems may require the complexity of heterarchy.

Just because heterarchy is complex does not mean that heterarchies cannot function effectively. The wonderful thing about the discovery of heterarchy in the human nervous system is that it functions like an existence proof (proving something is *possible* by pointing to an *actual* case that exists) to show that heterarchy can and does work. "That it has worked so well throughout evolution, without itself evolving," writes McCulloch, "points to its structure as the natural solution of the organization of appropriate behavior." Contrary to Lyndon Johnson's claim that Gerald Ford could not walk and chew gum at the same time, we *are* able to walk and talk and think and chew at the same time. We do not fall on our faces when one activity overlaps another.

Anarchy is not the only alternative to hierarchy. Only an overly strong attachment to the hierarchical paradigm sees any compromise of hierarchy as a fall into anarchy. As McCulloch puts it, "Circularities in preference, instead of indicating inconsistencies, actually demonstrate consistency of a higher order than had been dreamed of in our [hierarchical] philosophy." Putting your right foot in front of your left foot may not be strictly "consistent" with completing a sentence about the problems of tax reform, but the ability to talk about tax reform *while walking* is thoroughly consistent with the full context of the demands on the time of a busy congressman. He cannot afford to wait to talk about tax reform until he is comfortably seated behind his desk. He must be capable of multitasking and parallel processing.

Heterarchical models are finding their ways into thought patterns across a range of disciplines, from neurophysiology and artificial intelligence to political science. The pattern picks up cultural resonances from Douglas Hofstadter's discussion of "strange loops" in his widely read *Gödel, Escher, Bach,* in which the Moebius strip becomes an emblem for heterarchical structures looping back upon themselves. Inside becomes outside and outside becomes inside. The way up becomes the way down in Escher's strange graphics.

As different disciplines serve up different examples of hierarchies looping back on themselves to become heterarchies, two different but closely related aspects of heterarchy come into focus. The first is the circularity represented in Hofstadter's phrase "strange loops." The second is a pluralism of first principles. Because the priority system loops back on itself, different principles, neurons, containers, or authorities come to play the role of "first." Sometimes it is the circularity of relationships that is most salient, sometimes the plurality of principles.

Part of the trick in living with heterarchy lies in learning how to serve several masters. But isn't this multiplicity of authorities a central feature of the postmodern condition? Just as patriarchal authority is giving way to feminism in the postmodern family, so the power of the boss in business is yielding to other powers: from regulators to consumer activists, from unions to foreign competitors, from stockholders to antitrust lawyers.

We hear increasing calls for accountability precisely because it is often difficult to tell just who is in charge. Knee-jerk hierarchy tempts us to identify one source of all authority, but anyone who knows the ways of a complex corporation will be able to tell you that one officer will be able to help you with one kind of problem while another officer will be better at helping you with another kind of problem. One person is good at improving press relations, another is better with the shareholders, a third is an authority on marketing, and a fourth is the expert on new product development. In serving several masters it's best to know who's who, and what they value.

APPLYING THE NEW TOOLS TO THE NEW RULES

We need a purchase on values, because it is not good enough to develop scenarios only for what *might* happen. We need scenarios for what *ought* to happen. We need *normative* scenarios, scenarios for *better* futures. But who's to decide what counts as *better*? Pat Robertson, William Bennett, Saddam Hussein? You see the problem: too often, as soon as you leave the cool neutrality of scientific objectivity, you seem destined to worship at the altar of one or another claim to absolute, eternal Truth.

There is a third way beyond fundamentalism on the one hand, and the ethical neutrality of value-free, objective science on the other. We do not have to choose between the Eternal Absolute on the one hand and pernicious relativism on the other. It is possible to base distinctions between better and worse upon a careful articulation of the *shared hopes of the community*—and here we are thrown from content back to process, for it is the process of scenario planning that can bring to light the shared hopes of the community: *its* vision of a better future, which may not be the same as some other community's or corporation's vision.

By basing the definition of the good on the shared hopes of the community, we accept the democratization of meaning and give ourselves an immediate escape hatch from the pretentiousness that haunts philosophy; for in many a community, particularly many corporate communities, the shared hopes of the community are no loftier than making money. But is that *all* that corporate executives want? The cynical view would say, yes, that's all they want. But experience, as well as close attention to the historical evolution of the business environment and the legitimacy of the corporation in the economic era, suggest otherwise.

I must pause here for a moment to recall and extend what's already been said about the legitimacy of the corporation, ethical pluralism, and the ethics of business—not business ethics in the sense of keeping individual executives from lying, cheating, or stealing, but the ethics of doing business in general, the increasingly close relationship between *adding value* on the one hand . . . and *values*, on the other. What could be more obvious: if you want to get paid, you had better deliver the goods! If you want to do well, you had better *do good*. Now that information gathering and dissemination is getting better and better, it's no longer possible to "make a killing." You can't take the money and run when you're illuminated by the light of the World Wide Web.

To succeed in business over the long haul, you've got to deliver the goods; to deliver the goods, you've got to know the good. It's not easy doing good better than the next guy, at lower cost and higher value to the customer. For one thing, you've got to know your customers' values. That's why I spent five years with SRI's Values and Lifestyles program conducting empirical studies of American values—first, because you've got to know *their* values in order to deliver what *they* judge to be good; second, because as anthropology tells us, different cultures and communities have different values; and third, because, as Hegel and the Existentialists tell us, those values can change over time.

To do good scenario work, you've got to know the values of the consumers you want to serve and the values of the organization that wants to serve them. By triangulating the values of these two communities with a third corner—what science tells us is physically possible—we can frame scenarios that tell us not only what *might* happen, but what *ought* to happen. If you then figure out how to do the good, I'll guarantee that you will do well. Find a better way to help people communicate, and they will pay you. Find a better way to help people organize their lives, and they will pay you. Find a better way to help people educate their children and, even for that, they will pay you.

Tap into people's values, find out what they value, and you will know what they will pay for. But don't leave it at short-term whims and wants. Yes, there is a market for chocolate and televised mind-candy, but over the long term you will have to supply something more sustaining if you want to stay in business. In order to provide something more sustaining, you will, eventually, run up against the profoundly philosophical question: What is necessary in order for human beings to live fulfilling and deeply satisfying lives? Answer that question, and help other people find their answers, and you will have a good business.

To summarize the new tools: Part Three began with a chapter on social creativity. A social philosophy of *some* rather than *one* (individualism) or *all* (collectivism) gives us new players for a new game that features an economic logic over a political logic.

What are the new tools that these new players will employ in the new economic game? The first of those tools is scenario planning—a team sport that calls for creativity and a capacity to see the same old stuff in new ways. A second tool for seeing anew is a paradigm or worldview. We saw how and why Americans have been slow to appreciate the power of paradigms. Third, we pulled together seven features of a relational worldview by reviewing the paradigm shifts that have rocked a range of different disciplines.

Now I want to apply these tools to several tasks. The first chapter of Part Four, *New Rules, New Tools,* is entitled, "Facts, Values, and Scenario Planning." I want to look at ethics through the lens of the relational worldview. The point is to give just enough but not too much force to the word *better* in better futures: just enough to escape nihilism and pernicious relativism, but not so much as to be guilty of utopian evangelizing.

After giving teeth—but not fangs—to the meaning of *better* in better futures, the concluding chapters will pull it all together by sketching the kind of scenario planning we need to improve health care, education, and politics in the new millennium.

Part Four
New Rules,
New Tools

CHAPTER NINE

FACTS, VALUES, AND SCENARIO PLANNING

The seven features of the relational worldview have import for our understanding of norms. Let's turn now to a more sustained reflection on the ethics of the relational worldview, a new look at norms, and a fresh look at values. Rather than trying to identify a new approach to norms, in each of the disciplines, I'll wind the seven features of the relational worldview into a thicker thread called *ethical pluralism*.

The point is to see how we can save the force of norms from the corrosive power of time, difference, and democratic leveling, but do so without relying on timeless absolutes or transcendent values. In order to marshal the collective will needed to build better futures, we need to find a moral fulcrum for prying the present toward a better future. We need the leverage of moral critique as a motive for improvement. But a relational morality can neither rest on the firm foundations of timeless absolutes nor suspend itself from the hierarchical sky hooks of transcendent values. Where, then, is a fulcrum for moral critique to be found?

In this chapter, I develop an idea that I call *ethical pluralism*. In the next chapter, I'll show how it can be a powerful tool when communities join to plan scenarios for their futures.

A NEW LOOK AT NORMS

In both a premodern religious context, and in a modern, liberal, progressive context, the idea of a normative scenario is likely to connote some common understanding of some transcendent values. In the premodern context those values would be derived and legitimated by reference to the will of God. What is good, everywhere and for all time, is

what conforms to the will of God. In a more modern, secular, human-
istic regime, norms may be legitimated by reference to a science of human nature or a timeless structure of rationality. The secular enlightenment substituted the universality of science for the universal reach of a
monotheistic God. In both contexts—premodern religion and modern
science—there was a way to legitimate norms that could transcend the
particular interests of private individuals and local customs and practices. There was a way of referring to a higher authority, an Absolute
that transcended the relative perspectives of different individuals and different cultures.

Now, for better or worse, we live in a postmodern era. Part of what
defines the postmodern condition is the lack of definitive criteria—religious or scientific—for progress toward a more perfect humanity. In
place of the Christian heaven on earth we are confronted with a plurality of religions: Muslim, Buddhist, Christian, Jewish, and any number
of sects. In place of the modern idea of secular progress we find a plurality of standards for a more perfect humanity: feminist, multicultural,
Native American, you name it.

So it's hard to name a norm and claim that it applies to everyone
everywhere. And if a supposed norm does not apply to everyone everywhere, then perhaps it is not a norm at all, but just one more custom
peculiar to a particular tribe. Jews don't eat pork. Southern blacks like
pig's feet. WASPs cultivate the stiff upper lip, and so on.

To reduce the normative to the sociology of taste seems to rob the
normative of the obligatory, imperative power that premodern and modern norms possessed. These postmodern "norms" seem pale and impotent compared to the commandments of the Lord or the universality of
science.

No wonder normative scenarios seem out of date. No wonder that
reference to norms seems naïve. No wonder that futurists are tempted
into the bad faith of suppressing their wishes for a *better* tomorrow and
instead devote their best efforts to worst–case scenarios. The premodern and modern sources for legitimating transcendent norms have been
delegitimated by a more sophisticated recognition that we live in postmodern times when absolutes like God or a universal human nature have
lost their credibility.

How, then, is it possible to reconstruct a normative discourse after
the deconstruction of transcendent values? How can we justify normative scenarios when norms are, "to borrow W. B. Gallie's by now famous phrase, essentially contestable"? Part of the answer, I believe, lies

in *entering the contest.* A normative scenario can articulate the force of widely accepted values without requiring either the omnipotence of a Lord of lords or the universality of mathematics. Norms need not be absolute in order to transcend the relativity of individual opinion. Norms need not be completely unambiguous to exercise some force of obligation.

In addition to entering the contest, though, we need to reappraise and reframe our understanding of just what the contest is about, and just what values *are.* In the remainder of this chapter I want to use some of the features of the relational worldview to reframe the challenge of reconstructing normative discourse; then I'll take a fresh look at values. What *are* values such that we can honor them? How do we experience values? How do we develop a mature sense of values? Building on both a descriptive and a developmental approach to values, I'll conclude with a theory of values that can satisfy the requirements set by the relational worldview's reframing of this new look at norms.

Before unfolding the argument, let's consider the difference between *norms* and *values.* Though it's too early in the course of my argument to offer precise definitions, it's not too soon to note general distinctions. Putting it in crude terms that will have to be refined, norms are relatively more objective, values more subjective. Norms set the standards toward which we aspire; values are the decision criteria we use to get there.

While this distinction is easy to make in theory, it gets pretty muddy in particular cases. A just society may be the norm toward which political action aspires; a sense of justice may be the decision criterion we use to get there. I'm not particularly concerned with finding or drawing precise boundaries between norms and values. Not only popular usage, but also academic scholarship, tends to be fairly sloppy in mixing talk about what I'll call norms and what I'll call values, so I'm perfectly ready to acknowledge that the distinction I'm drawing is to some extent stipulative. I'm using these terms in my own way to talk about a real distinction; but others often use these terms in slightly different ways to map some of the same territory.

It's not as if we're distinguishing between tungsten and manganese here. We'll get no help from experimental science. Nor are we dealing with a distinction as arbitrary as that between, say, hillbilly and bluegrass music. I am stipulating the way I will use the terms *norms* and *values,* and I will do my best to remain consistent to the use I am stipulating. My stipulations are not arbitrary. I think they are fairly close to popular and scholarly usage, but since that usage is itself fairly slippery, I want to preempt the sorts of rejoinders that say, "No, that's not what values are! You've confused values and norms," as if we were talking about classes of entities as objectively distinct as tungsten and manganese.

Granting the ambiguity of the terms we're using, let me now draw on some of the features of the relational worldview to take a fresh look at values. What would count as a *better* humanity must differ from actual humanity in ways that are speculative, creative, risky, artistic, and never definitive or obvious. The gap between what *ought to be* and what *is* cannot be closed by the force of law. It can only be closed by a human will that could have acted otherwise.

Now that we have fallen into time we must figure out how to moralize in time—how to find, create, and maintain norms and values that are appropriate to the times. Rather than imagining that norms must derive their obligatory force from some timeless foundation that would transcend any particular conditions, we must see how the moral dimension of our existence is intrinsically tentative—stretched across a gap between what *is* in any given present, and what *ought to be* in a better future.

The definition of what would count as a better future cannot be read off from the past or from some great blueprint in the sky that would transcend past, present, and future. Instead, the criteria for what will count as a *better* future, like the criteria for what would count as better art, are bound to contain some reference to the recent past and present. Like all cultural movements, the evolution of ethics will depend on an interplay between individual creativity and an evolutionary selectivity that operates on a level that transcends the individual.

Knowing this much about the necessary tentativeness of norms and values, what can we derive from the recent past and present of the human sciences? What hints toward a normative scenario can be drawn from recent developments in the human sciences? The influences that determine one's sense of morality in twenty-first century America cannot be said to constitute a well-ordered, internally coherent whole. We inherit a dialogue that posits the rights of the individual even as it posits the need for social justice. The dialectic of individualism and collectivism is not about to be settled once and for all, even after the demise of Marxist ideology.

The case of Salman Rushdie, the author forced into hiding by the Ayatollah's threat of death for his blasphemy against Mohammed, offers a poignant example of the difference between moralizing within a culture and the attempt to moralize between cultures. Salman Rushdie got into trouble by trying to straddle two cultures. As a Westerner he embraced the value of free speech and the liberty of the individual; but as a Muslim he committed blasphemy. He now claims obedience to Islam. It is hard to see how his piety toward Mohammed can be squared with the words that he has written and published so freely.

Am I arguing for the death of Salman Rushdie? No. I am only pointing out the *difficulty* of ethical debate across cultural boundaries. For those who acknowledge the cultural relativity of values, there can be no simple appeal to standards that transcend all cultures. You can appeal to norms that operate within and work to constitute a culture. But once you step outside that culture, or try to stand between two cultures, then you risk the betrayal of one culture for another. Once you become a cultural double agent, the rules become very messy—which is not to say that there are no rules; only that they will sometimes conflict with one another. Salman Rushdie's guilt in the eyes of Islam cannot be redeemed by an equal and opposite innocence in the eyes of a Western tradition preaching the right of the individual to free speech. For even in our Western tradition we acknowledge the needs of the collective and the demands it can make for individual sacrifice.

Most of us do not span radically different cultures in most of our day–to–day activities. Our values derive from the interplay between the norms of the culture we were reared in and our awareness of a larger, newer world that calls to our sense of concern. To say that we derive our sense of morality from the culture we are reared in is to admit a vast panoply of influences, given the range of texts we may have been exposed to in our formal education and the range of stories we have internalized from years of television and movies.

Literary critics then help us to read the text of our culture to determine the inventory of meanings upon which we can draw. By deconstructing the authority of the author, literary critics remind us of the shared work of constituting and maintaining meanings within a culture. Reception Theory reminds us of the importance of a literary selectivity in which readers participate in the evolution of meaning.

Critics are the preeminent *prosumers*, Alvin Toffler's term for proactive consumers who influence the shape of a product by making sure the producers know what they want. Through the wonders of modern technology and information processing, prosumers actually participate in product development by feeding their preferences into the design and production software. Critics have been doing as much ever since Milton read Virgil. Critics help to determine the shape of the literary "product" of a society. The rest of us participate as well each time we "vote" with the purchase of a book, contribute to an opinion survey, or tune in to a particular show on television. In the metabolism of the symbolic economy, we all play a role every time we engage in dialogue, read a newspaper, respond to a new movie, or use words in ways that bend their meanings in new directions.

As with the literal ballot box, so also the symbolic ballot box of cultural production and consumption of images selects only those options it can understand and appreciate, whether candidates or referenda. Part of the role of futurists in this system of cultural metabolism should therefore be to articulate in an understandable and appealing way some images of better futures.

To summarize the combined significance of the semiotic turn and the fall into time: we now know that the sources of *meaning* to be found in the myths and values of a given culture can be called upon to give form and structure to an individual life; but further, we know that these sources of meaning can transcend the individual without being absolute or eternal. Norms can be obligatory and contestable at once. This is how norms *are*. They are not to be confused with will–o'–the–wisp opinions at one extreme, or necessary laws at the other. The human sciences show us how to move beyond a laws-and-causes approach to human nature, and still hold on to the role of culturally conditioned *meaning* as influential for an individual life.

If this is indeed how norms are, then what must values be such that they can serve as decision criteria for helping us live up to the norms of our societies? The next section takes up this question. We need a fresh look at values that correspond to this new look at norms.

A FRESH LOOK AT VALUES

We postmoderns are at an awkward age: old enough to question authority, young enough to be unsure of autonomy. A little like teenagers, we suffer the growing pains of rapid transitions, both internal and external.

If I may push this analogy between teenagers and our adolescent millennial society a little further, consider the ideas of development and maturation as they relate both to individuals and to societies. In both of its applications, the idea of *development* has itself undergone rapid development.

Modernist theories of historical and psychological development presumed a single path of growth for both societies and individuals. For societies there was the linear theory of social and economic development: from ancient to modern according to the idea of progress; from less developed to more developed economies according to the naïve hopes of the World Bank during the 1970s and 1980s. For individuals, the dominant theories of development were equally linear. Freud defined a fixed series of biologically driven stages: the oral stage, the anal stage, the Oedipal stage, latency, adolescence, and finally a mature personality whose character was largely determined in the first three years of life. Likewise, the theories of economic development defined by theorists like Walt Rostow and Robert Heilbroner spoke of a "Great Ascent" from poverty and primitivism to modern industrialism. Modernization was for countries what maturation was for individuals: a single-lane highway ascending toward a fixed destination.

In both cases the goal of development had a comforting familiarity for mature, successful, American males. Not only had we made it; the *it* we had *made* was really it. Our values defined the meaning of normality. We set the norms to which all others were expected to aspire. Like masters of the universe, we perceived the rest of the world in our own image. Our values were not just *our* values; they were The Values. Intelligence? Of course. Courage? Certainly. And on down a list including efficiency, punctuality, and many other virtues often frustratingly absent in children, wives, and the workers of the Third World. But we of the white male West would educate them. They could be *developed*.

Looking back, some of us admit an appalling arrogance of power in that ethnocentric developmentalism. But let us be generous. That arrogance was also a kind of innocence. In their calm confidence in adopting that image of individual and national maturity, those older white males were as much childlike as godlike. They had not yet really grappled with the fact of human freedom. They had not fully entertained the possibility of many possibilities: that women might not *want* to be like men, that Muslims might not *want* a Western version of modernization. Such thoughts were very nearly unthinkable. And who had time, much less respect, for mere feelings?

Things have changed, and with them, values. I want to capture some of those changes and suggest their implications for the present and future. But before launching into a glib list of "new values for a new morality," I want to pause a little longer on preliminaries to note how the game board has changed before going on to describe new rules.

The rest of this chapter is divided into three sections. The first section draws out the *developmental* model in its psychological context. The second section takes a candid look at the way people actually talk about values. It is more *descriptive*. The third section turns from the developmental approach of the first section and the concrete description of the second section to present different *theories* of morality to see how they measure up against both developmental and descriptive approaches.

A summary of points drawn from the developmental, descriptive, and theoretical approaches will then allow us to locate values in a matrix of features that define what values are and are not. Equipped with the discoveries made along the way, I'll then return to the subject of better futures, by then better able to say just what I mean by *better*.

1. THE DEVELOPMENTAL MODEL OF MATURATION

To capture the sea change surrounding particular shifts in values, the situation of the adolescent is instructive. For the child, the image of maturity consists in being just like the parent. For the adolescent, just the opposite, at least sometimes. The drama of oedipal rebellion, like most dialectical struggles, presents a play of identity in difference. Different values may be entertained, but often with the hope of finding a certainty and absoluteness that resembles the certainty that children perceive their parents as possessing.

Let me offer an all too familiar example. Dad says material success and membership in The Club are important. Sonny says, "Not on your bourgeois life, Pops." Spiritual enlightenment and the non-exclusive brotherhood and sisterhood of humankind—an all-inclusive "club" very different from Dad's exclusive country club—are the correct values according to Sonny. Sonny and Pops may differ in the values they espouse, but Sonny is identical to Pops—or at least to his perception of Pops—in being sure that his values are The Values.

This dialogue may go through further familiar stages. Disillusioned by the philandering of his spiritual guru—his substitute father—Sonny may reach the certainty that there are no values at all. He may turn from his childish assumption of morality, and his adolescent discovery of a new morality, to a cynical dismissal of all morality: nihilism. "It's all relative. Do whatever feels good."

The formulaic quality of Sonny's dismissals should be a tip-off to the fact that Sonny has not completely outgrown the kind of childish morality that seeks a simple answer for every question. The adolescent may question the answers that were accepted in childhood, but new answers will have to be equally simple as long as adolescence persists. Nihilism is a very simple answer, however sophisticated its European statements may sometimes sound. Woody Allen can tell you everything you ever needed to know about nihilism and about the value of valuelessness when it comes to scoring on dates.

Values! You just can't escape them. But the game board changes as the developmental dialectic unfolds. In the first stage of childhood and innocence, the values at hand are The Values. There are no other contenders. If questions arise about the justification of those values, the answers lie with authority: Daddy's authority, God's commandments, or the sacredness of what was learned at mother's knee.

At a second stage—adolescence—authority is no longer sufficient. Quite the contrary. But the answers sought must have the certainty and simplicity that earlier resided in authority. At this stage, people who no longer trust the Ten Commandments are nonetheless looking for a kind of great blueprint in the sky, a more or less rational account that tells what's right and wrong for everyone everywhere. Just as rationality is supposed to take the place of authority, so philosophy is supposed to replace religion.

Having taught philosophy for many years, I can attest that many young students turn to philosophy in hopes of finding a replacement for religious beliefs they've come to doubt. They want to replace the orthodoxy of religious belief with the clear-eyed rationality of philosophy. The goal is to retain some certainty about the values that lend meaning to life, but without the mumbo jumbo of miracles and superstition. The motives of most students in introductory philosophy courses are not so very different from the motives of those who join esoteric religious cults. They want to find some basis for moral certainty. But good teachers of philosophy, from Socrates on down, differ from cult leaders in refusing to serve up simple answers to satisfy that wish for certainty. Rather than providing simple answers, good teachers pose hard questions.

There is a third stage, beyond the first stage of authority, beyond the second stage of rebellion against authority and its replacement by simple formulas, nihilistic or cultish. This third stage consists in the creation, adoption, and choice of values: moral autonomy.[1]

No one is utterly free. You can't create or choose different values every day. Whims are not values, however much they may serve a similar function as criteria for choice. Both values and whims can play the role of criteria for discriminating among options. But the closer values come to whims, the less they play the role of rational criteria. If you choose your standards afresh every day, then the choice itself is made willy-nilly: the choice of criteria can be judged by no prior criterion. You just choose! That kind of voluntarism seems terribly close to having no values at all.

Values cannot be so quick to change. Once adopted, they must persist for some time. Not necessarily forever. But if values can be traded in for new models every year, then they seem more like fads or fashions, less like what we usually think of as *values*.

2. A CONCRETE DESCRIPTION OF VALUES IN EVERYDAY LIFE

The effort to clarify the half-life of values, to pin down the difference between a whim and a value, carries us from the developmental approach to values to the descriptive approach. How do we usually think of values? Let us look at the everyday experience of values. We won't assume anything about what values *are*. We won't even assume that there is any such thing as a value. As the founder of the philosophical movement known as phenomenology, Edmund Husserl, put it, we "bracket" the existence of values, and then take the experience of values at face value: let it reveal itself on its own terms.

How, then, do we *experience* values? Let us count the ways.

First, we feel them as constraints. Let's face it—if we are going to take the experience of values at face value—values can cramp your style. In what kinds of situations is someone likely to say, "But where are your values?"—when you are about to do something you're not supposed to do, like cheat on your taxes, tell a little white lie, or cut in line in traffic. Values can act as severe limitations upon desire. Values place limits on self-serving motives.

Second, values can act more positively: beauty can delight, reverence can inspire. Holding beauty as an important value can lead one to experiences that lift the self above self-serving motives.

Third, we tend to think of values in an honorific sort of way. Values are invoked as a secular version of the sacred. They have a certain halo effect. When people speak of values, men straighten their backs and women pull their knees together.

Working backwards from our actual behavior—the phenomenology of human behavior with respect to values—what do we learn about how values must work to account for their capacity to limit, elevate, and inspire reverence?

Clearly, values must somehow transcend individual interests. To be able to stand over and above our private desires, to be able to genuinely *oblige*, values must stand above and beyond individual and transitory wishes. How can values possess such obligatory force if that force does not derive from the power of an authority figure or the universality of law? Referring back to the idea of stages of ethical development, we can put this question another way: beyond fear of punishment or reverence for authority, what would motivate someone to restrain desires or engage in noble activities?

3. THEORIES OF VALUE

A number of theories have been proposed to answer this question about the source of the force of obligation: first, enlightened self-interest (with the stress on *enlightened* to distinguish it from the short-term self-interest of whims and desires); second, a utilitarian calculation of the greatest good for the greatest number; third, an appreciation for whichever choice renders the will consistent with itself by avoiding logical self-contradiction. These three answers to the question of the obligatory force of values are known to the trade as Epicurean ethics, utilitarian ethics, and Kantian ethics, respectively. There have been variants aplenty.

One variant (the intuitionist tradition extending from Hutcheson to G. E. Moore) holds that we have a kind of ethical intuition, that we just *know* right from wrong by virtue of a peculiar faculty that is neither wholly rational nor wholly emotional or instinctual. You could think of this as a kind of instinctual school of ethics: there's nothing you can say about how this strange faculty of ethical intuition works. We just know that it does work. Of course, sometimes it doesn't work. Some people don't seem to know right from wrong; they simply lack the right instincts. Of such people, we say, "They have no values." If we insist on regarding ethical decision making as such a mysterious phenomenon, we can imagine a Presbyterian distribution of instincts: like grace, you've got it or you don't; and if you don't, there's not much you (or society) can do about it.

A second variant that seems to remove individual responsibility from ethical decision making is sociobiology: instead of the Devil, my genes made me do it. Edward O. Wilson, Richard Dawkins, and their followers would have us believe that values are like thumbs: useful tools for the perpetuation of the gene pool. If we didn't have them, we would perish as a species. Altruism, which may not be in the interest of an individual, may serve the tribe very well. Some may have to take risks in order that others might survive and carry on. All very well and good for those automatic decisions that we attribute to motives like maternal instinct. But what about less automatic cases? What about those situations in which it is by no means clear which course of action you ought to take? Attributing particular decisions to genetic makeup is a little like blaming the collapse of a roof on gravity. Sure, gravity made the roof fall down rather than up; but what we want to know is why this particular roof collapsed while others remain intact. Like gravity, sociobiology offers explanations at a level of generality that ignores precisely those specifics that occupy center stage in concrete descriptions of values: the conflicts, the attempted excuses, the guilt, the whole messy process of moral deliberation.

SUMMARY AND SYNTHESIS

To summarize the last two sections on concrete descriptions and various theories of values: I took a look at some familiar features of moral crises and then reviewed some of the major theories purporting to explain how we make our way through such moral crises. Some of the theories, particularly the Kantian and the utilitarian, offer rules and laws for calculating the correct answer for questions of value; other theories minimize the role of deliberation and choice. Instead, they present human valuation as either intuitive or as variations on a biological theory of instincts. They present man as a creature of instincts, or a mechanism for perpetuating a gene pool.

Now I want to pull together several of the insights to be derived from both the concrete descriptions and the theories. Two major quandaries emerge from this quick review of values–related behavior and the theories proposed to explain them. First, we find a spectrum from the particular to the general in many different forms: particular whims as opposed to general principles; individual wants and desires as opposed to universal needs; the customs of a particular tribe as opposed to general laws of biology or anthropology that might pertain to all human beings; particular situations with their mitigating circumstances as opposed to a general description of the human condition. In the Kantian imperative to make sure that the motive of your action can be universalized without self-contradiction (listen to mothers saying, "But what if *everyone* were to do that?") you hear this test of the particular against the universal. Likewise in the utilitarian calculus of the greatest good for the greatest number, the good of the whole prevails over the good of the particular individual. And when the individual feels the constraint on his individual will that comes from thinking about the good of the community, again, the general will is prevailing over individual will or impulse. These several oppositions can be summarized under the rubric, the particular versus the general.

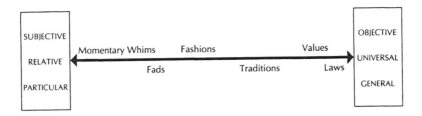

A second quandary, or set of quandaries, can be summarized under the rubric, the voluntary versus the involuntary. Here we find instinct versus choice, necessity versus freedom, compulsion versus deliberation, and automatic behavior versus autonomous behavior.

Now let us take these two scales, from the particular to the general and from the involuntary to the voluntary, and consider them as axes defining a conceptual "space." The point of this exercise is to locate the domain of values.

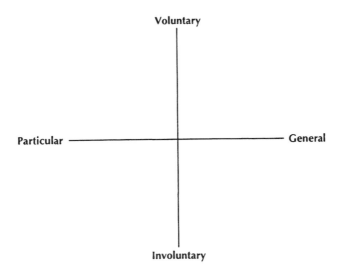

Given this space in which to locate different decision criteria and motivations, we can see some exemplary occupants in various quadrants:

- In the *general/involuntary* quadrant belong some of the motivations for some of our decisions:
  - instincts
  - laws of nature
  - the laws of the state (a little toward the particular)
  - universal needs: food, water, shelter, etc.
- In the *particular/involuntary* quadrant belong other drivers of choice:
  - habits
  - fetishes and compulsions
  - disabilities: deafness, blindness, learning disabilities
- In the *particular/voluntary* quadrant belong still other decision criteria:
  - wants and desires
  - whims and impulses (further toward the particular)
  - choices that are artistic or aesthetic
- In the *general/voluntary* quadrant belong:
  - values (finally), the kind that oblige one's choice, but do not constrain or determine with necessity

Summarizing both the spectrum from the particular to the general and the "space" that values occupy:

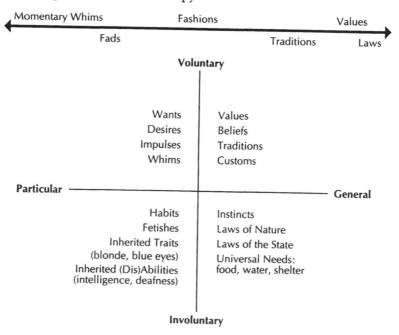

Values occupy the general/*voluntary* quadrant for two reasons: first, because you *can* decline to do what you ought to do. Second, on a level relating to cultures rather than to individuals, the multiplicity of different value systems proves that different cultures are not involuntarily constrained to conform to just one value system. Values are part of a system of which free will or voluntary choice is another, mutually implied, part. Values and volition are mutually required parts of a system. Values cannot force their compliance; they are not natural laws. They are general—or they are not values, but wants or desires. They are voluntary only by comparison to laws. They are less voluntary than the particular choices of an individual. You can't choose new values every day or for every occasion. Nonetheless, different value systems are chosen by different peoples; there can be more than one system of values. This is important. It will color our approach to the evolution of politics, the institutional systems we have developed for mediating among different and competing systems of values.

The fact that values are to some extent voluntary, the fact that different peoples choose different value systems, necessarily entails a plurality of value systems. For the likelihood of all peoples choosing the same value system is about as great as the likelihood of all tribes inventing the same language.

The stage of childlike innocence tends to revere a single authority and to regard all conflicting beliefs as simply mistaken. A second, or adolescent stage, is ripe for the nihilism implicit in descriptive neutrality. Fixated on the rebellious power of the budding ego, the adolescent is all too eager to undercut any attempt at moral restraint by challenging the obligatory force of all morality.

Part of the process of maturation to a third stage of adulthood involves gaining the ability to acknowledge uncertainty, to accept the frailty of even one's loftiest ideals. One's highest values suffer when many different values are high on different orders of rank. To accept the significance of one's own choice is to acknowledge the degree to which the world does not make the choice for you. Values beckon but do not drag the will. The will needs values to guide its choices, to differentiate important choices from mere impulses. But if the guidance of values were strict enough to command 100 percent compliance, then "choice" would not be voluntary. It would not be choice at all, but forced compliance.

The third stage of development—adulthood for the individual, postmodernity for our culture—consists in the ability to live with real choices and with the ambiguity and uncertainty imposed by an awareness that

other people make different choices in similar situations. Movement toward moral maturity for a whole nation would then imply pluralism,
but without the indifference toward values suggested by mere relativism.

In the final part of this chapter, I want to develop this notion of pluralism without indifference—*ethical* pluralism—by showing, first, how particular values can persist through different stages of moral development; second, how their force and rationale changes within those different contexts;
third, how attitudes toward the future relate to values; and fourth, how
some recent shifts in values fit into the pattern I've been developing; finally,
I'll draw some conclusions about what we are likely to see in the future.

FROM THE MORAL MAJORITY TO MORAL MATURITY

Any particular value, such as honesty, can be endorsed and acted on
within a range of different ethical systems. Honesty may mean conformity with the commandment, "Thou shalt not bear false witness."
Honesty may have nothing to do with divine authority, but may instead
derive from an inner-directed desire for personal integrity, sincerity, and
authenticity. Or, honesty may find its rationale in a pragmatic, outer-
directed, institutionally based argument for honesty as the best policy.
Finally, honesty may be chosen out of reverence for the possible rather
than a pragmatic appreciation for what is actual: say, for the ideal of
undistorted communication as a condition for a social integrity that transcends both individuals and particular institutions. To understand present values, much less anticipate future values, you have to appreciate the
considerable range of perspectives and explanatory systems surrounding any particular value, like honesty.

I press this point about the alternative contexts for values because I
want to get behind empirical poll data to a deeper appreciation for what
many have interpreted as a recent shift toward more traditional values,
such as the strength claimed by the Christian Right and by Shi'ite Muslims. I believe that some of what we are seeing is not a regression to an
authoritarian stage of morality, but an advance to a more responsible
adoption of values. Greater prudence in sexual habits and a declining di-
vorce rate may look like a return to authority and obedience on their
face; but in fact, the shift toward what looks like more traditional behavior may be the result of greater maturity and autonomy rather than
a new subservience to old traditions.

This new prudence is partly a function of changing attitudes toward
the future. In keeping with the idea that we postmoderns are emerging

from an adolescent distrust that followed a modernist faith in progress and confidence in the future, I want to suggest another parallel track to this three-stage logic. Correlated with the movement from childhood through adolescence to maturity, consider a movement from optimism through pessimism to a more realistic assessment of both problems and opportunities. I am suggesting an interpretation of recent decades as moving from the innocent optimism of the forties and fifties through an adolescent, antiauthoritarianism during the sixties and seventies toward a more mature assessment of problems and opportunities in the eighties and nineties. This is, of course, a very broad-brush picture, but facts can be found to support its logical cogency and intuitive appeal.

In the early eighties it was truer than ever that, as Paul Valéry once put it, "The future isn't what it used to be." Americans' expectations for a better future had fallen dramatically over earlier decades. This fairly dramatic turn from optimism to pessimism was provoked in part by a series of objective events: the ignominious withdrawal from Vietnam, the Watergate scandal, and OPEC and the oil embargo. Perhaps the closest correlation between objective conditions and subjective attitudes was that between inflation rates and pessimism about future business conditions. But I think it would be a mistake to seek wholly mechanistic explanations linking public opinion to objective conditions.

During the sixties and seventies, a decline in faith in our leaders paralleled a decline in faith in the future. Again, it could be argued that this dramatic decline was solely attributable to mistakes made by leaders, Watergate being the prime example. But again, I would reply that such an argument misses the subjective side of the social system, a maturation beyond childlike trust in authority.

The argument I am making, that the antiauthoritarian sixties and seventies marked a period of adolescence in American social psychology, a period that was preceded by innocence and will be succeeded by greater maturity, gains further support from three more pieces of evidence: the demographics of the baby boom; a rebound in confidence since the eighties; and the almost European sophistication with which Americans responded to President Clinton's sexual adventures. The social-psychological maturation process is assisted by the literal aging of the baby boomers.

Note, however, that confidence levels are nowhere near what they were back in the innocent age of the 1950s. Nor, I would argue, are they likely to regain such heights. I say this not out of pessimism, but from a guardedly optimistic appreciation for a greater maturity in the American people. Just as an adult rarely regains the same sense of infinite possibility characteristic of youth, so a more mature America is unlikely to regain a modernist faith in progress as automatic.

In considering a one-dimensional confidence scale, we have another example, like the Right/Left spectrum, in which one-dimensional thinking can be misleading. My remarks have been directed toward the insight that the so-called return from Left to Right, or from pessimism to optimism, is not just a return. Rather, the same old values are modified by their new setting:

> *Not an automatic faith in the future, as if it were foreordained that Americans must reap the harvest of being number one, but a hardwon confidence in our abilities to overcome competition and adversity.*
>
> *Not a defensive retrenchment to the safety and simplicity of authoritarian, fundamentalist beliefs, but a conscious choice and mature affirmation of the values and gratifications of family life, despite its limitations on sexual freedom.*

The far-out life of total liberty to do your own thing is giving way, not to the puritanism of a Mrs. Grundy, but to a more mature freedom, a freedom grounded in discipline, like the freedom exhibited by Yo Yo Ma as his fingers dance on the neck of his cello, free to create any sound a cello can make, but free only after hours of disciplined practice.

Greater psychological maturity means greater psychological sophistication. As I put it earlier, the symbiosis between values and volition can appear as something of a paradox. I want to point the way to the resolution of that paradox and to do so in a way that moves beyond trend data to an understanding of moral maturity.

	I	II	III
STAGE	I	II	III
DECADES	1940s-1950s	1960s-1970s	1980s-1990s
AGE OF	Innocence	Adolescence	Maturity
STANCE TOWARD FUTURE	Optimism	Pessimism	Realism
STYLE	Authoritarian	Antiauthoritarian	Participatory
MODE	Monistic	Relativistic	Pluralistic
MOTIVATION	Absolute commands	Voluntaristic impulses	Moral choices

At Stage I, moral crises are eliminated by the power of the One True Moral Order, a monistic hierarchy that commands obedience and brooks no dissent. Optimism is appropriate to this order, for the power of the Good appears uncontested and invincible.

At Stage II, moral crises don't arise since the power of the individual recognizes no restraints. Despite an initial sense of euphoria that comes with liberation from authority, Stage II ends in tears caused by nihilism and pessimism, for without values that transcend the impulses of the individual, life has no meaning.

Only at Stage III is there tension between the individual will and transcendent values; therefore, only Stage III provides the necessary conditions for genuine morality.

From the perspective of Stage III, we can see how the apparent conflict between values and development toward pluralism can be resolved. If values had to be general or universal in order to transcend and restrain the impulses of the individual will, then whittling away at the general scope of values seemed to diminish their halo effect. From the pluralistic perspective of Stage III, however, that whittling is not a diminishment, but instead stands as proof of genuinely human responsibility. Though the individual may not be utterly free to value anything at all, collectively we are responsible for the value systems we set over ourselves. The proof of our collective choices consists in the cultural differences that result from those choices, for example traditions that favor individualism or collectivism, materialism or spiritualism.

Now to return from the logic of values to present realities, I want to harvest the hybrid crop we have planted with this mixing of normative, descriptive, and developmental perspectives. Let me recall that my philosophizing is not entirely abstract, but rooted to several trends: attitudes toward the future, confidence in institutions, rising educational levels, shifting church memberships, and attitudinal data drawn from nitty-gritty market research.

Based on this empirical appreciation for the present, combined with a recollection of past stages and a sense of the possible future, I believe we are entering a time when values—real values, not authoritarian commands or mere whims—will assume increasing importance to more and more people. Nobel laureate Roger Sperry is right when he speaks of human values as "the most strategically powerful causal force now shaping world events."[2]

Still, you may ask, "Which values?" I've begun to give an answer by suggesting a move away from the hang-loose liberation of the "me decade." But I must stress the thrust of the entire argument, which is that particular preferences are far less important than the general context in which they are found, and the change of context now underway is not just a shift back toward conservatism on a one-dimensional scale, but a development toward a moral maturity which, if anything, will give the traditionalists less to get upset about.

Of course this development could get sidetracked. A war in the Persian Gulf or some environmental disaster could upset the general mood of optimism Peter Schwartz calls "The Long Boom."[3] But sidetracks aside, American society seems to be poised for a transition from anti-authoritarian, anti-institutional values to a more participatory concern for values that transcend the individual will. The issues that call for our attention are no longer issues of individual freedom, such as prayer in the classroom, sexual preference, or abortion. Instead the issues at the turn of the millennium are moral crises—such as the environment, racism, and economic inequalities between the rich and the poor in developed economies and between the relatively rich economies of the northern hemisphere and poorer economies to the south—that cannot be settled by individuals acting alone.

The main moral conflicts at the turn of the millennium are social, not individual. Yet our postmodern, multicultural, globally wired human species no longer subscribes to any single ethical hierarchy. Hence, we are thrust, like it or not, into moral crises that create genuine tensions between the individual will and transcendent values. This may be an awkward age, but it is also a time in which we are experiencing the conditions for genuinely moral choices. No longer naïve about the authority of our fathers, those dead white males who purported to be masters of the universe; no longer dancing to antiauthoritarian tunes that end in a dirge of nihilistic tears; this middle age of mature, millennial morality grants the messiness and complexity of a world where different peoples have different values. And this doesn't mean that different individuals can value whatever.

Now older and just a little bit wiser, we can concede a measure of *cultural* relativism without falling into the immoral maw of *subjective* relativism. We don't need the universalism of our modernist fathers. We don't want the antiauthoritarian arrogance of adolescent sons. We are finally able to choose—genuinely and responsibly—to value our commitments to better futures. There might just be meaning to life, without reliance on The Values of gods or masters.

We've left the calm confidence of modernity and its certainty of having made progress over the ancients. We are entering into what some call, looking backward, the postmodern condition. But wouldn't we rather look forward? Wouldn't we rather take the tools of the relational worldview and turn them to use in framing futures that are, if not quite utopian, at least *better* than the present?

The following chapters take a closer look at how scenario planning works in general, and how, more specifically, the tool of scenario planning can be applied to creating better futures for education and health care.

CHAPTER 10

SCENARIO PLANNING:
A TOOL FOR SOCIAL CREATIVITY

With a few interesting and important exceptions, like Alvin Toffler, Charles Handy, Peter Drucker, and John Naisbitt—all of whom spurn large office staffs or consultancies, but give credit loud and often to their wives with whom they actively collaborate, navigating the future turns out to be a team sport. This is not an accident. To the extent that navigating the future occupies an uneasy place between rigorous research and science fiction, it requires contributions from many minds, not just one or two.

The practice of scenario planning is not all that difficult to describe, even if it is fairly difficult to do with skill and expertise. The process begins with the definition of a problem. We are not interested in the future of everything, but the future of a particular company, community, country, or industry. Once the problem has been identified, then it takes a group of a couple of dozen people to brainstorm a long list of key factors and environmental forces that might influence the outcome of the focal issue. It helps if the group is fairly diverse—young and old, male and female, of different ethnicities, with different jobs, and from different parts of a company or community—so that the list of key factors and environmental forces is long and varied. In thinking about possible futures, there is a sense in which you have to *think of everything!* Who knows, today, what might turn out to be important? Experts are not always the best resources for thinking outside the box, and often what we are looking for is the unexpected, the unlikely, the key factor that will blindside us if we remain locked in the tunnel vision of received wisdom.

Having done its best to think of everything (limited only by the criterion of relevance to the focal issue), the group then needs to settle on a small number of scenario plots.[1] This is not easy, for once you have acknowledged that the future is not predictable, then it would seem that one could spin any number of stories. Why choose just those plots that eventually get developed as detailed scenarios? It takes a subtle blend of artistry and method to settle on those stories that will shed the most light on the focal issue. It also takes a subtle blend of the concerns of individuals and the range of the group; facilitation of the form by an individual and provision of content from the group; and the idiosyncrasy of individuals and the collective judgment of the group.

Once the scenario team has settled on two to five basic plots, then the challenge is to return to the long list of key factors and forces and use that list to give relevant content to the stories. Each scenario is a story with a beginning, a middle, and an end. Scenarios are not simply state descriptions of the world on some particular future date. It's important to see how we get from here to there, what has to change first, and what next. Settling on a set of scenario plots and populating those scenarios with events and forces drawn from the list of key factors is usually the work of a two-day scenario workshop. After that workshop, a smaller team undertakes the task of turning a set of scenario outlines into narratives as long as several thousands of words each. The group can come up with the basic ideas, but writing in committee is famously impossible. So it falls to just a few to take the outlines generated in the workshop and turn them into full–blown stories.

The task of writing good scenario narratives usually demands research. One of the achievements of an initial scenario workshop is to identify those areas about which we don't know enough about the present and past, much less the future. So it will take at least a month, and probably more, before the core team can come back to the larger scenario team with a set of well-written, well-researched narratives. At a second scenario workshop, the larger team addresses two challenges: first, are these the stories we wanted to tell? After reading the scenarios, the members of the larger team have an opportunity to correct simple errors, supply new plot elements, or modify the directions of the stories. Once the set of scenarios has been approved, the second challenge consists in asking the question, So what? If our community or company faces a future in which any one of these scenarios could come true, what should we be doing today to prepare?

Addressing this second challenge is different when confronted with a range of scenarios rather than a single–point forecast. If we knew what the future held, we could place all of our bets on strategies appropriate to that one future. Given a range of futures, however, the challenge is compounded. First you want to know which strategic options would be appropriate to which scenarios. Next you want to see whether there are some options that are robust across the range of scenarios. In the end what you are after is a strategy for all seasons. Sometimes you can find such a strategy; sometimes you have to depend on early indicators to tell you which scenario is about to unfold and which strategic options you should implement.

So much for this very brief description of the practice of scenario planning. Whole books have been written on what I've compressed into a few paragraphs.[2] For our purposes here, it is enough to give a sense of how the practice of scenario planning calls for both the breadth of experience represented by a group as well as the unique talents of particular individuals.

For all its talk of competition and rugged individualism, the business world at its best is far more team–oriented than academia. This is not to say that business executives are molded to the model of the man in the gray flannel suit. The mythology of conformist executives marching in step to the beat of the corporate drummer is, these days, obsolete. Entrepreneurship and skunk works are in; groupthink is out. In an era of information-intensive products and services, the need for top-down standardization of mass-produced replaceable parts is giving way to calls for bottom-up innovation and creativity. Produce the same old information over and over, and standardization produces redundancy, not more information. Repetition may be fine on the assembly line, but not in software design.

The need for innovation creates a role for individuality. But not just any old innovation will do. New products or new services must serve some want or need if they are to survive in the marketplace. Here's where teamwork becomes important. The creative individual left to his or her own devices may be nothing more than a crackpot. Just as most mutations are monstrous rather than adaptive, so not all innovations find a market. Part of the role of the scenario team will be to articulate different scenarios that define plausible market needs, hopes, or desires. By balancing both the creativity of the individual with the reality testing of a team, scenario planning rewards both individuality and collaboration.

The business design of Global Business Network (GBN) included from day one a reliance on a network of individuals chosen for their ability to offer unique perspectives on a range of issues. Pierre Wack, himself the remarkable guru of scenario planning at Royal Dutch Shell, made a point of drawing on a network of what he referred to as "re-markable men," following (in the pre-feminist fifties and sixties) the language of one of his mentors, a mystic named Gurdjieff.[3] At GBN, we include many women in our network, from performance artist Laurie Anderson to anthropologist Mary Catherine Bateson. The men are as iconoclastic as these remarkable women: from sci-fi author William Gibson to rock star Peter Gabriel; from Harvard Business School professor Michael Porter to virtual reality inventor Jaron Lanier. When conducting scenario development workshops, we like to seed the group with a few individuals selected from our hundred or so network members. The point of including these individuals is not so much to draw on their expertise in any particular field as to provoke unconventional thinking, perspectives that are out of the ordinary, jolts to incipient groupthink, and idiosyncratic reflection that can reframe the issues and redraw the mental maps that executives use to chart their futures.

There is a role for individual idiosyncrasy in this work. Wouldn't it have been helpful to the Big Three in Detroit, and to the American economy as a whole, if there had been a few more iconoclasts to counter the consensus view of the fifties and sixties that Americans would never buy small cars? Since the mid-eighties, Detroit has been using alternative scenarios to introduce new car concepts. A few unconventional voices broke through the groupthink to inspire scenarios in which small cars, light trucks, and minivans might compete with the more conventional cars that carried mom, dad, buddy, and sis down the highways of Middle America. Now the roads are filled with a range of hybrids that have boosted Detroit's sales much more than the catalogue of traditional family autos could have done.

Another example illustrating the role of the individual in promoting unconventional, alternative scenarios: a single voice in a scenario workshop back in 1980 led to the development of a scenario that kept Colorado from jumping headlong into the synfuels industry. When virtually every policy maker in Denver was worrying about how to build infrastructure and concrete trailer beds fast enough to accommodate the rapid growth of an oil shale industry, one man raised his hand in a scenario workshop and said, contrary to everyone else in the room, "You know what I'm worried about? I'm worried about what we're going to do with all that freshly poured concrete if Exxon decides to pick up its marbles and go home," which is precisely what eventually happened. Because one individual voiced this contrarian scenario, the Colorado policy makers tapped the brakes on the infrastructure development program just enough to avoid a lot of sunk costs and environmental damage. There is a role for contrarian individuals in alternative scenario development.

There is also a role for teamwork. Not every contrarian is a genius, and individuals operating alone are not as good as a team at assembling a bundle of divergent scenarios. Further, there is that stage in the development of scenarios when brainstorming a whole spectrum of possibilities calls for diverse perspectives and a range of imaginations. At their best, scenario workshops turn into intellectual jam sessions with diverse perspectives, like different musical instruments, complementing and provoking one another in phrases combining both dissonance and harmony. Soloists sometimes emerge to grab attention for a few bars, but a successful workshop is an ensemble performance.

Granting the fact that both the individual and social models of creativity have their good and bad sides, how is one (or some, or all) to know when one or the other is most appropriate? To leave this question up to the individual, or to the group, is to prejudge the answer, and thus to beg the question.

I can think of two criteria that could be used by either the individual or the group. First, and fairly obvious: does the challenge at hand call for a minor modification or for a major transformation? If things are going pretty well and you just want to make them better, then look to an in-house team to come up with incremental improvements. If the system is going critical and anomalies suggest fundamental disorder, then you may want to call out for a renegade consultant to take an entirely fresh look.

Second, is a solo performance possible in the particular arena at hand, or are we looking at a situation where only an ensemble can get the job done? It's hard to perform symphonies or make movies all alone. Movie–making is a paradigm case of communal creativity. Sure, there is a place for individual genius, but at the end of the day, if the ensemble doesn't work well together, even geniuses can look bad.

Assuming that the application of these two criteria suggests the need for social rather than solo creativity, what is necessary for communal creativity to be possible? At GBN, there is a spirit of generosity such that we each see the benefit of making sure that the others are enjoying themselves as much as possible, not in the self-indulgent sense of taking time off from work, but in the self-actualizing sense that sees the doing of the collective work as the realization of the individual self. We do not always succeed in this noble and playful endeavor. But when we do, it has the feeling of a jazz ensemble jamming up a storm. The leadership shifts as one or another takes the lead. We don't work from a fixed score. There is a premium on improvisation. But at the end of a project, the whole thing has to fit together.

What is necessary for jamming to be possible?[4] For one thing, trust. In order to allow yourself or others to risk deviating from the norm, instead of repeating received wisdom, or spouting the party line, you have to trust that what you or someone else is saying is said in a spirit of goodwill. No one is trying to trick anyone else. Unlike the graduate seminar or boardroom shoot-out where people are trying to argue each other to the ego-death, our meetings usually have the feeling of a good conversation that builds, circles back, allows itself to wander into the unknown, then leaps to new connections. No one is in charge. Everyone (or almost everyone—we all have our slow days) contributes. And in the end the product bears the overlapping fingerprints of many hands. But you need to trust the other people in order to place in their hands the infants of your own intellect, the children of your dreams.

Another requirement: In addition to trust in others, you need enough confidence in yourself that you don't have to keep proving your worth to others. Insecure people can wreck a team. Those who are desperate to prove themselves worthy are liable to grab the ball at the wrong times and take shots they have no hope of making. Desperate to prove themselves, they make fools of themselves. I've come to admire most those who can remain silent the longest until, at just the right moment, they make an economical remark that puts a new spin on everything that has gone before.

Patience, respect for others, a sense of humor, a reservoir of knowledge and experience, the ability to listen closely to what others have to say—all of these individual and team skills are important in contributing to an ensemble performance. But the one I come back to as most important, or at least most significant to me in my limited experience is a spirit of generosity. If each member of the team is genuinely committed to giving more than he or she expects to get; if each member of the team is ready to extend the benefit of the doubt to others, always construing their remarks in the best possible light, never becoming defensive or sullen, then the ensemble performance will show each and every one to advantage.

It's so simple, really. As simple as love. But I don't want to romanticize what is often an arduous process: long days and nights, the discipline of learning skill, sheer stamina, and a perseverance that does not wander too far afield.[5] These are the ingredients of communal creativity, and they are not easy to come by, especially in large groups. The more people that you have in a meeting, the more patience, close listening, and conciseness is required. There is some upper limit to the number of people that can jam. I don't begin to know what that number is, but I think it's somewhere in the neighborhood of 15–25. Beyond that you're no longer an ensemble. Big bands need a conductor and a score, and any deviation from the score is not an improvisation; it's a mistake.

This numerical upper limit on the size of a scenario workshop poses an important challenge in the use of this tool: whose futures get drafted by a scenario team of 15–25? Just the future of the workshop team? Or does each member of the team act as a representative for others? How many others, and how is "accurate" representation to be achieved? Here the issues of Chapter 4, "Rethinking Representative Government," come back to haunt us. Scenario planning for an entire nation calls for careful attention to issues of representation, and to the means for public deliberation over scenarios that may have been created by a small group.[6] To the extent that a nation is bound to include very different groups with different interests, discussions of different scenarios are bound to uncover conflicts of interest. This is precisely one of the advantages of scenario planning: a range of scenarios provides a very broad tent to accomodate many views. This diversity and potential for conflict should be present in a scenario team of 20 people as well as in a nation.

You don't have to be close friends with everyone on the team, but it helps if you are friends with at least a few. You don't even have to like everyone on the team; chances are, if you've assembled a group diverse enough to bring different talents, knowledge, and experience to bear, then some people won't see eye-to-eye with others, which is why patience and respect become all the more important.

Precisely to the extent that you allow others to be *other* and not corporate clones, to just that extent you need to challenge your own sense of completeness and self-sufficiency. You cannot be a know-it-all and function well in a team; and the more you think you know, the less well you will listen to others. This business of teamwork requires more than the warm fuzzies of self-confidence and the love of others. You need to be hard on yourself, and subject yourself to others whom you do not always like.

What does it feel like to engage in communal creativity? You're not in control. If you already know where the conversation is going, then you're not going to hear anything new. But if you're not in control, you may sometimes feel confused, as if you're hanging on to the conversation by your fingernails. Sometimes you feel more like a predicate than a subject, or maybe like a dangling participle. You have to stay alert or you'll lose it. There is some risk that you will fail to follow, much less contribute to, the stream of collective consciousness. One's peers are sometimes so smart and eloquent. The feeling is very much like that of being one of the sub-personalities described in James Hillman's polytheistic psychology. You are not Zeus-like, in charge. Instead your consciousness is possessed by one of the lesser deities—subjective, idiosyncratic, and characterized by an identifiable personality, to be sure, but only one among the several personifications that make up the entire pantheon. You listen for the ways that others contribute, and you ask them to add a riff where you know they can help. You look for places to jump in yourself, but not unless no one else plays the notes you know. I often play notes from the philosophers because almost no one else knows what those obscure voices were talking about. And I listen for the insights of my colleagues, who know far more than I about any number of subjects. Together we try to come up with scenarios of the future that are enough like and enough unlike the past and present that real problems can be solved without pretending that we are radically better than we are.

What does it feel like to lead a scenario workshop, or to take part in one that is led by a master? I learned my lessons watching Peter Schwartz, the author of *The Art of the Long View* which, as of this writing, is the definitive text on scenario planning. In watching Peter conduct scenario workshops, I was often intrigued at the similarity between his way of working and that of an existential psychoanalyst: lots of questions, but more about the present and future than about the deep dark past.[7] The difference between facilitating a scenario workshop and conducting existential psychoanalysis is that the analysand is not an individual but an institution or a community. So the practice begins to look more Socratic than psychoanalytic. Taken off the analyst's couch and relocated into a meeting room with 20 people, the scenario workshop becomes a testing ground for the aspirations of a community. What do we want? How might we succeed in attaining what we want? What could happen that would open up opportunities? What dangers are lurking just over the horizon? Many of these questions are absurdly simple to pose: What are people worried about? What keeps you up nights? If you could ask an oracle just one question about conditions five years from now, what would you most want to know?

The leader of a scenario workshop is not there to teach but to listen. Just as good therapists are not very directive, so the scenario workshop facilitator is not there to tell people what to do or think, but to *draw out (e-ducare)* the concerns of others. Of course the questions are often leading questions. Like Socrates, the good facilitator will be a midwife bringing other people's intellectual children into the world. Also like Socrates, the good facilitator will need to know quite a lot about the subject under discussion in order to ask those questions that lead in the most productive directions.

Sooner or later there may be a literature as extensive as the annals of the psychoanalytic societies that does for scenario workshop facilitators what the Freudians and Jungians have done for psychotherapists, namely, that describes all the resistances, denials, transferences, and counter-transferences that can occur in the course of community "therapy." We are still awaiting the social Freud, the theorist who can open up the realm of the social unconscious and chart a path from social sickness to social health. For now all we have, in addition to our rummaging about among various sources, is the practice, and there is much to be seen, as Yogi Berra once said, by just looking.

In looking at many scenario workshops, I've been amazed at the number of revelations, the epiphanies that come with seeing the world in new ways. As in psychotherapy, it's no good just telling people the answer. They must discover it for themselves, whatever the "it" may be. As Socrates insisted, the truth is in the learner. Hence his rather bizarre notion of learning as *anamnesis*—recollection from memories implanted in the soul in some former life. I consider this theory well worth forgetting. To take it literally is to accept dubious ideas about the recollection of former lives. The important point expressed by this theory is the pedagogical point, the process imperative: better to question than to lecture.

Why is it so important that a process of questioning encourage the aspirations of a community to be articulated in the form of normative scenarios? Because *shared hope* then takes the place of human essence or holy commandments as the fulcrum for moral critique. Here is where we find the answer to the challenge of ethical pluralism. Once a community makes the effort to articulate a scenario worth aspiring to, then there is a standard for measuring the distance between what is and what ought to be—without relying on a theory of alienation from an ahistorical essence, or on a utopia as yet unrealized. In the past, most such standards have been drawn down from heaven rather than built from earth. Religious commandments and ideological principles have been invoked as sources for the meaning of *better* in organized attempts to create a better future. The peril of the postmodern era is the deconstruction of all of the old absolutes, whether religious or ideological. Does this condemn us to a nihilistic acceptance of whatever *is*? Not if we can find some other purchase for prying *ought* away from *is*.

The standards presupposed by our communities are not all the same. The Japanese and Chinese place more weight on the importance of social relationships, while English-speaking societies place more weight on the importance of individual liberty, for example. These cultural differences among fundamental values make it difficult to defend the idea that values, in order to *be* values, must be universal in their reach, applying to all people in all places at all times. As shown in the preceding chapter, if values are to have any force in restraining subjective wants and whims, they must derive their obligatory force from something less individual and private than wants and whims. That does not mean that only universal laws will do the job. Democratically endorsed hope will do as well. Because differences are possible in the details of our hopes, it's worth taking care to articulate with some precision the future we want to inhabit. This is what successful scenario planning accomplishes.

Without having set out to solve all of the theoretical conundrums left behind by Marxist theory, the practice of scenario planning nonetheless fulfills the hope for better futures. Without relying on the conservatives from the religious Right, or the thought correctors from the ideological Left, scenario planning can help a community articulate its hopes and its fears and, in so doing, define the values it holds dear. Best–case and worst–case scenarios are inevitably value–laden. In the corporate world, the most salient value is often profitability. But the larger the organization, and the longer–term the scenarios, the more important *sustainability* of profits becomes. As soon as sustainability becomes an important criterion for normative scenarios, planners are thrust into thinking about the web of interrelationships among our economic, social, and natural systems. Even the fittest cannot survive if they destroy the environment upon which they feed. To cite Gregory Bateson yet again, the minimum unit of evolutionary survival is neither the individual, nor the species, but species *plus* environment.

As we cast the net of scenario thinking ever wider and longer–term, there is virtually no significant corner of life that escapes its reach. Scenario thinking is inevitably systemic. As such, it is strategic. Strategy tends toward "big think", but not necessarily *universal* think. Our method is, above all, eclectic. We draw upon sources in the fields of psychology, anthropology, and philosophy.

The *process* involves a balance between listening to the client and drawing on research. Through interviews and workshops, we make sure that we understand the mental maps, the values, and the aspirations of our clients. In this sense it sometimes feels as if we are practicing a kind of analysis of the group mind.

We borrow from the tradition of psychology the insight that most of the important truths lie already dormant in the mind of the "patient," and that any new insights must be *their* insights, not ours. *They* must come to the stunning realizations and the epiphanies that lead to change and new behavior. It does no good for us to look smart if they don't recognize the insights as their own. What we leave behind is psychology's emphasis on pathology and sickness rather than improvement and health; its emphasis on cures—which rarely happen; and its emphasis on the individual psyche rather than the group mind.

For more help with groups, we draw upon the discipline of anthropology with its emphasis on cultures, its insights into pluralism and diversity, and its conviction that there are many ways, not just one way, to play the human game. We borrow from anthropology its talent for observation, and for what Clifford Geertz calls "thick description," the many layered webs of meaning, rich with telling details, that are necessary to weave a good scenario narrative.

What we leave: Lévi-Strauss' claim to a single, deep structure at the heart of human nature—a One beneath the Many cultures that would, if we found it, tell us the final truth about human essence; and second, we leave behind an ethical neutrality that shadows anthropology with a dark shade of relativism and nihilism.

If we are to take seriously the idea of citizenship in a democracy, then the setting of a community's direction into the future *must* be an act of communal creativity, not just the steering of a community by a few individuals. If a community is to take responsibility for its forward direction, and not just arrive in the future by force of happenstance, then there must be a means for setting that direction in a way that calls forth the creative impulses of that community in a coherent and thoughtful way.

Simply voting on options that have been scripted by others is a less creative form of choice than the collective shaping and fashioning of the options themselves. The scenario planning process provides a format for the collective shaping of alternative futures from which a community can then choose its eventual path. If the choice that is made is a choice of a strategy that was not *given to* the community but *created by* the community, then the community will more likely assume *ownership* of that choice.

Over two decades ago, Paul Hawken, Peter Schwartz, and I published a book entitled *Seven Tomorrows: Toward a Voluntary History*. The book contained seven scenarios for the United States from 1980 to 2000. Most of the scenarios were fairly pessimistic. Our main point in publishing that book was to warn our readers of the dire consequences of irresponsible and unwise policies and behaviors. Our real objective was captured in the subtitle: *Toward a Voluntary History*. Rather than "backing into" our future thoughtlessly and haphazardly, why not marshal the collective will to frame a set of alternative futures and then choose the one that best captured our values and delivered on our hopes? The book sold reasonably well but never became a runaway best-seller. It was too pessimistic. Many readers told us that they found it depressing—not the sort of thing you wanted to pass on to a friend.

Since that time, and partly as a result of that experience, I've become convinced that positive scenarios, normative scenarios, and scenarios that lift our sights and inspire our hopes are far more effective than pessimistic morality plays are at moving people toward a voluntary history. Negative scenarios are psychologically difficult to entertain, but intellectually easy to create. You just take a description of the present and then tear it apart. Positive scenarios are psychologically easy to entertain—we all like a happy ending—but intellectually very difficult to draw in a plausible and convincing way. The reason for this is fairly simple: In order to write an optimistic yet plausible scenario, you have to imagine solutions to problems that no one has yet solved. If those problems had already been solved, we would already by living in that better future. Think, for example, how difficult it would have been to write a plausible scenario for the end of apartheid in South Africa in, say, 1980. Think how difficult it would have been to convince others of a scenario for the end of the Cold War prior to the fall of the Soviet Union.

The following chapters apply the tools of scenario planning and the rules of the relational worldview and ethical pluralism to the vexing issues of education, politics, and health care. Let me hasten to say that I make no claim whatever to having *solved* the problems of education, politics, and health care. I won't paint a utopian picture of a future in which all problems have been solved and everything works perfectly. My objective is to show how scenario planning can help us to produce better futures, not the best future. By engaging many stakeholders in a scenario planning process that shows some pitfalls on the downside while raising our sights toward normative scenarios on the upside, many stakeholders can make history voluntarily.

Part Five
Scenario Planning
in Action

CHAPTER 11

BETTER EDUCATION

Back in the early 1980s, well before the Cold War had ended, a very brainy group from the John F. Kennedy School at Harvard convened other experts like Robert MacNamara, the late Representative Les Aspin, and a former Ambassador to Austria for a week in Wyoming. The agenda: to entertain alternatives to nuclear deterrence 50 years into the future. I was asked to attend not because I knew anything about strategic arms, but to help manage the process of alternative scenario development. Over the course of five days of intense discussion, however, I was unable to bend the collective wisdom of that group to entertain seriously any scenario that would contain less than 50 percent of the then–current force structure—still enough megatons to make the rubble bounce and render the earth uninhabitable. Two decades later we now take for granted what was then unthinkable to some very good thinkers.

Surely there is a lesson here about the impotence of hope among intellectuals seized by an acceptance of the intolerable. We intellectuals would err on the side of pessimism rather than be accused of naïveté. World-weary pessimism seems so much more intellectually respectable than even the most educated hope.

However, I would argue—and it has been the aim of this book to do so—that the fashionable face of all-knowing despair is finally immoral. Granted, the bubble-headed optimism of Pangloss and Polyanna are equally immoral. A refusal to look at poverty or oppression can contribute to their perpetuation; but so can a cynical commitment to their inevitability.

Let's not forget that radical change for the better *is* possible. Dictatorships in Haiti, Nicaragua, the Philippines, and the USSR, *have* been toppled in recent decades—which is not to say that their successors are without problems. Real per–capita disposable income in the United States *has* grown over tenfold in the twentieth century—which is not to say that no poverty remains. Finally and most emphatically, the parting of the Iron Curtain and the end of the Cold War must offer lessons of hope regarding other seemingly intractable issues.

In this last part on scenarios in action I'll apply some of the themes that have been running throughout this book. In this chapter I'll weave several themes into sketches of possible futures for education. We and our children need to learn the components of a relational worldview, the tools we need in order to see, imagine, hope for, and create better futures.

Imagine a scenario in which educational reform is finally taken seriously, not as the imposition of some new religion on the young, but as the cultivation of human potential. The tools are at hand, but today we have not yet applied those tools in our schools. Instead we expose our children to teachers who are drawn from the lowest quintile of our universities' graduating classes. No wonder. Teaching is not a high–status job. Teachers get neither the pay nor the respect their profession deserves. Now imagine what could happen if education became the leading mission of the new millennium, much as civil rights and the Vietnam War preoccupied the sixties, feminism and the environment motivated so many in the seventies, and greed obsessed the eighties and nineties. It could happen. Social agendas do change.

The mission of the Christian Brothers of the Lasallian Schools is "the education of the young, especially the poor." They currently educate 750,000 children around the world. During a workshop with the Christian Brothers in which our focal issue revolved around enlisting the rich to support the education of the poor, one of our network members, Robert Fuller, broke his silence of several hours to say, "I've been sitting here listening to your worries about the challenges you are facing, but I can't help thinking that you might be sitting on the number one mission of the twenty-first century. What the spread of democracy was to the twentieth century, the spread of education could be to the twenty-first. Just as access to a vote spread from under 20 percent of the world's population to over 80 percent during the twentieth century, so the spread of access to a decent education could be the big story of the twenty-first century." It could happen.

If education became the cause of the new millennium, if teachers' salaries were raised and the respect paid to educators enhanced, then we might be graduating students who could build better futures, both for themselves and for their children. But in order to get from here to there, we need to be clear-eyed and realistic about just how far we have to go. James Traub tells a tale of life in the Hartford school system where 92 percent of the students are non-white and 65 percent come from single-parent households.

> Gladys Hernandez, who taught at an elementary school called Bernard-Brown, spoke of the school's grimed-over plastic windows and recalled that in twenty-three years she could never get the proper writing paper for her students. Most of the children, Hernandez said, were Puerto Rican, and spoke neither Spanish nor English properly. "They called everything a 'thing,'" she testified [in trial testimony in the case of *Sheff v. O'Neill*, a case concerning illegally segregated public schools]. "Even parts of their body they didn't know. They didn't know their underclothing, what it was called. If they had a grandparent, they didn't know that they were a grandson or a granddaughter." Once a year, Hernandez said, the school permitted her to take the children on a trip, to a zoo or a farm. "The most extraordinary thing happened when they came to the river," she testified. "They all stood up in a group and applauded and cheered, and I was aware they were giving the river a standing ovation. And they were so happy to see the beauty of the river, something that most of us go back and forth [across] and never take time to look at."[1]

Children are capable of enthusiasm and delight. How, why, do we persist in wringing out of them their inborn capacity for learning? Despite the well-intentioned and often heroic efforts of school boards, administrators, teachers, and parents, public education cries out for thoroughgoing, systemic reform. The practice of education has not kept pace with social, economic, and technological change. Though there have been piecemeal reforms aplenty—from the new math through the whole language approach to reading, to bilingual education, charter schools, class–size reduction, peer review, exams based on national standards, and countless other experiments—the overall record of educational reform is disappointing. In *Tinkering Toward Utopia*, David Tyack and Larry Cuban document the dismal record of educational reform over the past century. They show how every effort at tinkering with one part of the educational system—whether by down-from-the-top policy or up-from-the-bottom experimentation—eventually gets pulled back into the equilibrium of the larger system of public education.

An issue of the journal *Daedalus* was devoted to the question of public education's resistance to reform. In the lead essay, Yale professor Seymour Sarason argues that only a systemic approach that looks at all parts of the very complex system of public education has any hope of making lasting changes. "What are the parts of the system?" asks Sarason. "Teachers, school administrators, boards of education, state departments of education, colleges and universities, state legislatures and executive branches, the federal government, and parents."[2] So some of us in California have been convening a series of meetings at Global Business Network to engage each of those constituencies in taking the long view on the very complex system that is public education.

The tool to be employed, scenario planning, is uniquely suited to the task. Because scenarios look at the future as a whole, they are especially appropriate to understanding and changing large, complex systems in turbulent environments. If there's one thing I've learned in 30 years of work in and around education, it's this: There's no easy answer. There's no one thing to learn that will improve education. The closest metaphor for education is parenting. Both parenting and education are directed toward the growth and cultivation of human beings. Most parents will agree that there's no silver bullet for parenting. It's a day in, day out, year in, year out challenge. The human mind is a complex thing. Growing and cultivating human minds is a systemic task. You have to get a lot of things right, not just one.

At least 23 issues have to be addressed and aligned if you want good schools. First, I'll list them, and then I'll paint a couple of scenarios that suggest how you can get some of them right or wrong. The main driving forces include:

Standards and Accountability

Outcomes more important than inputs—Test scores and school rankings increasingly dictate school funding for a variety of reasons, such as real estate competitiveness, and emphasis on outcomes rather than inputs in other industries like health care.

Merit–pay movement—There is increasing pressure to link teachers' and principals' pay to student achievement, as measured by standardized tests.

Raising aspirations—For many, the standards movement has less to do with standardization for comparative purposes than with raising the bar and asking more of students so that they will achieve more of their potential.

Privatization

Choice and deregulation—In industries from electric utilities to airlines, there is a broad move away from the regulated–utility model featuring one monopolistic provider and toward deregulation and competition among different and competing providers of services. Problems encountered with the deregulation of electricity—high prices and rolling blackouts—must give pause to advocates of the privatization of education.

Voucher initiatives—This legislation allows students (parents) to use tax dollars toward private and parochial school tuition.

Parochial schools—Religious and denominational schools are likely recipients of vouchers.

Corporate training programs—Corporations are offering courses to make up for what their employees failed to get in their public school education.

Technology

Locus of learning: home schooling, distance learning—Physical schools are being replaced as we see increasing capabilities for decentralized instruction through computer, video, and other interactive communications links.

Educational hardware and software—There is increasing use of educational computer software, including sophisticated simulations, in school.

Self-paced and self-styled learning—Software is available that adjusts not only to different speeds of learning, but also to different styles. There is increasing recognition that different students have different types of intelligence, and that software can adjust, as a good teacher would, to suit their different learning styles.

School Finance

Federal, state, and local balance—The federal government needs to devote more money to public education to help ease the tension between state and local funding: where most of the funding is local, as in New Hampshire, inequalities abound; where most of the funding is from the state, as in California, there's usually not enough of it.

Public funding—Should the trend toward the privatization of everything carry over to schooling? Should school budgets be hostage to rising and falling tax revenues?

School Governance

Role of the school board—Some school boards have become stepping stones for political careers, at the expense of the children, and, as such, have become highly politicized. Yet the community needs a say in how its schools are run.

Charter schools—There are increasing opportunities for creating niche and parent-created schools inside the public system, but evidence to date does not demonstrate the superiority of charter schools.

Staff development—There is growing dissatisfaction with existing staff development and the rising costs of training.

Curriculum design—Do current curricula prepare students for the future or the past? Do state codes inhibit curriculum reform?

The Public Agenda

Education and national culture—Do Americans care as much about education as Chinese, Japanese, Germans, or Israelis?

The women's movement—Fewer two-parent households and more opportunities for women are leading to fewer highly skilled women choosing teaching as a profession.

Education for what?—Educators speak of the "school–to–work transition," but little attention is given to the future needs of society. Like generals preparing for the last war rather than the next, our schools often prepare students for yesterday's jobs, not tomorrow's.

Special education/Inclusion—While working with a group of educators in Illinois, a school bus driver challenged the rest of the scenario team with a question: "What are the voters going to say when they discover that I spend 30 percent of my budget on 3 percent of the students I serve? How are they going to view that expenditure, especially when they come to understand that those 3 percent are far less likely than the rest to gain meaningful employment and contribute to the tax rolls?" Special education is important. It's a good thing. But it's a possible time bomb in shifting resources away from the needs of the many toward the special needs of the few.

Demographics

Decline of the nuclear family—With the increase in the number of single–person, one-parent, step-parent, and childless households, the percentage of households with children in school has dropped from 45 percent to less than 25 percent, thus diminishing the proportion of people immediately interested in, and voting in favor of, public schools.

Ethnic mismatch between teaching staff and students—In California, for example, the majority of students—60 percent rising toward 70 percent over the coming decades—are "minorities," while the teaching staff is only 20 percent minority. This mismatch makes it difficult for children of color to find role models of their own ethnicity.

Aging student body for lifelong learning—Parents for whom English is their second language are increasing their demands on public schools to help them, especially in states like Arizona, California, and Florida where they are a large part of the tax base.

Before anyone offers you an easy answer for saving education, run a quick check against all of the above and see whether each and every one of these issues has been addressed. If you neglect any two or three, your solution will likely fail.

To give some indication of how solving one problem can create others, let me sketch just two scenarios. I've constructed these scenarios with two goals in mind: first to show the real promise of some potential reforms; but second, to show how one-dimensional solutions fail when the rest of the larger whole of the education system is neglected for the sake of some single part.

The Technology Fix

Imagine a day only 10–15 years hence when all students have what Alan Kay once called "the Dynabook." Any text in any language can be accessed. The book will contain educational programming enabling students to learn at their own pace and in their own style. As we've learned from Howard Gardner, there are at least eight types of intelligence.[3] Until now most of our schooling has emphasized just one—the logical/analytic—thus creating one game with a few winners and a lot of losers. What if we have educational programming that caters to all types of intelligence, thus creating a lot of games with a lot of winners?

Greater use of educational technology will allow more home schooling, more distance learning, more learning and on the job, thereby easing the school-to-work transition. Good news for employers who now complain that schools aren't teaching what they want their employees to have learned.

This scenario sounds great . . . but what about the following roadblocks? First, if technology and distance learning empty the schools, then who's going to do the baby-sitting for all of those two–income families? The women's movement, shifts in the workforce, and the new opportunities available to working women have dealt a double blow to education. First, if mom's not home when junior gets out of school, how much worse is it if junior never goes to school? Second, while teaching and nursing were among the few good career opportunities for bright women 50 years ago, today there are plenty of great jobs luring intelligent young women out of teaching.

Second, for all the promise of customized educational programming, how are we going to get these changes past our state education departments, local school boards, and standards and accountability systems? If you think that textbook selection has been over-politicized, wait till you see the rhubarbs that will result if we rely on a software free-for-all as our substitute for textbooks.

Third, who's going to retrain our teachers, many of whom know less than their students about computers? As information technology has been introduced into the corporate world, we've learned that training tends to be about twice as expensive as hardware and software combined. Staff development is already a sore point for most teachers, who view in-service training as comparable to root canal work.

Fourth, who's going to pay for all of this new technology and the training to use it? Most public school classrooms today don't even have a twisted pair of copper wires for attaching a phone, much less a computer. We'll need to fix broken windows and leaky roofs before we can buy educational hardware and software for every kid in public school.

Let's take this objection as a segue to a second scenario.

The Corporate Fix: Privatization

Imagine a world 10–15 years hence in which Chris Whittle and the Edison Project have flourished; where Michael Milken and his for-profit company, Knowledge Universe, have prevailed. Imagine a world in which voucher initiatives have helped to empty public schools by allowing tax dollars to follow children into private and parochial schools.

Privatization could help pay for educational technology alright. And it would probably ease the school–to–work transition by putting the curriculum in the hands of future employers. But what else might we see in this scenario? Let's look first at the way voucher initiatives would probably play out. Vouchers look like a great deal for the first people who take them. They can use tax dollars to subsidize at least part of the cost of a private school education that is probably better than what was offered in the public school they left. But what about the next round of vouchers, and the rounds after that? And what about the kids left behind in public schools?

As good as vouchers look for the first takers, there simply aren't enough private and parochial schools for all of the later takers. Market mechanisms will kick in. Prices for the private schools will go up. The vouchers will help mainly those who have enough money to supplement them. Those who are left behind—the later takers and the poor—will be left in public schools from which the cream of students and funding has been skimmed.

Market mechanisms create winners and losers—albeit more winners; the market is a positive-sum game, but there are some losers nonetheless. In those industries that have a mandate to universal service—communications, health care, public safety, and education—market mechanisms alone will not be adequate to the task. Despite the headlong rush toward the privatization of everything, from hospitals and prisons to education, a moment's thought about the mandate to universal service tells us that we're all worse off if our phones don't connect everyone to everyone; we're all worse off if some of our neighbors are sick; and we're all worse off if some of our neighbors are illiterate. There *is* an abiding role for government, taxes, and the delivery of public services, including public education.

I haven't painted a positive scenario in which all of the pieces work successfully together. Nor have I covered all of the issues listed above, such as special education—a great cause which, like the women's movement, has some unintended consequences like the siphoning of billions of dollars from the rest of the educational system. But I hope this brief listing of issues, and just two scenarios showing the consequences of firing just one silver bullet—whether educational technology or vouchers and privatization—will give some sense of the systemic nature of education, and the need to get *all* of the pieces in place before education, as a whole, improves.

Just as we are beginning to do in California—there's a new Master Plan in the making for which we hope to develop a set of scenarios—each state needs to convene all of the major players listed by Sarason. Only by engaging all of the major players in scenario planning can we (a) generate the political will needed for change, (b) cover all of the bases needed for a genuinely systemic approach, and (c) achieve the legislative initiatives necessary to enable schools to change.

The 50 states are the appropriate units of representation to engage in scenario planning for educational reform—not the federal government, which is too remote from local school districts. While "site-based management"—the self-management of individual schools by the teachers in those schools—has a lot to recommend it, the first steps must happen at the state level, if only to change laws that make site-based management impossible. In most states there are volumes of state education codes that make local initiatives illegal at worst or unlikely at best. Like the Berlin Wall, those state codes need to fall before local innovation and creativity can flourish. But the state codes will not be eliminated unless they can be replaced through legislation that provides guidelines with which school districts might work.

The 50 states are the right places to begin scenario planning for educational reform for a range of reasons consistent with the relational worldview. First, they are *different*. What students in North Dakota need to know is not entirely the same as what students in Texas need to know. Sure, the basics of reading, writing, and arithmetic may be universal. But just as Clifford Geertz observed that the differences among cultures may tell us more about them than their similarities, so the differences among states create opportunities rather than barriers to effective learning. Does this reasoning carry all the way down to each local community? Yes and no. Yes, to the extent that face-to-face education is inevitably local. But no, to the extent that there need to be restrictions on religious extremists who would eliminate the teaching of evolution, or racists who would practice segregation.

See how the politics of education plays out the logic of the social philosophy of *some*, and serves as an example of ethical pluralism. Yes, we want to grant a degree of decentralization in public education in order to accommodate differences among different parts of the country; but no, we don't want to go to atomistic extremes of allowing any individual school or school district to use tax dollars in any way that a majority of the locals pleases. By fixing on the 50 states as intermediate between federal and local control, we can practice appropriate representation on the one hand and appropriate guidance on the other.

Scenario planning for educational reform is both necessary and possible at the state level. I know because I've had an opportunity to participate in scenario–planning projects in California, Florida, Hawaii, Illinois, and New Hampshire. I've also had an opportunity to generate scenarios for the National Council of State Education Associations where representatives from Iowa, Minnesota, Oklahoma, Virginia, and Wisconsin all reported very different trajectories toward different scenarios. I've seen up close the play of identity and difference in different states, and I've become convinced that only at the state level is it possible to enlist the participation of all of the players needed to achieve a systemic perspective. It is rare that local school boards, much less individual schools, have the resources, either in cash or in talent, to take a fresh look at education. Even if they did, they would be hamstrung by existing state education codes if they tried to do anything radically different.

Scenarios provide an appropriate tool for educational reform because a set of alternative scenarios provides a broad tent under which the many interests having a stake in education can be heard, be they parents, teachers, administrators, students, educational support people, politicians, or employers. Scenarios can facilitate public debate among all of these interests better than some analytic research report precisely because scenarios are stories that are easy to communicate. In this way, education scenarios exemplify the shift from explanation to narration. Further, by involving many stakeholders, scenario planning takes account of the *democratization of meaning*. Scenarios accommodate the *fall into time* to the extent that they help us educate our children for their future, not our past. To the extent that scenarios show how the many moving parts of our complex educational systems interact with one another, scenarios reveal the *heterarchy* of interests and authorities at play in education.

While the state is the appropriate locus of deliberation for running scenario workshops on the future of education, the nation is the appropriate locus for health care reform, and the globe the appropriate locus for environmental issues like the care of the oceans. I'll address the issue of health care reform in the next chapter, but first I want to pick up several of the threads woven through earlier chapters in order to re-view politics through the lenses of the relational worldview. Both education reform and health care reform will require new legislation. Because both education and health care deserve a mandate for universal service, neither of these major industries can be expected to improve as a result of marketplace mechanisms alone. As we move from the political to the economic era, we can introduce market forces into some aspects of health care and education, by providing choices among an array of competing providers. But marketplace mechanisms alone will produce winners and losers, and we're all worse off with more illiterates and sick people among our neighbors.

The public sector still has a job to do. How can we recast that job in light of the shift to the economic era? How might a new politics look through the lenses of the relational worldview? And how might that new politics help to improve health care?

CHAPTER 12

BETTER HEALTH CARE

This chapter returns to the role of government in a post-political, economic era. The key to a better politics will be rethinking representation. The relational worldview gives us the tools we'll need to reframe representation. Health care will provide the testing ground for a reframed politics, because the marketplace alone will not give us the health care we need.

The key is the concept of representation. A worldview isn't just a picture of what is represented. It's also a way of representing. The relational worldview represents the world differently from the way the ancients represented their world, or the Enlightenment rationalists represented their world. What if we take what we've learned about epistemic representation—the epistemology or theory of knowledge behind the relational worldview—and apply what we've learned to political representation?

Assume, just for the sake of a playful hypothesis, that epistemic representation *can* serve as a model or paradigm for political representation. Then what are the implications for politics in our post-political, economic era, and, more specifically, what role should residual government play in health care?

In order to explore the implications of taking epistemic representation as the model for political representation, let's first describe the features of epistemic representation that are to serve as the model for political representation. First, representation is not simple, not one-to-one. Second, representation alone is insufficient to account for knowledge.

The significance of the first point—representation is not simple—is just this: If one-thing-one-thought proves to be an impoverished and simplistic view of epistemic representation, then one-person-one-vote may be equally inadequate as the last word in political representation. Further, if one-to-one correspondence of any kind is the real casualty of an appreciation for the complexity of epistemic representation, then one-dollar-one-vote cannot, in the economic era, save democracy following the demise of political legitimacy. The cash register cannot simply replace the ballot box by substituting dollars for votes as markers of preferences. Even if the marketplace *could* replace the ballot box as the locus for registering preferences, the refutation of simplistic one-to-one linkages in epistemology suggests that single dollars are no more adequate than single votes as tokens for guiding social policy because the mandate for universal service requires that even those with no dollars should still have votes.

This point becomes even clearer in the case of health care. For unless you believe that the sufferings of the rich are somehow more acute due to their highly refined sensibilities, then you have to conclude that a poor person's pain deserves as many dollars spent toward its relief as a rich person's. But if health care policy is left to marketplace mechanisms, either directly through a fee–for–service system, or indirectly through a government policy that is not driven by one-person-one-vote, then you can bet that the rich person's pain will get more relief than the poor person's.

So much for the import of the first point: One-to-one representation is as inadequate in politics as it is in epistemology, even if you substitute dollars for votes in the economic era. Testing the truth of this implication by extending it to its import for health care policy only helps to prove the point.

Now let's draw out the implications of the second point: representation alone is insufficient to account for knowledge. The force of this point is simply that *knowledge demands doing as well as seeing.* To know is not simply to see at a distance; to know something or someone demands that you *interact* with them. Knowledge is participatory and interactive; it is not just spectatorial. Any truly adequate theory of knowledge must complement its account of *knowing that* with an account of *knowing how.* Granting once again that we are riding roughshod over intricacies that remain to be explored, it's worth observing that a long philosophical tradition from Plato through Descartes to contemporary representationalists has systematically and repeatedly obscured the pragmatics of knowledge. Theoreticians have downplayed the importance of *praxis*—doing, action, and experience as both the means and the ends of sensing, seeing, or knowing. Any theory of knowledge worth its salt must overcome the representationalist bias by supplementing its account of semantics (how signs *represent* things) with an account of pragmatics (how signs help us to *do* things).

Taking this point about epistemology as a model for representative democracy, what are we to conclude about its import for politics? Crudely speaking, representation isn't enough! Simply gathering the opinions of the electorate (whether by one-man-one-vote or by more complex systems of representation) is as insufficient to political philosophy as representationalism alone is insufficient to epistemology. Something more is required to make politics work. But what is that *something more?* If we take our guidance from the model provided by an enriched theory of knowledge—a theory of know-how as well as know-that—then the answer would seem to lie in the direction of *praxis* and all that it implies. And what might that be?

One of the things we've learned in epistemology is that Lockean empiricism doesn't work. It's too simple. The idea that things outside the mind leave their impressions in the mind in a simplistic, one-thing-one-idea representation fails to capture the complexities of the mapping relationships between knowledge and reality. Not only is representationalism inadequate from the point of view of one-to-one mapping of what is outside the mind to what is inside the mind, as if each single thing *out there* created a single impression *in here;* further, beyond the simplistic notion of one-to-one mapping, *the polarity of influence is too one-sided.* What Kant and his many heirs have contributed to our understanding of knowledge is the insight that the knower plays a major role in constituting knowledge. The knower is not simply a passive recipient of perceptions. As Kant put it, the categories of understanding and the forms of intuition play a major role in shaping our knowledge. Hegel's history of successive forms of consciousness and Nietzsche's perspectivism are both nineteenth-century legacies of Kant's reversal of the polarity between knower and known. In the twentieth century, the idea persists in the phenomenology of Husserl, Heidegger, and Merleau-Ponty, and in the hermeneutics of Hans Georg Gadamer. For the phenomenologists the key concept is *intentionality.* For Gadamer it is *pre-understanding (Vorurteilung).* For all of these heirs of Kant, the passivity of empiricism has been reversed toward a more active role for the knower. Whatever is merely presented to the knower will be re-presented in knowledge in ways that are significantly determined by a form of consciousness, or by a particular perspective, or as a function of intentionality or pre-understanding. Representation is not simply a passive recording of impressions, as Locke thought. It is, instead, actively shaped by the mind, the consciousness, the perspective, and the intentionality or pre-understanding of the knower.

If we take as our guide for the reframing of politics not simply the deconstruction of one-to-one mapping but also this reversal of polarity evident in the last two centuries of epistemology, and if we follow that guide into a politics reframed for the economic era, what we should expect to find there is a comparably activist political leadership—not one that passively follows poll data on public opinion, but leadership that shapes public opinion, leadership with vision (read intentionality), leadership, in short, that leads rather than follows. *This* is the import for politics of the reversal of polarity in epistemology.

There will be much more to say at lower levels of abstraction to keep this insight from being misused as a rationalization for tyranny or a relapse into the activist central state of the political era, just as there is much more that needs to be said (and has been said) to keep, say, phenomenology from falling into the absurdities of claiming that *thinking something so* is enough to *make it so.* To speak of a simple reversal of polarity is to overstate the case. In both politics and epistemology, we are finally discovering, after centuries of slamming back and forth between dialectical extremes, that there is a third way, not a compromise, but a dialectical synthesis of extremes between the activity and passivity of both the knower and the known. In both politics and epistemology we are discovering that representation is neither passive nor active but both at once: *interactive.*

Nowhere are the subtleties of this dynamic between leadership and democracy more salient than in health care. The next section serves as a demonstration for many of the ideas that run through this book: the new game—economics; new players—different *groups* that need representation, not just individuals; new rules—each of the features of the relational worldview that can contribute to creating better health care, and, finally, the new tool of scenario planning. I want to make a case for how and why we need to engage in scenario planning on a national level in order to break the logjam over health care reform.

BETTER HEALTH CARE

Left to marketplace mechanisms alone, American health care will continue to rise in price even as it underserves large segments of our population—currently the number of uninsured is around 44 million and rising at a rate of about 750,000 per year. Granting that we've reframed this question from the political to the economic era, we know that the answer does not lie in heavy-handed political regulation. Neither Canada's single–payer plan nor England's National Health Service can provide the model for America in the economic era. Marketplace mechanisms should play a major role in the allocation of health care resources. But knowing what we know about markets—namely, that they will produce losers—and believing in a mandate for universal service for health care, there is a role for political leadership and government action in compensating for what the market cannot do, namely, limit prices at the top end and enhance access at the bottom end of the health care market.

The shift from fee-for-service toward prepaid managed care is sweeping America. Driven by employers' needs to limit increases in expenditures for the health of their employees, it is hard to see how the trend toward managed care could be reversed. But its direction can be shifted. While the initial impulse toward "managed care" turns out to be *managing costs*, the dangers of overzealous cost cutting leading to reduced care and adverse outcomes has led a number of large employers to look more closely at cost effectiveness in terms of *improved outcomes*. That is to say, the meaning of "managed care" is shifting from "managing costs" to actually "managing health."

A related component of the shift from fee-for-service medicine to prepaid managed care is the shift from the medical care model to a health-enhancement model. This latter shift can be described as a shift from "Don't fix it if it ain't broke" to "Keep it fit so it doesn't break."

A little bit like education as it shifts from an emphasis on teaching and inputs to learning and outputs, health care, too, is undergoing a massive paradigm shift from an emphasis on medical care performed by doctors (producers) to an emphasis on healing that is centered in patients (consumers). Just as we hear talk of standards and accountability in education, we hear similar talk about "outcomes research" in health care. Both professions are following other industries along the broad path from "producer-push" and an emphasis on inputs to "consumer-pull" and an emphasis on outcomes.

As with education, health care is also ready to be examined with a view toward the future, in several senses, and for its own industry-specific reasons. Part of the rationale for using scenario planning to examine education lies in the ineluctable fact that the future will be populated by the people now in school. If we want to improve that future, we'd better populate it with well-educated citizens. For health care the reasoning is equally compelling, even if the medical care model does its best to suppress it. In the medical care model, you don't fix what isn't broken. Disease-oriented medical care works after the fact, after the onset of disease. All this is changing, and in ways that make the future orientation of scenario planning ever more timely. As health futurist Clem Bezold so succinctly puts it in the opening paragraph of an article in *The Futurist:* "Over the next decade, the focus of health care will widen to include greater emphasis on preventing diseases rather than allowing them to develop until treatment is required. Doctors will become more concerned about syndromes of risk because they will better understand the influence of genetics, environment, and behavior on disease."[1]

Preventive care is future–oriented. It aims at better health in the future rather than fixing what went wrong in the past. Preventive care calls for the kind of future–oriented mentality that scenario thinking promotes. But it's worth asking—to pick up a theme from rethinking representation—whether the solitary individual is the appropriate unit of representation when making investments in healthier futures. In addition to the future orientation of preventive care, the quote from Clem Bezold also points toward the increasing importance of environmental and behavioral issues. This shift lends itself to the application of the relational worldview and the social philosophy of *some.* Disease is increasingly understood as a function of social relations and behavior. Tom's lung cancer may reside in Tom's lungs, and once he's got it, Tom's the one who needs therapy. But Tom's smoking habit was the behavior that increased the likelihood of his contracting cancer, and years of political support for the tobacco industry contributed to the likelihood of Tom's unhealthy behavior.

As early as 1977 the Surgeon General estimated that behavior accounts for fully 50 percent of variation in disease over the course of one's life, environment another 20 percent, genes 20 percent, and medical care just 10 percent. These figures suggest just how out of whack our very expensive dependence on the producer-push, doctor-centric, fix-what's-broken, past-oriented medical care model is. Assuming the obvious—that better futures are healthier futures—it's not enough to invest in my own individual fitness through improvements in my own individual diet and exercise regime. Preventive health care for individuals is a big step in the right (future–oriented) direction. But the Surgeon General's estimates of the importance of both behavioral *and* environmental factors calls for social action as well as individual action, public health in addition to private health, and population-based medicine in addition to individual-based medical care. This call can be answered by scenario planning for health care reform.

Groups of people need to get together to frame scenarios that demonstrate different constellations of trade-offs between cost, quality, and access to health care. Alternative scenarios can provide a broad tent under which different interests can get a hearing. By rehearsing different futures, we can optimize across a balance of competing interests and generate the political will necessary to enact national health care reform.

We had a shot at health care reform in the early years of the Clinton administration. For a while it looked as though the Clintons were exercising the kind of leadership that a better politics demands. The Clintons convened several meetings of experts on health care and fashioned a plan for switching from a fee–for–service model that featured cost-unconscious consumers and third–party payers to a managed–care model that would keep costs down and offer access to everyone. Part of the problem with the Clinton reforms lay not so much in the design of the new model but in the manner of its deployment. The Clintons and their top aide on health care reform, Ira Magaziner, failed to practice a politics of inclusion. They failed to honor that feature of the relational worldview labeled the *democratization of meaning*. They thought that if they got the best thinking of a few dozen leading experts and designed a solution to the crisis of increasing health care costs, they could then shove that solution down the throats of Congress and the American people. They thought that they had ascended to the peak of a hierarchy of power, and could therefore impose their solution top-down. They were not sufficiently sensitive to a *heterarchy* of competing interests, most notably the power of the pharmaceutical industry, which paid for the creation and airing of the infamous Harry and Louise ads. Those simple and highly communicative 30-second stories showed how the Clinton reforms could turn out wrong for ordinary citizens. While the reformers were busy trying to explain the complexities of the health care system with the charts and graphs beloved by policy wonks, the pharmaceutical industry beat them in the battle for public opinion through a skillful reliance on the power of *narrative*.

If the Clintons and Ira Magaziner had been more respectful of the *democratization of meaning*, they might have explored what the people mean by managing health, rather than relying on a few dozen experts for a definition of managed care. The Clinton health care reforms foundered for lack of an adequate *politics of representation*. Consumers were not adequately represented in the politics of health care reform under the Clintons, either in the design of the reform package, or in the politics of its vexed and vain failure at passage through Congress.

Defining *health* is not easy. Keeping abreast of the shift from *things to symbols*, surfing the *fall into time*, we'll do well to see *health* as *ambiguous*. To the old medical care model, health is the absence of disease. To the new relational worldview, health is something positive, not just a lack of disease. Psychologist Abraham Maslow added to Freud's picture of the psyche by basing his psychology on peak performance rather than pathology. So, likewise, a richer understanding of the symbol, *health* will include health enhancement as well as the relief of disease. And when it comes to *enhancing* health, then what's outside of my body—the air I will breathe, the water I will drink, the food I will eat—becomes the focus of attention, not germs, viruses, or dysfunctions inside my body.

When it comes to enhancing health, attention shifts from the tendency of most people to think only about their own health needs and to the environment that affects everyone's. Attention swings 180 degrees from focusing inward on the individual self to focusing outward on the *environment*, those "environmental factors" that, according to the Surgeon General, account for twice as much variation in healthy outcomes as all medical care put together. Once the spotlight swings toward the environment, then health care ceases to be something I can manage by myself. Social action is necessary to manage the environment. And scenario planning can provide the tools we need to balance different interests, create a consensus, and achieve the political will necessary for federal legislation and systemic health care reform.

This is not a book about health care, and I do not claim to be an expert on the health care system. But I've had enough experience running scenario planning projects in the health care arena to see how well health care serves as a test case for the ideas that *are* central to this book. The last decade of headlines about health care illustrates the shift away from a (political era) government monopoly toward more privatized (economic era) marketplace dynamics. But the dissatisfaction with HMOs, as well as the 44–million-and-growing uninsured demonstrate the limits of the marketplace. The game has changed, and so have the players. In place of the solitary general practitioner making house calls on a horse and buggy, we see increasing consolidation of for-profit hospital systems and large pools of employees seeking group rates from third–party payers. Health care calls for the *social philosophy of some* with its attention to different interest groups as sources of innovation and creativity.

The rules have also changed. A paradigm shift in health care parallels the paradigm shift we've traced through the human sciences—as paradigm shifts are wont to do, given that they are like the shifting of tectonic plates underlying *all* of what we see, say, and do. There will be less emphasis on acute care and more emphasis on chronic care (consistent with an aging population); therefore fewer jobs for medical specialists and more jobs for primary care generalists; and finally, there will be a paradigm shift from a medical care model favored by the American Medical Association to a growing respect for alternative or complementary care. Each of these points refers to a recognizably distinct trend, but they are all related in a single paradigm shift that reflects the *fall into time*, a *heterarchy* of competing interests and practices, and the *ambiguity* of the very meaning of *health*.

Given the current ferment in health care, it's easy to imagine several alternative scenarios for the future of American health care. I'll sketch the elements of two scenarios just to illustrate the range of possibilities, but my real intent is not to *solve* the problems of health care by imagining different solutions; I don't claim to be an expert with "the answer." Rather, my hope is that, once confronted with a range of possibilities, and once aware of the fact that if we do nothing but let market mechanisms take their course, we will all suffer from a sub-optimized system, then readers will be inspired to engage in the kind of scenario planning that would generate a consensus and the political will to enact the necessary reforms.

As with education, there is no easy answer. Many players need to agree on many issues before we can restore some coherence to our health care system. Let me describe just two of many possible scenarios in order to illustrate the range of possible solutions, the complexities involved, the applicability of the new tools of the relational worldview and scenario planning, and, finally, some of the trade-offs between the different hopes of different communities.

Defined Contribution

The meaning of this phrase comes by way of contrast with the current system of "defined benefits." Many employers offer their employees health plans that *define the benefits* that can be received given different diagnoses. That definition of benefits includes what is and is not covered—kidney stones but not cosmetic surgery—as well as a list of physicians "in the plan." Such defined benefit plans have been described as paternalistic insofar as they provide for employees, but leave the choice of benefits and providers up to the employer.

Defined contribution plans would define the amount that an employer would pay into a health plan, but they would leave up to the employee more of the choices as to how to spend, or not spend, the contribution. As one wag put it, employers offer vacation days, but they don't tell you where to go on your vacation. So why should they tell you which doctors you must use, and which therapies are payable?

Choice can mean more than a choice among providers. It can also mean a choice among models of medicine (Western or Oriental; traditional or alternative/complementary), procedures, therapies, or drugs. Physicians may scoff at the ignorance of consumers: what does an accident victim in a coma have to tell the brain surgeon? But apart from such acute–care emergencies for which the authority of medical science is clearly superior to consumer preference, physicians will be hard pressed to resist a juggernaut trend toward increasing consumer choice.[2] And when improved education systems link up with improved Internet access to outcomes research on different procedures, we'll come closer to meeting the need for the informed consumers that a working marketplace in health care requires.

Wouldn't you like to be able to make your own choices, not only about doctors, but about entire medical regimes? Maybe you'd like some acupuncture, massage, aromatherapy, diet regimen, exercise program, or a weekend at the "health spa." All of it can be arranged using your own medical savings account. No more having to get authorizations from some insurance company. *You* make the choices that will best enhance your health. Once having accepted a greater degree of responsibility for your health, you might get more interested in your health. After all, up to now, you pretty much left it up to your doctor. He or she is the expert. You just bring in the chassis and let them poke and prod, pretty much the way you bring your car to the mechanic, except that with the doctor you can't leave it for a day while you go about your business. However, if you're managing a medical savings account which you know you'll need to draw on fairly heavily sooner or later, then you might start to think about your health as an *investment* that you want to manage. Do a good job of managing your health, and you will have more money to spend on health spas rather than CAT scans.

Managing health like an investment was the theory behind so-called capitation, the practice of taking a certain amount of money per year per head and guaranteeing to treat what ails any of the "heads" during that year. Many of the early HMOs used capitation. It's really very much like an insurance policy, but involves less paperwork. Instead of insuring a person event by event, doctor visit by doctor visit, capitation has just one unit: the person-year. Everything is a cost, so the more you treat, the higher the costs. The thought was that this obvious fact would lead HMOs to invest in keeping their plan members healthy to avoid their needing expensive treatments later. But marketplace mechanisms actually discourage investments in preventive health. How?

If an HMO—let's call it HMO-A—chooses to spend money on forward-looking preventive care, they might well anticipate lower costs in the future. Preventive care looks like a good investment. Their customers will be healthier, and their stockholders will be happier. Nice theory. But in the meantime, prior to the "harvest" of both health and financial benefits, HMO-B might avoid the costs of preventive care and then use the savings to lower its prices. Years after HMO-A has invested in the health of its members, a significant number of those healthy people may notice the lower prices offered by HMO-B. They then take the health paid for by HMO-A across the street to HMO-B, which takes a free ride on the investments made by HMO-A. In the highly competitive world of managed care, marketplace mechanisms have introduced a perverse disincentive for future-oriented preventive care. For HMO-A in a competitive marketplace there is a first–mover disadvantage that comes from doing the right thing.

The theory of introducing marketplace mechanisms and a greater awareness of costs didn't work out well for HMOs or their members, but it might work out better if each individual could see the consequences that disease can have for his/her portfolio. This would have a major impact on what Alain Enthoven identified early on as one of the major weak points of our current health care payment system, that is, "cost-unconscious consumers." As long as consumers have no concept of the costs involved in different therapies, you can guarantee that prices are going to go up. As long as consumers remain clueless about the lack of significant difference between prescription drugs and generics, you can guarantee a tilt toward more expensive prescription drugs over generics. Give the consumer some clues in the form of repeated whacks at his or her medical savings account, and consumers will take a greater interest in their health and the costs of things that help their health.

Consumers will not only feel some incentives for accepting defined contribution rather than defined benefit, but further, if we give in to the incentives that give us defined contribution, then the nature of defined contribution should create further incentives for individuals to keep themselves healthy. In the old days if they got sick, it sure made a difference to their health, but it didn't make that much difference to their pocketbooks. The insurer chosen by the employer had to take the hit, whether it was $5,000 or $50,000, and whichever it was didn't make much difference to the individual. Under defined contribution, that would change. Now you are your own insurer, with maybe some help from your employer in paying the premiums.

Employers have an incentive to accept defined contribution. Acting as the intermediary between their employees and the providers of health care is an immense administrative hassle. As corporations return to their core competence and outsource other functions to professionals for whom that function is *their* core competence, the management of health care is a natural candidate for outsourcing, along with janitorial services, food service, and pension management. By cutting the employer and insurer out of the loop that binds you to whatever doctors you want to use, some analysts estimate that we might save $18 billion in marketing and administrative costs.

The defined–contribution scenario has a lot to recommend it, but a truly scenaric perspective will look beyond the first wave of intended consequences to the second and third waves of the consequences of the consequences, including unintended consequences. When you start to tell some stories about the beneficiaries of defined contribution, it's not hard to imagine that some people will spend their medical savings accounts unwisely. Some will splurge on massages and have nothing left when cancer strikes. What then?

Critics of defined contribution often describe it in extreme terms. Quite the opposite of paternalism, defined contribution has your employer writing you a check and then saying, in effect, "You're on your own." Defined contribution, they say, looks great to "the young immortals"—employees in their 20s and 30s who would like to amass savings in their medical accounts rather than cross-subsidizing their elders with premiums toward insurance policies the young immortals rarely tap. Defined contribution may not look as good to older employees who risk tapping out the contribution as defined—and capped.

The debate over defined contribution will bear similarities to the debate over the privatization of Social Security: Should we mandate the privatization of Social Security so that individuals can manage their own savings for retirement? Should we allow smart investors to raise the ceiling of their retirement incomes, accepting that some investors will risk losing all? Or should we guarantee every citizen a minimum floor of retirement income? Like defined contribution, the privatization of Social Security appeals to rugged individuals who are confident in their own abilities to make wise choices with their investments. The privatization of both Social Security and defined contribution share an ideological tilt toward a conservative individualism and away from a more liberal commitment to social solidarity. Like vouchers for education, defined contribution needs to be tested in scenarios that show the consequences of the consequences in a range of different future circumstances.

Relationship-centered Care

A very different scenario for the future of health care follows from a worldview that is less individualistic and more relational. This approach is called "relationship-centered care."[3] The idea behind relationship-centered care is to focus attention on the importance of the relationships between doctor and patient, as well as the wider circles of relationships to family, job, society, and environment.

Ian McWhinney, one of the leaders of this movement, is explicit about the influence of the Enlightenment paradigm on our current medical care model.

> As is always the case, this development in clinical method was associated with a change in the perception of disease. Since classical times, Western medicine has used two explanatory models of illness . . . According to the *ontological model*, a disease is an entity located in the body and conceptually separable from the sick person. According to the *physiological* or *ecological model*, disease results from an imbalance within the organism and between organism and environment: Individual diseases have no real existence, the names being simply clusters of observations used by physicians as a guide to prognosis and therapy. According to the latter view, it becomes difficult to separate the disease from the person and the person from the environment.[4]

Rather than leaving the patient on his or her own as in the defined contribution scenario, relationship-based care calls for attention to context. Rather than viewing disease as localized in a single individual, like a faulty carburetor in the body/chassis of a car, the relational worldview of relationship-centered care sees illnesses as imbalances arising from and affecting a larger context. For that reason, the practice of medicine can't be left to subspecialists alone. Both prevention and cure demand atten-tion to a nested field of relationships: between a single symptom and the whole person with their hopes, fears, and past medical history; between the person and the physician; and outward to family, community, job, and environment.

Taken to extremes, this view of medical practice will seem impossi-bly daunting, as if you can't cure anything without curing everything. As McWhinney acknowledges, relationship-based care "requires noth-ing less than a change in what it means to be a physician." But if you talk with doctors now laboring under the strains of the current system, you will find that they are not happy to have their medical judgment compromised by coverage decisions made by bureaucrats at the health plan. Like many patients, many doctors are ready for a change in what it means to be a physician.

How might change happen? Will marketplace mechanisms alone take our health care system in a direction we want it to go? Not if the per-verse incentives currently characterizing the system are any indication. In order to level the playing field so that HMO-A does not suffer a first–mover disadvantage for doing the right thing, we need national health care reform. But the failure of the Clinton reforms shows the need for a broad-based political will to get a comprehensive and coherent set of reforms through Congress. How might such political will be gener-ated? Answer: by framing and publicly debating a set of alternative sce-narios for the future of health care.

I don't know the answer to the question, what is the best way to de-liver health care? I do not claim to be an expert on health care. But I am reasonably sure that we can do better than we are doing today on a whole host of measures like cost, quality of care, and access. Because not all good things go together, because there are bound to be trade–offs between cost and quality, or cost and access, we need a way to enter-tain options, and scenarios are an excellent means for articulating the options.

Are we willing to limit expensive therapies for the few in order to ex-tend greater access to the many? Do we want a system that rewards healthy behaviors and penalizes risky behaviors? These are questions that scenario planning can help to answer. Narrative scenarios can il-lustrate, with all the vividness of the Harry–and–Louise ads, the conse-quences of different policy decisions. Rather than "backing into" some future that just *happens to us* as a result of marketplace mechanisms, Americans can democratically and voluntarily *choose* one future or another. But such choice is impossible unless the options are articulated. Scenarios are the ideal tools for articulating those options.

Like education, the health care mess provides a test case for the several ideas running throughout this book: the transition from the political to the economic era that threatens to push markets toward what they cannot do; the social philosophy of *some* that sees groups as agents of purposeful change; and the features of the relational worldview that allow us to see things like health and disease differently in different scenarios.

All of these pieces come together, as they must, in holistic pictures of what it will take to create futures better than the present. Scenarios provide a way of seeing all the parts working together in narrative wholes. Further, those scenarios that show constellations of the parts working more effectively together can serve to lift our sights toward better futures. The measure of better is not some table of values handed down from on high by some latter–day Moses. One group need not impose its values on another. Instead, different communities of different sizes can use scenario planning as a tool for articulating the shared hopes of the community, and those shared hopes then become the fulcrum for lifting better futures away from the actual present.

As becomes clear from even the cursory reviews of the key factors and forces affecting education and health care, building better futures calls for a systemic perspective—a holistic approach that respects the complex interrelationships among many players and many factors. In the past, the threat of complexity has usually been met by appeals to scientific expertise. Leave it to the technical experts. You don't design power plants democratically. So, likewise, we've delegated the design of our schools and hospitals to technical experts. But are we willing to leave the design of our lives, of our futures, to technical experts?

Lately we are discovering that if you leave the design of large, complex systems to the experts, you run the risk of writing large checks to support fiefdoms built by specialists. Whether it is special ed students claiming 30 percent of the busing budget for 3 percent of the students, or medical research specialists pulling resources away from public health, the demands of the special and partial have a way of draining and obscuring the health of the whole. Leave problem solving to the specialists and you will get technical solutions to partial problems, but the whole system that results from those partial solutions may not reflect the values of those who are supposedly being served.

Scenario planning offers a way to see things whole, and to do so in a way that honors both the theoretical knowledge of the experts as well as the practical interests of ordinary citizens. The scenario team can *represent* both theoretical and practical interests. The logic of representation in scenario planning doesn't follow a simplistic one-person-one-vote process. Instead the team is composed to represent a whole range of different interests, as with the panoply of interest groups listed by Sarason, or the range of stakeholders in the health care system.

Further, the decision–making procedure used in scenario planning does not rely solely on technical solutions that are expected to be free of bugs—as if it were possible, according to some Enlightenment ideal of rationalistic science, to get it right the first time and then impose the perfect solution from the top down. Instead the decision–making procedure characteristic of scenario planners is more pragmatic, less rationalistic. Let's imagine a solution like vouchers or defined contribution, and then let's wind-tunnel that solution through a range of possible futures. What seemed like a good idea initially might not seem so when one looks at the consequences of the consequences. When you allow many different interests to be represented, as can be done using a range of different scenarios, then you greatly reduce the likelihood of unintended consequences. You are less likely to be blindsided by unanticipated problems.

Scenarios turn out to be good tools for testing technical solutions against the well–represented interests of many different stakeholders. This is why we want to take another crack at national health care reform using scenarios. This is why we want to wind-tunnel California's new Master Plan for public education through a set of scenarios shaped by representatives of all of the groups listed by Sarason. Scenario planning allows us to integrate the technical expertise of the specialists and the values of ordinary citizens to create futures that reflect the shared hopes of communities.

CHAPTER 13

CADENZA: EARTH MIGHT BE FAIR

Throughout this final chapter, the musical leit-motif that justifies the title is the playful dance of freedom rather than determinism, play as opposed to work, art as opposed to science, creativity as opposed to engineering, freedom as opposed to necessity. This business of better futures cannot be a grim calculation of the necessary. Instead, scenarios are stories about what might be possible. Don't expect a rigorous proof for what *must* be done; only some suggestions for what *might* be done, and why, given all that has gone before, that's the best we should hope for.

Despite the lure of pagan polytheism and my allegiance to Hermes the messenger, I'm nonetheless drawn to the sheer poetry of the Christian hymns. "Earth might be fair and all men glad and wise . . . " What a wonderful idea, even in its sexist language. "All persons glad and wise" wouldn't exactly scan. *Earth might be fair:* the richness lies precisely in the ambiguity between ethical and aesthetic interpretations of *fair.* We could certainly do with a little more justice; we could also do with more beauty, the Shakespearean meaning of *fair.*

Even with the wonders of modern science there never seems to be enough: enough love, enough attention, enough respect, enough dignity. So we make too much of the things we know how to make: war, toxic waste, bad television. Perhaps there is a better way to organize our lives and our relationships, one that does not pit the demands of work against the delights of love. Perhaps there is a way to reconstruct our world, as Brown and Lyman invite us to do. But in doing so we cannot base our reconstruction on the firm foundations of science, because science cannot tell us what we want, or how we should exercise our freedom. Further, scientific laws like the constant conservation of matter and energy may mislead our imaginations to underestimate what is possible for humanity.

I know of no law of the constant conservation of laughter, or any limitation on joy. I see no reason to limit our sense of what is possible for the distribution of delight. These human *goods* need not be subject to a law of constant conservation. If I have more, you needn't have less. Quite to the contrary, there might be a virtuous circle of mutual reinforcement in the spread of sublime delight, like a ripple of laughter that gains momentum in a crowd. According to the economics of the sublime, there *can* be enough for all.

Still, there is no universal understanding of the best way to live a deeply fulfilling human life. On the contrary, there is a rich and variegated ecology of customs and mores. Further, there is a constant risk of *transgression*. Precisely to the extent that people have learned that *being good* is not necessarily about conforming to timeless norms, but rather more about exercising human freedom in the service of creativity and delight, there is a constant danger of decadence. Like creativity in art, creativity in life sometimes requires a bending of the rules for the sake of beauty. But not all novelty in art is successful. Some slides over into the decadent and ugly. How is one to know where to draw the line?

There are no rules for how to break the rules safely, though *games* can be seen in this context as ways of limiting play to only those moves that are safe, moves that limit the risks to contestants. The spread of human freedom means a spread of risk taking, and risks are not risks if they never fail.[1] The close bond between freedom and transgression means that some confrontations with evil are virtually inevitable. Though it may sound as perverse as Freud's uncovering of infant sexuality, I see the origin of evil in the play of innocents, in the horsing around that got too rough, in the joke that went wrong. "I didn't mean it that way," he said. Because ambiguity allows for multiple interpretations, the Symbolic Turn can end in tears.

The very thing that renders the information economy possible—the Semiotic Turn—also renders transgression unto evil virtually inevitable. Earth might be fair, and almost all glad and wise, but human beings will not be angels, and evil will not be eradicated. Ambiguity—the potential for multiple interpretations of anything that serves as a symbol—is the name of the snake in the garden. The snake is wise. The snake offers the promise of wisdom from the tree of knowledge. The snake is generous: he offers more than just one interpretation of every symbol. He gives us more for less. But the price we pay for the play of symbols, the gain of ambiguity, is the loss of certainty.

Watch the play of cute little kittens and you will see a rehearsal for the brutality of the tiger. See in the tussling of adorable little puppies the vicious attack of the wolf. But there is no viciousness or brutality in the animal kingdom, really. The moral overtones come only from minds that can add an interpretation of cruelty to what, in nature, is a mere act of survival. It takes a twisted mind to turn nature's metabolism into acts of evil. It takes a Symbolic Turn to add cruelty and evil to innocent, if sometimes violent, nature.

It takes a twisted parent to convince a child that he was "being mean" to his younger sister when all he was doing was playing. This move is called attribution by psychologists. "Don't pinch your sister," is one thing. "Don't be mean," is another. By the latter I may learn not only how *not* to be mean, but also that, deep down, I *am* mean. Innocence disappears so quickly.

The gift of symbolic play is a condition for freedom . . . and a sentence to the inevitability of evil. Human beings can be more truly human, more free, more creative, and less subject to the uniform necessities of nature. We have struggled up through the realm of necessity and now stand, more and more of us, on the brink of the realm of freedom. The shift to an information economy is the crucial instrumentality for this transition.

WHY THERE CANNOT BE ONE BEST FUTURE

Here at the end, I'd like to suggest, to intimate, to whisper, to sing if I could—but hardly to argue—a set of relationships between several of the other threads that have been woven through this book, and suggest a pattern for normative scenarios: ambiguity, the information revolution, and ethical pluralism.

Precisely because the very nature of information is to differentiate, precisely because information theory defines information as a difference that makes a difference—news, not noise or redundancy—an information economy can thrive only where mass-market conformity breaks up into highly differentiated niche markets.

There was a fine match between industrial mass manufacturing and the conformist values of the mass market. If keeping up with the Joneses meant having the same car, and the genius of the industrial economy lay in producing lots and lots of the same car, then the match between supply and demand was, as it were, made in heaven. But this match is coming unglued with the transition from the industrial to the information economy. As Arnold Mitchell, creator of SRI's Values and Lifestyles (VALS) program, used to put it, the Belongers (we used to capitalize the names of our lifestyle segments) like to "fit in," but those who lead the new lifestyles "prefer to stand out rather than fit in." Individuation is the name of the game in the new economy. But individuation is (a) precisely what becoming more human is all about, according to every wise psychologist from Carl Jung to Erik Erikson, and (b) precisely what an information economy, as opposed to a mass-manufacturing industrial economy, is prepared to deliver.

The VALS program was all about charting the breakup of the mass market into segments or lifestyles that were not, strictly speaking, better or worse than one another, just different. But now the segments are shattering still further as individuals internalize the diversity of multicultural mores into the depths of their own souls. There was a time when Achievers could be trusted to behave in all situations like Achievers, and Belongers would remain true–blue Belongers, and the try-anything-once crowd, the segment we called Experientials, could be trusted to shop around. But now you see people who are Achievers by day and Experientials by night; ladies who shop Bloomingdales one day and Price Club the next; men who wear black tie one night and a black motorcycle jacket the next. In short, people aren't staying true to type. A marketer's nightmare: people are becoming less predictable. But a humanist's dream: people are becoming more free.

In our work with alternative scenarios, we constantly come up against several interrelated questions having to do with human values. It is clear that one of the most important factors affecting the demand for energy is people's willingness to conserve. Will people be willing to drive a "green" car that is smaller than an SUV? How much air pollution are we willing to breathe? How many homeless will we allow on our doorsteps? These are questions about values. They do not turn on questions of technological feasibility but on the very human question of what people will want in their lives in 10–20 years. What part of a full human life will be scarcest and therefore most valuable? Time? A sense of community? Meaning? Money? If we could know that a sense of meaning will be more important than money, how would that skewing of the ecology of values tend to revalue other parts of life? If business wants to deliver the goods, businesspeople need to know what people think is good. For anticipating fundamental shifts in economic *value*, anticipating changes in *values* is essential.

It is however very difficult, perhaps impossible. Because if anything is a function of human freedom, it is the revaluation of human values. If our values are like a hardwired, read-only program, then we are pretty mechanical creatures, hardly free at all. Only if we can overwrite at will, only if we can reprogram the human biocomputer, can we be said to be free.

To the extent that freedom defines the human condition, the prediction of human values is in principle impossible. As Aristotle formulated the paradox over two millennia ago, if you can know the future, then you can't do anything about it; if you can do something about the future, then you cannot know it in advance.[2] This paradox lies at the self-contradictory heart of traditional attempts at scientific strategic planning, which supposes, on the one hand, that you can predict the future, but on the other, that energetic implementation of a vision can change the future to a corporation's advantage.

You can no more predict human values than you can predict movements in contemporary art. It is the artists who will do something about the future of art, and it is free human beings who will revalue their values. If either one is predictable, then she is not an artist, he is not a human being. Both beauty and humanity share an inherent unpredictability.

This unpredictability should be cause for joy among humanists because it is precisely this unpredictability that we can just as well interpret as freedom flexing her muscles. The old shell of oppressive conformism is breaking. The constriction of Smalltown's norms is being broken all over the globe and, one by one, individuals are emerging from the realm of necessity—what nature or nurture tells them they *have to do*—and stepping forth into the realm of freedom toward what they want and hope to do. A new technology, an information technology whose essence is to differentiate, will be there to greet them.

Of course human freedom is very playful, even capricious. And as I've mentioned, in the play of innocents the seeds of evil and transgression are born. But as playwright, poet, and philosopher Friedrich von Schiller pointed out in his *Letters on the Aesthetic Education of Man,* "Man is most truly human when he plays, and when he plays, most truly man." In our playfulness we will keep remaking human life as we go along, better and better for the most part, but occasionally worse.

How might some of the other characteristics of the relational worldview play out in normative scenarios? The fall into time will be more widely acknowledged. Imagine a world where people are able to swim in the tides of change rather than drown in confusion. Employers will be looking for swimmers, people who can keep up with time's current. They are the best at coping with change. In a scenario where most people were comfortable with a certain amount of change, there would be less reactionary insistence on the sanctity of tradition, and less certainty about the justification for punishing transgressors.

The democratization of meaning will take the form of an evolutionary survival of the most resilient interpretations of family life, romance, and success. There will not be just one pattern of perfection toward which all would aspire in some recrudescence of industrial standardization. Instead the paradigmatic preoccupation with *difference* over identity will encourage differentiation and experimentation, if not transgression. There will not be one best way of being human, but a rich ecology of species in the gardens of the sublime.

There is no clear *end* to the creation of better futures because embracing the fall into time means that there will be no unambiguous finality, no goal which, once reached, would mark a conclusion. In this sense, too, the reach for better futures is not utopian. I have not drawn a blueprint for an ideal society. Instead I have tried to reinterpret parts of the present—such as education, government, and health care—through the lenses of a relational worldview already evident in the human sciences. I believe that some of the phenomena that others lament—the decline of traditional orthodoxies, the melting into air of firm foundations—can be reinterpreted in ways that could contribute to better futures. But it is clear to me that some better futures demand more than merely incremental improvements of the commonplace. A paradigm shift is required if we are to reinterpret the present as the prelude to better futures.

Scenario planners can contribute their stories without having to invent a new worldview out of whole cloth. Rather, we need only look around and see what is already happening in the human sciences. There we find the symbolic turn already accomplished, a preoccupation with difference over identity already evident, the fall into time already acknowledged, and the democratization of meaning well under way. With a new look at norms, a respect for the way ambiguity drives us toward pluralism, and an appreciation for the resultant heterarchy of values, we ought to be able to learn to live together in communities of communities. We can weave these threads into scenarios that have normative import, scenarios that carry the transition from explanation to narration further into the futures that we would like to leave to our grandchildren. Truly, Earth might be fair, and almost all glad and wise. If we could only use our imaginations to spin out scenarios of better ways to play.

NOTES
<hr>

CHAPTER ONE: AIMING HIGHER

1. James Oliver Robertson, *American Myth, American Reality* (New York: Hill & Wang, 1970), xv.
2. Thomas Berry, "Comments on the Origin, Identification and Transmission of Values," *Anima* (Winter, 1978).
3. Cf. James Ogilvy, *Many Dimensional Man: Decentralizing Self, Society and the Sacred,* (New York: Oxford University Press, 1977).
4. Cf. Richard Rorty, *Philosophy and Social Hope,* (New York: Penguin Books, 1999), esp. Chapter 3, "A World Without Substances or Essences," pp. 47 ff. See also Joseph Jaworski, *Synchronicity* (San Francisco: Berrett-Koehler, 1996), in which he attributes his understanding of a relational worldview to what he's learned from David Bohm.

CHAPTER TWO: RELIGIOUS, POLITICAL,
AND ECONOMIC PASSIONS

1. Cf. Norman O. Brown, *Life Against Death: A Psychoanalytic Interpretation of History* (New York: Vintage Books, 1959) for a reading of history as prolonged neurosis.
2. Clifford Geertz, *The Interpretation of Cultures* (New York: Basic Books, 1973), 29.
3. Cf. Arnold Mitchell, *The Nine American Lifestyles* (New York: MacMillan Publishing Co., 1983).
4. Cf. Karen Armstrong, *The Battle for God* (New York: Alfred A. Knopf, 2000). Armstrong argues that we need to appreciate different fundamentalist movements—Christian and Islamic alike—not so much as sim-

ple throwbacks to premodern belief systems, but as parts of a post-modern reaction to the pace and confusion of modernity.

5. Cf. James Ogilvy, *The Experience Industry*, Report No. 59, The Values and Lifestyles Program, SRI International, 1985; also, "The Experience Industry," in *American Demographics* (December 1986): 27–29, 29–30, 59–60. For a more recent and more fully elaborated treatment see B. Joseph Pine and James H. Gilmore, *The Experience Economy* (Boston: Harvard Business School Press, 1999).

6. See Sherry Turkle, *The Second Self* (New York: Simon & Schuster, 1984); and *Life on the Screen* (New York: Simon & Schuster, 1995).

7. Cf. Warren McCulloch, "A Heterarchy of Values Determined by the Topology of Nervous Nets," *Embodiments of Mind* (Cambridge, Mass.: MIT Press, 1965), 40–44.

8. For more on this idea, see also, James Ogilvy, *Many Dimensional Man: Decentralizing Self, Society and the Sacred* (New York and London: Oxford University Press, 1977; NY Harper & Row, 1980).

9. See Francis Fukuyama, *The End of History and the Last Man* (New York: The Free Press, 1992) for the most fully articulated statement of this nostalgic view.

10. Cf. James Ogilvy, "Greed" in *Guilty Pleasures*, ed. Robert Solomon (New York: Rowman & Littlefield, 1999), 87–116.

CHAPTER THREE: THE LIMITS OF THE MARKETPLACE

1. For a more recent statement of a similar thesis, see Daniel Jonah Goldhagen, *Hitler's Willing Executioners* (New York: Alfred A. Knopf, 1996).

2. Cf. Joseph S. Nye, Jr., "In Government We Don't Trust," *Foreign Policy*, n. 108 (Fall 1997): 99 ff. See also Seymour Martin Lipset and William Schneider, *The Confidence Gap* (Baltimore: Johns Hopkins Press, 1987).

3. Throughout 1999 and 2000, a series of articles in *Education Week* covered two trends: first, the succession of state supreme court rulings against voucher initiatives on the grounds that they failed to provide equal education to all children; second, the results of tests showing no significant advantages gained by students in charter schools. As of this writing, the case for the benefits of voucher initiatives has not been made.

4. Ernest Boyer, "School Choice," A Special Report for the Carnegie Foundation for the Advancement of Teaching (1992), 12 and 14.

5. E. D. Hirsh, *What Our Children Need to Know* (Boston: Houghton-Mifflin, 1989).

6. Arthur Schlesinger, Jr., *The Disuniting of America* (New York: W. W. Norton & Co., 1992), 43.

7. Howard Gardner, *Frames of Mind* (New York: Basic Books, 1983); *The Mind's New Science* (New York: Basic Books, 1987); *Multiple Intelligences* (New York: Basic Books, 1993); *Intelligence Reframed* (New York: Basic Books, 1999).

8. Gregory Bateson, *Steps to an Ecology of Mind* (New York: Chandler Publishing, 1972); *Mind and Nature* (New York: Dutton, 1979).

CHAPTER FOUR: RETHINKING REPRESENTATIVE GOVERNMENT

1. Cf. Kees van der Heijden, *Scenarios: The Art of Strategic Conversation* (West Sussex: John Wiley & Sons, 1996).

CHAPTER FIVE: BEYOND INDIVIDUALISM AND COLLECTIVISM

1. See Charles Hampden-Turner and Fons Trompenaars, *Seven Cultures of Capitalism* (New York: Doubleday, 1993) for definitive evidence showing the differences between American individualism and Japanese collectivism.

2. Henry David Thoreau, "Civil Disobedience" (New York: Dover Publications, 1993).

3. Alexis de Tocqueville, *Democracy in America,* ed. Mayer (New York) 506.

4. *Ibid.,* 508.

5. George Herbert Mead, *Mind, Self, and Society* (Chicago: University of Chicago Press, 1934).

6. David Riesman, *Individualism Reconsidered* (Garden City, N.Y., 1955), 26f.

7. *Ibid.,* 13.

8. *Ibid.,* 14.

9. Philip Slater, *The Pursuit of Loneliness* (Boston: Beacon Press, 1970), 9.

10. Richard Sennett, *The Fall of Public Man* (New York, 1977), 89.

11. Robert Bellah et al., *Habits of the Heart* (Berkeley: University of California Press, 1985), 76.

12. *Ibid.,* 7.

13. *Ibid.,* 8.

14. *Ibid.,* 79f.

15. *Ibid.,* 84.

16. Alfred North Whitehead, *Science and the Modern World* (New York: Macmillan, 1925).

17. Friedrich Nietzsche, *The Genealogy of Morals,* trans. Francis Golffing (Garden City, N.Y.: Doubleday,) 178f.

18. David Hume, *The Treatise of Human Nature,* Book I, Part IV, Section 6.

19. Erik Erikson, *Identity, Youth and Crisis* (New York: W. W. Norton, 1968), 15f.

20. *Ibid.,* 17.

21. Sigmund Freud, *The Ego and the Id,* trans. Joan Riviers (New York: W.W. Norton, 1962), 15.

22. *Ibid.,* 46.

23. *Idem.*

24. *Ibid.,* 45.

25. Cf. James Moore, *Care of the Soul* (New York: Harper Collins, 1992). See also the work of Moore's mentor, James Hillman: *The Soul's Code,* (New York: Warner Books, 1997).

26. James Hillman, *Re-Visioning Psychology* (New York: Harper Collins, 1975), 22.

27. *Ibid.,* 24.

28. *Ibid.,* 25.

29. Harry Guntrip, *Psychoanalytic Theory, Therapy, and the Self* (New York: Basic Books, 1971), 93.

30. *Ibid.,* 37.

31. *Ibid.,* 91.

CHAPTER SIX: SOCIAL FORCES AND CREATIVITY

1. Cf. Theodor Adorno et al., *The Positivist Dispute in German Sociology,* trans. Glyn Adey and David Frisby (New York: Harper Torchbooks, 1976).

2. Richard Harvey Brown, in *Structure, Consciousness, and History,* ed. R. H. Brown and Stanford M. Lyman (Cambridge: Cambridge University Press, 1978), 15.

3. For starters, see Bertell Ollman, *Alienation: Marx's conception of man in capitalist society* (Cambridge University Press, 1971); Robert Blauner, *Alienation and Freedom* (University of Chicago Press, 1964); Herbert Aptheker, ed., *Marxism and Alienation: A Symposium* (New York: Humanities Press, 1965); Leopold Labedz, ed., *Revisionism* (New York: Praeger, 1962); Nicholas Lobkowicz, *Marx and the Western World* (Notre Dame, Ind.: Notre Dame Press, 1967); Fritz Pappenheim, *The*

Alienation of Modern Man (New York: Monthly Review Press, 1959); Gajo Petrovic, *Marx in the Mid-twentieth Century* (Garden City, New York: 1967).

4. Howard Gardner, *To Open Minds: Chinese clues to the dilemma of contemporary Education* (New York: Basic Books, 1989), 250.

5. Harold Bloom, *The Western Canon* (New York: Harcourt Brace, 1994), 46.

6. Cf. Harold Blooms argument in his book *The Anxiety of Influence* (New York: Oxford University Press, 1973) that strong poets are those who survive the oedipal struggle with their greatest predecessors.

7. Cf. Charles Spinosa, Fernando Flores, and Hubert Dreyfus, *Disclosing New Worlds: Entrepreneurship, Democratic Action, and the Cultivation of Solidarity* (Cambridge: The MIT Press, 1997), 16–33, 162–175, for an insightful treatment of what 'making history' means.

8. Cf. Arthur Koestler, *The Act of Creation* (New York: MacMillan, 1964).

9. "In general, it might be said that the current awareness of a crisis in sociology focuses on three main issues. First, no available paradigm has achieved dominion in the discipline. Instead a plurality of approaches rooted in different and even opposed epistemologies compete for regency. Second, none of these paradigms appears to have attained internal consistency with respect to its own. . .assumptions. Finally, despite sociology's lack of preparedness, a host of moral and political issues demand from it both explication and resolution. As in earlier crises, the task confronting sociology is complex. . . .

   "Much of the writing in this volume is informed by what might be called a "symbolic realist" or "cognitive aesthetic" perspective. The two terms are not quite synonymous. Symbolic realism stresses ontology; cognitive aesthetics stresses epistemology. The first focuses on the possibility of our having symbolic worlds; the second provides criteria of adequacy for judging whether such worlds constitute knowledge." (Richard Harvey Brown and Sanford Lyman, in *Structure, Consciousness,* and History, ed. R. H. Brown and Stanford M. Lyman (Cambridge, 1978), 1, 2, 5.

10. *Ibid.,* 6.

11. *Ibid.,* 9.

CHAPTER SEVEN. FROM WORLDVIEWS TO BETTER WORLDS

1. One of the central tenets of Martin Heidegger's existential philosophy as expressed in his *Being and Time* is his thesis that care (*Sorge*) is what

differentiates human being-in-the-world (*Dasein*) from a merely calculative rationality. Computers may be able to calculate, but computers don't *care*.

2. George Lakoff and philosopher Mark Johnson, *Metaphors We Live By* (Chicago: University of Chicago Press, 1980), 5.
3. Claude Lévi-Strauss, *Structural Anthropology*, trans. Jacobson and Schoepf (New York: Basic Books, 1963), 203f.
4. Clifford Geertz, *The Interpretation of Cultures* (New York: Basic Books, 1973), p. 44.
5. *Ibid.*, 5.
6. *Ibid.*, 47.
7. *Idem.*
8. Clifford Geertz, *Local Knowledge* (New York: Basic Books, 1983), 3. See also *Available Light*, (Princeton: Princeton University Press, 2000).
9. *Local Knowledge,* op. cit., 20.
10. Edward Said, *Beginnings* (New York: Basic Books, 1975), 12.
11. Roland Barthes, *Roland Barthes*, trans. Richard Howard (New York: Hill & Wang, 1977).
12. Said, *Beginnings,* op. cit., 380.
13. *Ibid.*, 282.
14. *Ibid.*, 290.
15. *Ibid.*, 39.
16. *Idem.*
17. Paul deMan, *Blindness and Insight: Essays in the Rhetoric of Contemporary Criticism* (Minneapolis: University of Minnesota Press, 1985).
18. Cf. Nietzsche, *The Will to Power*, trans. Walter Kauffmann (New York: Vintage Books, Random House, 1967), Book One, "European Nihilism."
19. Jacques Derrida, "Structure, Sign and Play in the Human Sciences," in *The Structuralist Controversy*, eds. Macksey and Donato, Johns Hopkins University Press, Baltimore and London, 1970, 264.
20. Roland Barthes, *Roland Barthes by Roland Barthes,* trans. Richard Howard (New York: Hill & Wang, 1977), 92f.
21. *Ibid.*, 94.
22. *Ibid.*, 99.
23. Cf. Robert C. Holub, *Reception Theory: A Critical Introduction,* (London and New York: Methuen, 1984); and Hans Robert Jauss, *Toward an Aesthetic of Reception*, trans. Timothy Bahti (Minneapolis: University of Minnesota Press, 1982).
24. Manuel Castells, *The Power of Identity* (Oxford: Blackwell, 1997), 3.

CHAPTER EIGHT. THE FEATURES OF THE RELATIONAL WORLDVIEW

1. Warren McCulloch, *Embodiments of Mind* (Cambridge, Mass.: MIT Press, 1965, 44.
2. Tom Wolfe, *The Pump House Gang* (New York: Farrar, Straus & Giroux, 1964), Introduction, 3–14.

CHAPTER NINE. FACTS, VALUES, AND SCENARIO PLANNING

1. Cf. the extensive literature on the psychological stages of moral development, from the pioneering work of Erik Erikson to Robert Kegan, *The Evolution of the Self* (Cambridge, Mass.: Harvard University Press, 1982).
2. Roger Sperry's views on values can be found in his book *Science and Moral Priority* (1983; reprint, New York: Praeger, 1985) and in an earlier essay, "Mind, Brain, and Humanist Values," in John R. Platt, ed., *New Views of the Nature of Man* (Chicago: University of Chicago Press, 1965).
3. Peter Schwartz, Joel Hyatt, and Peter Leyden, *The Long Boom* (Reading, Mass.: Perseus Books, 1999).

CHAPTER TEN. SCENARIO PLANNING:
A TOOL FOR SOCIAL CREATIVITY

1. See Peter Schwartz and James Ogilvy, "Plotting Your Scenarios," in *Learning From the Future,* ed. Liam Fahey and Robert Randall (John Wiley & Sons 1998), 57–80.
2. Cf. Peter Schwartz, *The Art of the Long View,* (New York: Doubleday Currency, 1991); Kees van der Heijden, *Scenarios, the Art of Strategic Conversation* (New York: John Wiley & Sons, 1996); Gill Ringland, *Scenario Planning: Managing for the Future* (New York: John Wiley & Sons, 1998); and the many sources cited in these three books.
3. Cf. Gurdjieff, *Meetings with Remarkable Men* (New York: E. P. Dutton, 1991).
4. Here I refer the reader to a book called *Jamming* (New York: Harper Business, 1996) by John Kao, who showed the slides of China (see Chapter 6, p. 111) in the early 1970s when he was a student at Yale. He spent several years as a professor at Harvard Business School where he taught courses on entrepreneurship and creativity. He is now Chairman of The Idea Factory in San Francisco.
5. For a series of informative stories about the features of creative groups or, as he calls them, "great groups," see Warren Bennis and Patricia Ward

Biederman, *Organizing Genius: The Secrets of Creative Collaboration,* (Reading, Mass.: Addison-Wesley, 1997). See also *Social Creativity,* ed. Alphonso Montouri and Ronald E. Purser (Cresskill, N.J.: Hampton Press, 1999).

6. See Adam Kahane, "Changing the Winds: Scenarios for People Who Want to Change the World," in *Whole Earth* (Spring 1999): 82 ff., for a discussion of several examples of scenario planning for nations.

7. For the future orientation of existential psychotherapy, see Ludwig Binswanger, "Freud's Conception of Man in the Light of Anthropology," trans. J. Needleman, in *Being-in-the-World* (New York: Basic Books, 1963); Medard Boss, *Psychoanalysis and Daseinsanalysis,* trans. Ludwig Lefebre (New York: Basic Books, 1963); and Rollo May, ed., *Existence* (New York: Basic Books, 1958).

CHAPTER ELEVEN. BETTER EDUCATION

1. James Traub, in the lead article of the June 1994 issue of *Harper's,* entitled "Can Separate Be Equal?" See also Jonathan Kozol's *Savage Inequalities* (New York: Harper Perennial, 1992) for vivid descriptions of the decrepitude of public schools in East St. Louis and Camden, New Jersey.

2. Seymour Sarason, "Some Features of a Flawed Educational System," *Daedalus* (Fall 1998), 2–3.

3. See a growing list of books by Howard Gardner, including *Frames of Mind* (New York: Basic Books, Inc., 1983); *The Mind's New Science* (New York: Basic Books, 1987); *Multiple Intelligences* (New York: Basic Books, 1993); and *Intelligence Reframed* (New York: Basic Books, 1999).

CHAPTER TWELVE. BETTER HEALTH CARE

1. Clement Bezold, "Health Care Faces a Dose of Change," *The Futurist,* 1 April 1999, 30.

2. Cf. Regina Herzlinger, *Market Driven Health Care: Who Wins, Who Loses in the Transformation of America's Largest Service Industry* (Reading, Mass.: Addison-Wesley Publishing Co., 1997), esp. Chapter 2, "When Patients Won't Remain Patient," and Chapter 3, "Give Me Mastery or Give Me Death: The New Health Care Activist."

3. Cf. C. P. Tresolini and the Pew-Fetzer Task Force, *Health Professions Education and Relationship-Centered Care* (San Francisco, Calif.: Pew Health Professions Commission, 1994).

4. Ian McWhinney, "Why We Need a New Clinical Method," in Moira Stewart et al., *Patient-Centered Medicine: Transforming the Clinical Method* (London: Sage Publications, 1995). I am indebted to David Reynolds for bringing this work to my attention.

CHAPTER THIRTEEN. CADENZA: EARTH MIGHT BE FAIR

1. Cf. Roberto Mangabeira Unger and Cornel West, *The Future of American Progressivism* (Boston: Beacon Press, 1998) for a call for more experimentation and social creativity.
2. Cf. Aristotle *Nicomachean Ethics*, Book VI, especially chapters 2, 5, 9, and 12.

INDEX

some, 85, 100; social philosophy of, 15, 54, 66, 68, 87, 101–2. *See also* community
Soros, George, ix
Sperry, Roger, 171
Spinoza, Baruch, 89–90
Spitzer, Leo, 130, 132
SRI International, 80, 82
standards, of marketplace, 47–51, 52, 194, 207. *See also* consequences; outcomes
Starobinski, Jean, 62
State, and Church, 31, 32, 34. *See also* public sector
states, on education, 199–201
Steps to an Ecology of Mind (Bateson), 57
story, 7–8, 9, 26, 140–41, 176. *See also* myth; paradigm; scenario
strategic planning. *See* planning, strategic
Structure, Consciousness and History (Brown and Lyman, ed.), 229
Structure of Scientific Revolutions, The (Kuhn), 117
subjectivity, in sociology, 93–95
Surgeon General, U.S., 208, 210
sustainability, 184
"Symbolic realism and cognitive aesthetics: An invitation" (Brown & Lyman), 108
"Symbolic realism and sociological thought: Beyond the positivist-romantic debate" (Brown), 9
Symbolic Turn, 220, 221. *See also* ambiguity; interpretation
symbols, 26–27, 124, 138, 139–40. *See also* information; knowledge

teamwork, 175–77, 179, 180
technology, 26, 53, 195, 197–98, 221–22
telecommunications, 4–6, 42, 52, 53–54
theology, 22. *See also* religion
theory: on collectivism and individualism, 83–86; cybernetic systems, 108–9; Marxist, 97–100; Reception, 134, 135, 142–43; sociological, 95–97; on values, 163–64
thing, emphasis on, 139–40
Thoreau, Henry David, 78, 79
Thrasymachus, 143
time, 141–42, 156. *See also* future; history
Time and Narrativity (Ricouer), 141
Tinkering Toward Utopia (Tyack & Cuban), 193
tools, 3, 11–13, 16, 148–50, 180, 217–18. *See also* expertise; skills

"Transgressing the Boundaries: Toward a Transformative Hermeneutics of Quantum Gravity" (Sokal), 11
transgression, 220
Traub, James, 193
Tyack, David, 193

universality, 96
universal service, 52, 54, 59, 199, 207
utopia, 2–3

Valery, Paul, 169
values, 9–11, 80, 83, 135, 153–72; in applying tools, 148–50; change in, 159–62; and culture, 157–58; domain of, 164–67; and freedom, 222–23; and morality, 10–11, 156, 168–72; and norms, 14, 143, 153, 154–56; theory on, 163–64. *See also* better; good; improvement, progress
Values and Lifestyles (VALS) Program, xi, 80, 222
van der Heijden, Kees, 56
vision, of future, 12–13. *See also* scenarios
voluntary, *versus* involuntary, 165–66
voluntary history, 186
von Schiller, Friedrich, 223
vouchers, 43, 195, 198–99, 226n.3

Wack, Pierre, xi
Weber, Max, 93
Western Canon, The (Bloom), 104
Whitehead, Alfred North, 85
Wilkinson, Lawrence, xi
Wilson, Edward O., 163
Wittgenstein, Ludwig Josef Johan, 141, 145
Wolfe, Tom, 81, 146
workshop, scenario planning, 181–84
worldview, vi–vii, 16, 84–85, 86, 115; on collectivism and individualism, 73–74, 77–78; in psychology, 87–91. *See also* myth; paradigm; scenario; story
worldview, relational, 8–9, 14, 102, 108, 137–50; ambiguity in, 143–45; applying tools in, 148–50; hierarchy in, 145–47; holistic, 90; identity in, 139–40; and knowledge, 25–29; meaning in, 142–43; in normative scenarios, 137–38, 148, 223–24; semiotic turn in, 138–39; story in, 140–41

Yankelovich, Dan, 82
Yeats, William Butler, 132

Printed in the United States
85584LV00005B/13-24/A